Sexual Offending by Strangers

Exploring a specific type of sexual violence committed by a specific type of sexual offender, namely adult male on adult female stranger sexual violence, this book provides readers with an enhanced understanding of both the offences being committed and the offenders who commit them.

Although acts of serious stranger sexual violence are rare, they are important as they occur in the context of there being no pre-existing relationship between the offender and victim, meaning they present significant challenges to criminal justice practitioners who are required to investigate, assess, and understand such offending. Arguing for the importance of adopting an ideographic perspective, this book encourages readers to draw upon a variety of different theories and models as appropriate, such as considering the impact of a behavioural conditioning process, where sexual violence is a manifestation of prior learning or early life experiences. Divided into four sections, this comprehensive volume guides the reader through key concepts, different types of stranger sexual violence, and applications to criminal justice practice.

Sexual Offending by Strangers will be of use to police officers, prison officers, and practitioners working with offenders in either secure or community settings. It will also be of value to students and scholars researching the topic of sexual violence.

Paul V. Greenall, PhD, has spent most of his working life in secure hospitals. He started at Ashworth Hospital, near Liverpool, as an administrator before becoming a research psychologist there. He then worked in Forensic/Clinical practice within the secure units of Prestwich Hospital in Manchester. Dr Greenall is presently a principal forensic psychologist (HCPC registered) working within the mental health in-reach teams of several male prisons in the northwest of England. In all these roles, Dr Greenall has interviewed, researched, assessed, and worked clinically with a range of mentally disordered offenders, and from this he developed a particular interest in the assessment and formulation of sexual violence. Dr Greenall has also held academic posts at universities in Liverpool and Manchester and has lectured on Forensic Psychology to undergraduates and postgraduates. He is presently a senior lecturer in Forensic Psychology at Edge Hill University, a fellow of the High Education Academy, and a visiting fellow at the University of Huddersfield.

Sexual Offending by Strangers

Paul V. Greenall

Routledge
Taylor & Francis Group

LONDON AND NEW YORK

Designed cover image: gettyimages.com

First published 2025
by Routledge
4 Park Square, Milton Park, Abingdon, Oxon OX14 4RN

and by Routledge
605 Third Avenue, New York, NY 10158

Routledge is an imprint of the Taylor & Francis Group, an informa business

British Library Cataloguing-in-Publication Data
A catalogue record for this book is available from the British Library

Library of Congress Cataloging-in-Publication Data
Names: Greenall, Paul V., author.
Title: Sexual offending by strangers / Paul V. Greenall.
Description: Abingdon, Oxon ; New York, NY : Routledge, 2024. | Includes
bibliographical references and index.
Identifiers: LCCN 2024011220 (print) | LCCN 2024011221 (ebook) | ISBN
9781032109312 (hbk) | ISBN 9781032109305 (pbk) | ISBN 9781003217763 (ebk)
Subjects: LCSH: Sex crimes. | Sex offenders. | Criminal justice, Administration of.
Classification: LCC HV6556 .G76 2024 (print) | LCC HV6556 (ebook) |
DDC 364.15/3—dc23/eng/20240324
LC record available at https://lccn.loc.gov/2024011220
LC ebook record available at https://lccn.loc.gov/2024011221

ISBN: 978-1-032-10931-2 (hbk)
ISBN: 978-1-032-10930-5 (pbk)
ISBN: 978-1-003-21776-3 (ebk)

DOI: 10.4324/9781003217763

Typeset in Sabon
by codeMantra

To the three great loves of my life:
Louise, George, and Henry.

Contents

Figures

Tables

Boxes

Preface

The seeds of this book were sown over three decades ago when, by chance, I started working at what was then Moss Side and Park Lane (now Ashworth) Hospitals. Along with Broadmoor, Rampton, and the State Hospital, these unique hospitals detain and treat mentally disordered offenders under conditions of high security due to the risk they pose to themselves and/or others (see Greenall, 2023). Reading patient files and interviewing them on the wards stimulated a desire within me to understand the origins of their offending, which in some cases were very serious and deviant indeed. This desire was enhanced by some high-profile sexual murders in the early 1990s, especially those of Dr Elizabeth Howe on the campus of York University and Rachel Nickel on Wimbledon Common. Leaving aside the controversy of the Rachel Nickel investigation, I still consider Paul Britton's (1997, pp. 237–244) hypothesis about the then unknown sexual killer worthy of being on the reading list of any student of criminal sexual behaviour, as it bears more than a passing resemblance to some men I have worked with (see Greenall & Millington, 2021). My early experiences in high-security hospitals taught me an important lesson that I want to pass on to others.

The outward normality of serious violent offenders

Despite some individuals displaying high levels of deviancy and/or dangerousness, what struck me early in my career and again many times since was the outward normality of most serious violent offenders. This probably reflected naivete on my part, perhaps having its origins in how such offenders are portrayed within the media. Whilst we might expect secure hospitals to be full of '*monstrous*' men who would easily stand out from the crowd, as I report in this book, the reality is very different. On several occasions, for example, I have met men who have committed very serious and sometimes high-profile offences, and almost without exception, their striking feature was their outward normality rather than their violence or deviousness. One man, especially who had committed a very violent and deviant stranger sexual murder, simply did not live up to my media informed expectations when I met him. Rather than being some obvious '*monster*', he was meek, mild, and outwardly inoffensive, and I was left wondering how such a man could ever commit such an offence. These contradictions increased my motivation to understand the origins of such offending, and my subsequent studies and forensic practice ultimately focused on sexual offenders in general and strangers in particular. But here again, my experiences taught me another important lesson that I want to pass on to others.

A challenging area of research and practice

Those with aspirations of researching and/or working in this field should note that it can be very challenging. As I have learned through my own research, reading accounts of women being sexually assaulted and sometimes murdered is very unpleasant. That said, whilst researching sexual violence is challenging, interviewing the offenders responsible and/or working with several of them in group settings is even more so. On many occasions, for example, I have listened to men talk about their sexual assaults of women, girls, men, and boys, and not all of them were remorseful when recounting their offences, some of which appear in this book. Additionally, along with the violence and abuse inflicted on others, the accounts of violent, abusive, and traumatic childhoods which many (but not all) sexual offenders have experienced do not make for easy listening. Consequently, as this book illustrates, researching and/or working in this field is not for the faint hearted, but it must be done if sexual offenders are to be apprehended, prosecuted, and their risks understood and managed. And when it is done, regardless of your role in the criminal justice system, receiving adequate (practice based) supervision from a senior colleague is essential. Indeed, I would not work in this field, nor would I advise you to do so, without it. You should also be mindful that this work may impact on you personally. For me, apart from being an almost hysterically concerned parent when my children were young and out in public, my views, attitudes, and even sense of humour have changed, and the same might happen to you if you work in this field. My message therefore is that if you are not already, then you will need to become what Clarke (2013) calls a '*resilient practitioner*'. That will ensure your practice is safe and the impact this work has on you is limited. This leads me to the final lesson I have learned from my experiences that I want to pass on to others.

A duty to share

Those who research/practise in this field will, over time, become equipped with knowledge and understanding of one of the most feared and despised offences and the offenders responsible. This knowledge and understanding are used by criminal justice practitioners to investigate sexual offences and to assess and manage the risk posed by sexual offenders (Logan, 2016). However, we cannot expect those who work in this field to know everything about everything, and so multidisciplinary working and information sharing are crucial. What I have learned from my work is that those who have acquired knowledge and understanding of this area have a duty to share it with others, not just in formal meetings but in other ways too. That is why I have written this book. I do not claim to know everything about stranger sexual violence, or the topics covered in each chapter, and readers with more knowledge and experience may identify gaps. That said, this book represents my current knowledge and understanding of stranger sexual violence and what I consider to be its constituent parts. Once you have read it, you will know as much as I do. If your work allows, take what you have learned here and develop it further. Then do what duty demands, and pass your enhanced knowledge and understanding on to others.

Dr Paul V Greenall
Principal Forensic Psychologist &
Senior Lecturer in Forensic Psychology,
Lancashire, England.
August 2024

References

Britton, P. (1997). *The jigsaw man*. Corgi Books.

Clarke, J. (2013). The resilient practitioner. In J. Clarke & P. Wilson (Eds.), *Forensic psychology in practice: A practitioner's handbook* (pp. 220–239). Palgrave Macmillan.

Greenall, P. V. (2023). Forensic psychology and mental disorder. In K. Corteen, R. Steele, N. Cross, & M. McManus (Eds.), *Forensic psychology, crime and policing* (pp. 59–64). Policy Press. https://doi.org/10.51952/9781447359418.ch010

Greenall, P. V., & Millington, J. (2021). A sexual murder prevented? A case study of evidence-based practice. *The Journal of Forensic Psychiatry & Psychology, 32*(5), 759–775. https://doi.org/10.1080/14789949.2021.1889014

Logan, C. (2016). Risk formulation: The new frontier in risk assessment and management. In D. R. Laws & W. O'Donohue (Eds.), *Treatment of sex offenders: Strengths and weaknesses in assessment and intervention* (pp. 83–105). Springer. https://doi.org/10.1007/978-3-319-25868-3_4

Acknowledgements

I never thought I would author a book, but Routledge and my Senior Editorial Assistant, Medha Malaviya, have made this task possible, and I am grateful for their encouragement, assistance, and patience. As this book is influenced by my forensic and academic practice, I want to thank those who, knowingly or not, have contributed to my ability to undertake and complete it.

Within my forensic practice, I am fortunate to have worked with Dr Adrian West and Dr Caroline Logan. Over the years, their generous mentorship has taught me a great deal and greatly influenced my practice. Other colleagues I have been fortunate to work with include Drs Grace Crawford, Hannah Darrell-Berry, Claire Gately, Julie Hird, Naomi Humber, Richard Jones, Geraint Lewis, Kelly McCarthy, James Millington, Mark Swinton, Keith Whittle, Assistant Psychologist Dominic McConnell, Senior Mental Health Nurse Sherilyn Magee, and Art Therapist James Van-Lint. I also recognise the contribution of the countless offenders I have worked with in secure hospitals and prisons over the years. You learn something new from every offender you work with, and I have learned a great deal from these people, many of whom have generously shared their often dark and disturbing experiences with me.

From academia, I thank Professor David Canter, who I was fortunate to work with during 2005–2008. He too taught me a great deal and influenced my practice, and his work is cited throughout this book. I also thank Dave Selfe (formerly LJMU) for initiating my interest in sexual violence early in my career and Lee Rainbow at the National Crime Agency for facilitating my research into stranger sexual homicide. With the help of Dr Michelle Wright (formerly MMU), this research caught the eye of Routledge and led to this book.

Others to whom I am grateful include John Coulshed and his colleagues at Prestwich Hospital Library for doggedly obtaining references I never thought they would. I also thank officers from the Sex Offender Management Unit of Greater Manchester Police. Although their names are now lost to me in the mists of time, our collaborations provided a fascinating insight into the unenviable task of managing sexual offenders in the community.

Finally, and perhaps controversially, I acknowledge the contribution of two men I have never met but who, nonetheless, have influenced my practice: Robert Mone and Thomas McCulloch. In November 1976, when I was still a child, Mone and McCulloch escaped from the State Hospital at Carstairs. The resulting public inquiry (Reid, 1977) showed their planning was meticulous and coincided with some unfortunate security failures, and their escape involved the brutal murder of Neil McLellan (male nurse), Iain

Simpson (fellow patient), and Police Constable George Taylor. Having learned from them early in my career what some violent men in secure establishments are prepared to do to achieve their aims, Mone and McCulloch have been my imaginary companions for over three decades whilst working (and learning) in secure hospitals and prisons. This ensured that I have never been complacent within these institutions, and that has helped to keep me and those I work with safe.

Reference

Reid, R. (1977). *State Hospital Carstairs: Report of public local inquiry into circumstances surrounding the escape of two patients on 30 November 1976 and into security and other arrangements at the hospital.* Scottish Home & Health Department.

1   Introduction

> perhaps the single most important task which challenges
> forensic clinicians is that of understanding the causes
> of attacks and their meanings for the perpetrator.
>
> (MacCulloch *et al.*, 1995, p. 43)

Introduction

Of all the sexual offences, those committed by strangers are the ones that invoke much fear and leave victims, witnesses, criminal justice practitioners, and the media wanting explanations for the offender's behaviour. However, as indicated by the above quote, understanding why a man sexually assaulted a woman he did not know and what the assault meant to him is a challenging task. Despite there being several theories seeking to explain sexual offending (see Ward *et al.*, 2006), the diversity of sexual offences and the men who commit them means the best any criminal justice practitioner can achieve when dealing with a stranger sexual assault is to develop one or more evidence-based hypotheses that explain the offence in question, how/why the offender committed it, and ways to prevent further offences. However, when stranger sexual assaults also involve deviant sexual practices and serious physical violence, which, in some (albeit rare) cases, results in the victim's death, the task of developing an understanding of the offender and his actions becomes even more challenging. Although many people might assume that sexual offending by strangers relates to the offender's sexual needs and his inability to control them, research suggests this assumption is not always accurate, as other subjective needs can be satisfied within such offences. It is therefore essential for criminal justice practitioners working in investigative (e.g., police), institutional (e.g., prisons or secure hospitals), or community settings (e.g., probation) to enhance their understanding of sexual offending by strangers and the offenders themselves. Helping them to achieve this is the key aim of this book.

Terminology

The focus of this book is sexual offending committed by adult men against adult female strangers. Within this book, an adult is defined as being aged 16 or over, in line with the age of sexual consent within the United Kingdom. Whilst the sexual offences considered in this book are (mostly) legally defined, this book also draws upon a clinical definition which is well used within forensic/clinical practice. Boer *et al.* (2017) define *'sexual*

DOI: 10.4324/9781003217763-1

violence' as involving actual, attempted, or threatened sexual contact with another person without consent. Sexual contact includes various behaviours, which we shall consider in later chapters, such as sexual battery (e.g., rape or sexual touching), communications of a sexual nature (e.g., exhibitionism or obscene letters or telephone calls), and violating property rights for sexual purposes (e.g., voyeurism or theft of fetish objects). This broader definition captures some offences which, although not defined as sexual in law, are nonetheless clearly of a sexual nature (see Chapter 7). Consequently, throughout this book, the terms sexual violence, sexual offence(s), and sexual offending will be used interchangeably as appropriate, all referring to the same thing, namely sexual behaviour proscribed by law and/or that accords with the above clinical definition. Whilst sexual violence is legally and clinically defined, there is no universal and/or agreed definition of the concept of '*stranger*'. Consequently, criminal justice practitioners are left to apply either a definition used within their organisation (if one exists) or one from official publications or research. This situation, however, is problematic, and to address it, some clear definitions are presented in Chapter 2.

Stranger sexual violence and stranger sexual offenders

Although a more detailed exploration of stranger sexual violence is provided in volume two, at this stage, it is useful to consider the various ways in which this crime can manifest itself. The stranger sexual offender, for example, can be the man who steals women's underwear either from her washing line or, in more serious cases, from her home after breaking in (see Chapter 7). He could be the man, popularly known as a '*peeping Tom*', who secretly watches a woman bathe or get undressed whilst he masturbates, or he could be the man who jumps out from behind a bush in a park with his trousers and underwear around his ankles, exhibiting his erect penis to one or more unsuspecting women, perhaps even masturbating in front of them (see Chapter 8). He could be the man who gropes a young woman in a bar, a crowded train, or a public park, or the man who follows, attacks, and rapes a woman in an isolated location or again her home after breaking in (see Chapter 9). Finally, and most seriously of all, he could be the man who sexually assaults and kills a woman, again either in an isolated location or her home after breaking in (see Chapter 10). In any of these cases, the stranger sexual offender may be acting in accordance with his core values and beliefs, he may be influenced by a mental disorder or intoxication (see Chapter 5), or he may be attempting to satisfy his deviant sexual needs (see Chapter 6).

A dimensional aspect of stranger sexual violence

The nature of the offences described above suggests they exist along a continuum. A similar idea was proposed by Salfati and Taylor (2006), who found that rape and sexual murder existed along a continuum based on the level of violence. Here, however, the offences shown in Figure 1.1 exist along a continuum based on the levels of interpersonal, physical, and sexual contact that exist between the offender and his victim. At one end of this continuum, acquisitive offences (see Chapter 7) involve no interpersonal, physical, or sexual contact whatsoever. Non-contact offences (see Chapter 8) involve varying degrees of interpersonal contact, but no physical or sexual contact. Whilst contact offences (see Chapters 9–10) involve all three types of contact, a crucial point to note and which we

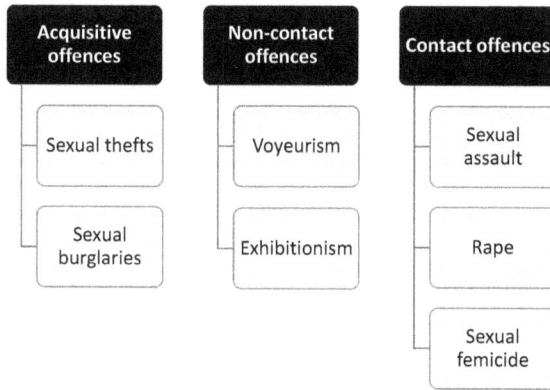

Figure 1.1 Dimensional view of stranger sexual violence

shall return to later in this book, is that stranger sexual offenders may not always remain within one of the boxes in Figure 1.1, or indeed at one point along the theoretical continuum, and commit the same kind of offence again. Rather, some of them will escalate their offending and engage in more serious acts of stranger sexual violence. Examples of this will be provided in later chapters, but for now, consider the case of the *'railway rapist'* John Duffy who was active in London during the 1980s (see Canter, 1994, 2003). He went from being a stranger rapist (see Chapter 9) to a stranger sexual killer (see Chapter 10).

But who are these men, and why do they act this way? The usage of labels such as *'perverts'* and *'nonces'* clearly shows that sexual offenders are viewed very negatively by many in society. Even among offenders in prisons, the masculine nature of these places ensures that sexual offenders are viewed very negatively (Sim, 1994). Consequently, they are often housed on separate wings (often called VP or vulnerable prisoner units) away from other prisoners, who would happily attack them given half a chance. Some people may assume that sexual offenders are unattractive, socially inept men who cannot *'get a woman'*. However, as any criminal justice practitioner who has worked with sexual offenders knows, these men do not stand out from the crowd, and you could easily walk past a sexual offender in the street or strike up a conversation with one in a bar without knowing. Equally, as any criminal justice practitioner who has worked with sexual offenders also knows, because of their early life experiences, psychological make-up, and criminal histories, sexual offenders are often some of the most complex and challenging offenders to work with (see Craissati, 2019). Having said that, as some of the best minds in this field remind us, there is no such thing as a typical sex offender, as no such profile exists (Boer *et al.*, 2017; Hart *et al.*, 2022). Within my own forensic/clinical practice for example, the sexual offenders I have worked with have included young lads who have sexually assaulted and raped young women whilst intoxicated on alcohol and/or drugs, antisocial men with varied criminal histories, men with one or more mental disorders, sexually deviant men who could not control their urges, sexual murderers, unemployed men, university educated wealthy middle-class professional men such as teachers and solicitors, ex-military men, young men, old men, black men, white men, men who targeted children, men who targeted adult women, men who targeted children and adult women, men who targeted elderly women, men who committed one sexual offence, men who committed several sexual offences, men who admit their guilt, and men who do not. Working in the field of sexual violence, you never know who you are going to meet next!

Intentional offenders – intentional offences

Whilst not every sexual offender I have worked with has targeted female strangers, many of them have. When trying to understand the mind of a stranger sexual offender, consider a question posed by Ward *et al.* (2006), who asked, how is it possible for a man to force a woman to have sex when she is clearly unwilling and/or distressed by this prospect and/or when she is drunk, unconscious, asleep, or otherwise unable to respond? On some occasions, the man may have made an error of judgement or an honest mistake, especially if he knows the woman, and the law acknowledges this. However, in my professional opinion, this cannot apply to stranger sexual offenders, as they would have clearly known that the women they were targeting were not welcoming their sexual advances. In such cases, sex was a weapon in a violent assault, and this fact further illustrates why the term sexual violence is an appropriate description of such behaviour. Moreover, stranger sexual assaults do not *'just happen'* as in order to be able to sexually assault a female stranger, an offender must engage in a decision-making process such as that presented in Figure 1.2.

Figure 1.2 summarises an offence decision chain presented by Proulx and Beauregard (2008), which includes factors that will be considered in later chapters. For example, the process commences with an individual who is motivated to commit a sexual offence (see Chapter 4). This motivation may have only just manifested itself in the offender's mind, or he may have had such an idea for some time. Either way, if not already in one, he needs to find and travel to (see Chapter 3) a location where suitable victims can be found (e.g., bars, clubs, and student areas) and be there at a time when they are likely to be available (e.g., evenings or weekends). Once there, he must find a suitable victim based on her desirability, vulnerability, and accessibility. Once she has been identified, he must decide on the most appropriate method of approach (see Chapter 2). In making this approach, he may have to adjust his behaviours to overcome any victim resistance, and he may have to evaluate the risk of negative outcomes such as passersby intervening or the victim being able to identify him afterwards (Proulx & Beauregard, 2008).

Another way to understand the mind of the stranger sexual offender is to consider the work of Kahneman (2012). He suggests people have two thinking styles: one fast, one slow. System one thinking operates automatically and quickly, with little or no effort and no sense of voluntary control. Examples provided by Kahneman (2012) include knowing that the answer to $2 + 2 = ?$ and detecting hostility in someone's voice. By contrast, system two thinking allocates mental attention to the task in hand and is associated with subjectivity, agency, choice, and concentration. Examples provided by Kahneman (2012) include looking for a woman with white hair and monitoring our behaviour in social situations. With this in mind, and looking again at Figure 1.2, each stage requires system two thinking, as the stranger sexual offender must pay attention to what is happening around him before deciding upon his next step. It is also clear that he must follow a decision chain – which he can break at any point – to the very end to achieve his sexually violent aims. This suggests that stranger sexual violence does not occur by accident but is the result of an intentional mental process, and this is exactly how it is viewed under English Criminal Law.

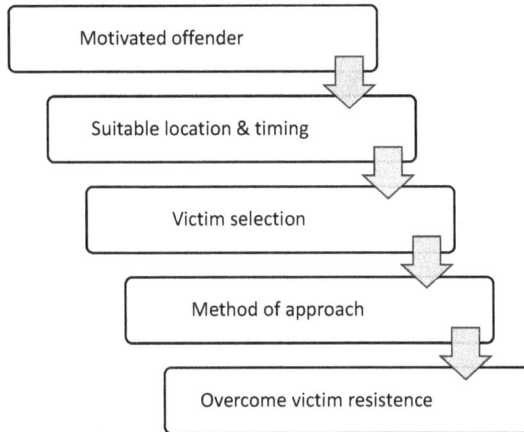

Figure 1.2 Offence decision chain

Source: Adapted from Proulx and Beauregard (2008)

Legal perspective

Under English Criminal Law, crime comprises two components that *must* be present for an offence to have occurred, namely the *actus reus* and *mens rea* (Cross, 2023). Although we can leave the finer details to our legal colleagues, criminal justice practitioners require a basic understanding of these two components and how they relate to stranger sexual violence, as they can help us to further understand the mind of the stranger sexual offender.

1 *Actus reus:* This is the guilty act and conduct element of an offence. This generally consists of one or more of the following components: behaviour (e.g., violence), circumstance (e.g., a fight), and consequence (e.g., injuries). Macdonald (2018) suggests there may not always be a consequential component within sexual offences, but there will be a behavioural (e.g., sexual activity) and circumstantial (e.g., victim not consenting) component.
2 *Mens rea:* This relates to the offender's thought processes and state of mind at the time the *actus reus* occurred. Under the Sexual Offences Act 2003, the *mens rea* generally includes two components. First, the offender intentionally engaged in sexual activity with his victim. Second, the offender lacked a reasonable belief that the victim was consenting to the sexual activity (Macdonald, 2018).

Macdonald (2018) suggests the *mens rea* concept of intention involves a choice to bring about a result because the offender wants it to occur. Understanding this is crucial, because it underlines the above ideas that the offender did not engage in sexual activity with a female stranger by accident. Rather, he *intentionally* engaged in sexual activity with her because he *wanted* to satisfy one or more psychological needs (see Chapter 4). Moreover, he did this *knowing* she was *not* consenting and did *not* want this to happen. Although a legal perspective focuses on the final stage of Figure 1.2, it shows that the stranger sexual offender not only intended to engage in sexual activity with his non-consenting victim, but he knowingly and intentionally followed a series of system two based decisions to achieve this. To understand how some men decide to behave in this way when most other men do not, we need to explore a range of factors that can influence their psychological make-up and decision-making (see Chapters 5–6). This requires an individualised approach (see Chapters 11–12), which brings us to the philosophy of this book.

Philosophy of this book

Although this book draws upon academic research, I also draw upon the lessons I have learned from my own forensic/clinical practice in secure hospitals and prisons. Whilst the following statement about my forensic/clinical practice may be obvious, it nonetheless illustrates the philosophy of this book and the challenge it seeks to help criminal justice practitioners address:

> Like other criminal justice practitioners, within my practice I work with individual offenders, and I try to assess and understand their behaviour.

What this means is that whilst I draw upon academic research to ensure my practice is evidence-based, in doing this, I, like other criminal justice practitioners, face the difficult challenge which is hardly mentioned. This challenge involves trying to apply research, often based on large groups of offenders, to the offender I am trying to assess and understand. Stating this is like poking a hornet's nest, as it relates to the age-old debate within the social sciences between quantitative (aka nomothetic) and qualitative (aka idiographic) approaches and whether and to what extent the findings of the former can be applied to the latter.

Nomothetic approach

Nomothetic research involves the quantitative analysis of groups of people who are meant to be representative of the wider population. The results generally comprise summaries of data and measures of difference or similarity tested by statistical tests, with significance indicated by p-values. As such, nomothetic research focuses on generalities, arithmetic means, and probabilities with a view to identifying *'laws'* of human behaviour, averaging out any individual variations or outliers. This allows predictions to be made about how people are likely to behave in given situations (Willig, 2022). Within the field of sexual violence, this approach has allowed various predictions to be made. Examples include that most stranger rapists are under the age of 30, most have previous convictions (Greenall & West, 2007, 2008), and most sexual offenders live close to where they offend (Beauregard *et al.*, 2005). Although these are reasonable evidence-based predictions, they belie the fact that not every stranger rapist is under 30 or has previous convictions (see Chapter 9), and some sexual offenders do not live close to where they offend (see Chapter 3).

From the group to the individual

The problems arising from applying group-based research to individuals have been highlighted within the field of violence risk assessment. As we shall see in Chapter 11, various risk assessment protocols have been developed from nomothetic research and are used to predict the likelihood of an individual offender violently re-offending. However, research by Hart and colleagues (Hart & Cooke, 2013; Hart *et al.*, 2007) found that when nomothetic-based risk assessment protocols were applied to individual offenders, the margins of error were so high as to render the risk estimates virtually meaningless. Consequently, they concluded that nomothetic-based risk assessment protocols could not be used to estimate the probability or likelihood that an individual would violently re-offend in the future with any reasonable degree of precision or certainty. Although these findings were disputed by some researchers (see Hart & Cooke, 2013), the problems of applying group-based nomothetic research to individuals were recognised decades ago by the famous behavioural psychologist B.F. Skinner, who in the 1950s made the following observations:

> A prediction of what the average individual will do is often of little or no value in dealing with a particular individual ... the actuarial tables of life-insurance companies are of no value to a physician in predicting the death or survival of a particular patient ... a science of behavior which concerns only the behavior of groups is not likely to be of help in our understanding of the particular case.
>
> (Skinner, 1953, p. 19)

Idiographic exploration of stranger sexual violence

Idiographic research involves a detailed examination of single individuals or small groups of individuals and aims to explore their uniqueness or how they experience a particular phenomenon in their own unique context. Ideographic research seeks to identify factors that operate at the individual level that contribute to that person's psychological functioning and their behaviour. This is achieved by gaining a thorough understanding of an individual or a small group, with the aim of this leading to a more general understanding of others (Willig, 2022). A popular idiographic approach is the case study (see Smith *et al.*, 1995; Yin, 2018), which has been used to explore actual (e.g., Brankley *et al.*, 2014) or attempted (e.g., Greenall & Millington, 2021) stranger sexual violence. In advocating an idiographic approach, I do not dispute the fact that nomothetic research can enhance our understanding of sexual violence at a macro level by providing details and/or theories about how and why *men* engage in sexual violence. However, criminal justice practitioners do not operate at the macro level, as they are required to focus their attention on the *individual* sexual offender they are working with. To understand how and why an individual sexually assaulted a female stranger, criminal justice practitioners will indeed draw upon nomothetic research, but to apply that research to the individual in hand, they must sift this through what I call an idiographic filter (see chapter 12).

Idiographic filter

This book is divided into four volumes. Volume one presents some key concepts which are required as a basis for understanding stranger sexual violence. These include exploring the concept of stranger violence, the journeys stranger sexual offenders take to engage in stranger sexual violence, the interpersonal and motivational dynamics that drive and underpin stranger sexual violence, the psychological factors that influence a stranger sexual offender's decision to engage in stranger sexual violence, and acts of sexual deviancy that may be included within such assaults. Volume two explores the offences in detail and follows the continuum idea of these offences presented above. Here each chapter follows a similar structure in that they firstly define the offence in question, consider how common the offence is, what typically occurs within such offences, what motivates such offences, and any future implications. Whilst volumes one and two are largely based on nomothetic research, volume three introduces ways in which the idiographic filter can be applied by criminal justice practitioners. This involves a process of formulation, not only of the offender but of the offence itself. This process involves drawing upon the research presented in volumes one and two and applying these findings to the case at hand, not in a blanket way but in a targeted way based on the professional judgement exercised by criminal justice practitioners.

Criminal justice practitioners

This book is aimed at those who work in three main areas of our criminal justice system, both professionals and students. First, those responsible for criminal investigations, such as police officers and civilians who assist them. Second, those who work in institutions such as prisons and secure hospitals, such as forensic mental health professionals (e.g., psychiatrists, psychologists, mental health nurses, and social workers), prison officers, and offender managers. Third, those who manage offenders in the community, such as probation officers. In trying to assist these diverse professional groups, this book is trying to ride two horses at once by helping those who know the identity of the stranger sexual offender responsible for a stranger sexual assault (i.e., those in institutional and community settings) and those who do not (i.e., police officers). Those who work in institutional and community settings will mostly have obtained the necessary professional qualification(s) to practice and should therefore be able to draw upon this book without necessarily having to consult others in their field. However, within the field of policing, there has been a tendency in recent decades to consult behavioural scientists – *'offender profilers'* – who draw upon their specialist knowledge, skills, and training to assist police with their investigations (e.g., see Alison & Rainbow, 2011; Bartol & Bartol, 2013; West, 2001). However, with the increasing professionalisation of the police (Kelly, 2023a) and with policing degrees now offered at many British universities (College of Policing, 2023b), graduate police officers may have less of a need to call upon these external advisors. Rather, moving forward, they may be able to utilise books like this to inform and enhance their own practice. So, whilst some readers may be surprised not to find a specific chapter on *'offender profiling'* this is because each chapter is designed to help police officers just as much as any other criminal justice practitioner.

Conclusion

Whilst several books have been written on sexual offenders and sexual offending, this book focuses entirely on one single type of sexual violence, namely those in which a man sexually assaults a female stranger in the real world, not cyberspace. Although statistically a minority of all serious sexual offences (Matheson, 2013), it is this same rarity that ensures these offences and the offenders who commit them present significant challenges to criminal justice practitioners who are tasked with dealing with them. This book therefore aims to provide those who work in this field with an enhanced understanding of both so that, in future, these challenges can be faced with confidence.

Part 1

Key concepts

2 Stranger violence

Stranger violence is frightening because we are often in the presence of persons who may launch an indiscriminate attack

(Riedel, 1993, p. 3)

Introduction

Stranger violence represents one of the most frightening forms of criminal victimisation and the idea of being sexually victimised by a male stranger is a prospect women fear more than any other crime (Scott, 2003). Scully (1994) suggests that from a woman's perspective, the fear of stranger sexual violence relates to the sudden and unexpected nature of such assaults, which leaves women at a tactical disadvantage. Given that the average man is bigger and stronger than the average woman, or at least the woman the stranger chooses to target, it is understandable how a sudden, unexpected sexual assault, which may include physical violence and a weapon (typically a knife), would leave many women feeling this way. Moreover, it is understandable why some women may feel inclined to modify their behaviour to limit their exposure to stranger sexual violence (Hickman & Muehlenhard, 1997) and why some organisations offer safety plans (Caledon/Dufferin Victim Services, 2023) and advice to women in this regard (e.g. see Patrick, 2017 and Box 2.1). Indeed, when looking at Box 2.1, one wonders how much of a negative impact it must have on women's lives if they incorporate such advice into their daily routines. Moreover, it brings home the fundamental point that such a routine is outside of the sphere of men's realities. With this in mind, we can understand why Scully suggested the fear of sexual violence *"restricts women's lifestyles in ways that fear of crime does not restrict men"* (1994, p. 172).

Box 2.1   Safety considerations to avoid stranger rape

At home

Use deadbolts; window locks; peepholes; timers for lights, radio, TV, and outside security lights. Never open your door to strangers; require ID from service or repair men. Plan several escape routes from your home. If you are a single woman, use only initials at your door and in the phone book. Pretend there is a man at home if

---

DOI: 10.4324/9781003217763-3

someone calls. If you come home and something looks wrong or different, do not enter; go to a safe place and call the police.

Out in public

Go with others. Vary your routines; go different ways at different times. Know where the safe places are; businesses that are open late, homes where people are up late, etc. If a situation feels wrong, get away fast. Stay away from bushes and parked cars; walk in the centre of the pavement or road.

In your car

Always lock your doors, when you are in the car and when you leave it, even if only for a short time. Park near lights at night. Have your keys in your hand when leaving a building for your car or leaving the car for a building. Drive with your windows mostly closed. Keep the car in good working order and keep the fuel tank at least 1/4 full. In case of a breakdown, stay in the locked car; if assistance is offered, request that police be called.

At work

Do not work late alone; keep company with others. Go to the carpark with others or ask security staff to accompany you. Vary your route (and time if possible) to and from work. Maintain assertiveness with colleagues.

Source: adapted from Staff (2019)

Chapter aims

This chapter introduces the concept of stranger violence and provides a clear definition of stranger sexual violence and stranger sexual offenders. The chapter then considers why the concept of *'stranger'* matters before exploring the interpersonal dynamics of this crime and the pathways that some men follow to access female strangers to sexually assault. Consideration of these ideas will provide a basis for the process of formulating hypotheses about individual cases of stranger sexual violence, a process that will be built upon in the following chapters.

Definition: *What is stranger violence?*

Initially, this may appear obvious: a violent assault committed by a stranger. However, as Riedel (1993) argues, the difficulty does not relate to how the violent aspect of this concept is defined, but what is meant by the term *'stranger'*. As will be shown, this is an accurate observation because defining the term stranger is not as easy as might first be assumed.

Although various sexual offences and some victim-offender attributes (i.e., child victim, family member, offender in a position of trust, etc.) are defined by statute, English Criminal Law does not define stranger. Within Britain, official reports exploring sexual violence have traditionally utilised narrow definitions. Examples include Harris and Grace, who defined stranger cases as *"where the suspect had no contact with the complainant prior to the attack"* (1999, p. 2), and Feist et. al., who similarly defined stranger cases as *"no prior contact whatsoever"* (2007, p. 12). Narrow definitions such as these view acts of stranger sexual violence as occurring in the context of no prior relationship between the offender and victim. Here we can hypothesise that the assault occurred with little or no warning whilst the woman was going about her ordinary business (Scully, 1994). By contrast, in the United States, official reports use a broader definition as *"incidents are classified as involving strangers if the victim identifies the offender as a stranger, did not see or recognize the offender, or knew the offender only by sight"* (Bureau of Justice Statistics, 2021). When applied to stranger sexual violence, this definition accommodates the possibility of some pre-crime victim–offender interaction. However, what happens, for example, if the victim is mistaken about her assailant's identity or her ability to see and recognise him is hampered by the tensions of the moment? Although broader definitions have the flexibility to include more cases, the danger is that some of them may be incorrectly identified as stranger assaults.

Police definitions

More recently, in Britain, official police reports have tried to accommodate both positions by recognising that stranger sexual violence may occur in the context of either no prior relationship between the offender and victim or a limited prior relationship. For example, Her Majesty's Inspectorate of Constabulary (HMIC) differentiates between *'stranger one'* cases where *"the suspect is completely unknown to the victim"* (2007, p. 49) and the more broader *'stranger two'* cases where:

> the victim and suspect have met for the first time (including those who were previously known to each other via the internet) or are known on first-name terms only or are known only through third parties such as mutual friends.
>
> (ibid.)

Similarly, the National Policing Improvement Agency (NPIA) later defined stranger rapes as:

> offences in which the victim has no previous knowledge of the perpetrator and has not knowingly met them before the offence. They are, therefore, unable to name them or to provide information about their identity. It also includes cases in which there were brief or single encounters within a short time period where the victim may be able to identify the offender but would not describe them as an acquaintance.
>
> (2010, p. 17)

Although the HMIC and NPIA have provided police forces with definitions they can work with, confusion as to what constitutes a stranger sexual offence remains. This is evidenced by the fact that the NPIA recognises that, on some occasions, it may not always be clear what the victim–offender relationship was. For example, when a man sexually assaults a woman he has only recently met, such as in a pub, this may need to be investigated as an acquaintance or stranger offence. Moreover, whilst the victim may regard the offender as a stranger, she may be unaware that he may have intentionally established a link with her to obtain information about her before assaulting her. This, the NPIA suggests, can allow the offender to present a picture to others that helps him to argue that the victim consented to sex. On other occasions, some offences that initially appear to have been committed by a stranger may, after investigation, be identified as domestic or acquaintance assault (NPIA, 2010).

A further problem was identified by an official review into rape investigation and prosecution (Criminal Justice Joint Inspection, 2012), which found that many police forces were not using the NPIA definition of stranger, and their crime recording systems did not distinguish between different victim–offender relationships. Moreover, police forces that did record victim–offender relationships were reliant on individual police officers to understand the different definitions and to tick the correct box on the form. This led to a wide variation (between 5% and 25%) in the number of stranger rapes recorded and an acknowledgement that the data was insufficiently robust to be used to assess the level of offending. Given that recommendation, one of this official review was that police forces *"should initially consider every stranger rape to be part of a pattern of serial offending, so that investigating officers consider the wider links to other crimes"* (ibid., 2012, p. 28), the investigative implications of not recording stranger relationships using a standard definition cannot be overstated. This is especially so, given that research suggests stranger sexual assaults are more likely to be reported to the police (Feist *et al.*, 2007; Flatley, 2018; Myhill & Allen, 2002) and result in conviction (Lundrigan *et al.*, 2019) than non-stranger cases. However, the benefits of recording stranger victim–offender relationships based on a clear definition extend beyond the realm of policing. Elsewhere within the criminal justice system, practitioners often use police records in their work with offenders. If these reports make clear that the offender they are working with has a history of sexually assaulting female strangers, practitioners can incorporate this important risk factor (Helmus *et al.*, 2021; Thornton *et al.*, 2003) into their assessment and formulation of the offender's history and future risk of sexual violence (see Chapters 11–12).

A clearer definition of 'stranger'

Previously, I presented a definition of stranger that dispensed with the need for narrow or broader definitions, as it included a standard timeframe for what constitutes a stranger. This was achieved by considering the level of victim-offender recognition, in particular, whether they knew each other the day before the assault (Greenall, 2018). Perhaps the best way to illustrate this is to consider the reality of the relationships in your life. There may, for example, be people who you know only by sight (e.g., a neighbour who lives down the road), or you may meet someone in a bar and be in their company for a few hours. If you did not know that person yesterday or only knew them by sight, you will know very little, if anything, about their history or current circumstances, their likes or dislikes. Upon meeting them today, therefore, the reality is that this person does not occupy a meaningful part of your life, because they are a stranger. And if, when you meet them today, that person physically and/or sexually assaults you, their status as a stranger would be amplified. Therefore, although originally referring to stranger sexual homicide, a slight modification of the definitions I previously offered (see Greenall, 2018) allows them to have more relevance to criminal investigations and forensic/clinical practice:

- *Stranger sexual violence:* A type of sexual violence that occurs in the context of there being little or no pre-existing relationship between the offender and victim, such that the victim would not have recognised her assailant the day before the assault or considered him to occupy a meaningful part of her life.

- *Stranger sexual offenders:* Men who commit acts of sexual violence against adult women with whom they had little or no pre-existing relationship, such that their victim would not have recognised him the day before the assault or considered him to occupy a meaningful part of her life.

Why does the concept of *'stranger'* matter?

Having presented a clearer definition of stranger sexual violence, a key question for criminal justice practitioners is: why does this concept matter? As will now be shown, it matters for two reasons, and both must be understood if stranger offences are to be successfully investigated and if the risk posed by stranger offenders is to be successfully managed.

The fear factor!

As stated in the opening paragraph, several researchers and organisations have found that the prospect of being sexually assaulted by a male stranger is feared by many women. Riedel (1993) suggests three components – *setting, behaviour, and people* – underpin this fear, and we need to examine them to enhance our understanding of stranger sexual violence.

1 *'Setting'* relates to where stranger sexual assaults occur, which is the focus of Chapter 3. However, because these assaults often occur in public locations, places such as bars, streets, and parks are where women feel more vulnerable to being sexually assaulted by male strangers. That said, we can only imagine the level of fear experienced by a woman when sexually assaulted by a male stranger in her own home, which my research suggests is not uncommon (Greenall & Richardson, 2015; Greenall & West, 2007, 2008).
2 *'Behaviour'* relates to the options available to avoid stranger sexual violence. Women who feel able to defend themselves due to, for example, being proficient in a martial art, carrying a weapon (e.g., pepper spray), or being out with friends may experience less fear than women who feel less capable of preventing such an attack.
3 *'People'* relates to those men who are predisposed to sexually assault female strangers. This highlights an important paradox, which is that although stranger sexual violence is feared by many women, much of their routine activities (e.g., shopping, using public transport, jogging, going for a walk, etc.) bring them into regular contact with male strangers. However, whilst most of these encounters are incident-free, women live with the knowledge that stranger sexual violence can happen anytime, anyplace, anywhere, and at the hands of any male stranger they encounter.

Limited exposure – limited experience?

As we shall explore in more detail in volume two, research suggests strangers account for a minority of serious sexual assaults. From a practical perspective, the rarity of stranger sexual violence is important, as it means most of the sexual offenders encountered by criminal justice practitioners will be men who have sexually assaulted women they know. This leads to a key question: will the ability of some criminal justice practitioners to investigate cases of stranger sexual violence and to assess and manage stranger sexual offenders be hindered by their limited experience of this crime? Logically, the answer is yes, because how can a crime be investigated or the offender assessed and managed if those charged with undertaking these tasks have limited experience with the offence/offenders in question? A similar point was made several years ago by Adhami and Browne, who, when focusing on police investigations, argued:

> although detectives bring much general investigative experience and expertise to a major crime enquiry, their ability to deal with specific types of low volume serious crime is hindered by their limited experience of that class of crime.
>
> (1996, p. 33)

Given that the targeting of strangers is a risk factor for future violence (Helmus *et al.*, 2021; Thornton *et al.*, 2003), criminal justice practitioners should develop an understanding of how sexual violence can occur between adult strangers. An excellent place to start is to consider the interpersonal dynamics of this crime.

Interpersonal dynamics of stranger sexual violence

There is one indisputable fact that all criminal justice practitioners should recognise when trying to understand acts of interpersonal violence; relationships matter, and the absence of a relationship matters even more!

This is not a new finding, as over five decades ago Amir (1971) suggested that most violent offences begin with some sort of relationship between the offender and victim, and these relationships are probably more important within acts of sexual violence than in any other crime. Indeed, making similar comments to the NPIA earlier, Amir suggested the existence of prior victim–offender relations may cast doubt on the victim's allegations, regardless of her behaviour prior to, during, or after the offence. The importance of victim–offender relationships has since been highlighted by others in the field. For example, Groth and Birnbaum (1979) included *'social relationship'* within the victim selection component of their protocol for the clinical assessment of an offender's sexual behaviour; the US Department of Justice suggested the victim–offender relationship was: *"one of the more significant dimensions of violent crime... [and] ...a key element to understanding crime and judging the risks involved for various groups in society"* (1984, p. 10); and Hanson and Bussière (1998) reported that the risk of sexual recidivism increased for men who had sexually victimised strangers; hence, as stated above, the targeting of strangers is now regarded as a risk factor for future sexual violence. Indeed, although presenting arguments that some may find challenging today, Amir suggested: *"criminology recognises that it is not always the offender alone who is to be blamed and condemned as responsible for the offence... [as] ...sometimes victims can be equally blamed"* (1971, p. 229). In highlighting the importance of victim–offender relationships and the role and possible culpability of victims in their own sexual victimisation, Amir left us some clues about the importance of strangers. For example, after explaining how men may misinterpret a woman's behaviour and draw the wrong conclusions, which leads them to commit a sexual offence, Amir cautioned us about one type of offender where knowledge of victim behaviour and the situation in which the offence occurred may not always be helpful, as *"he may indiscriminately and randomly attack any victim, no matter what her behaviour"* (1971, p. 262).

Amir was referring to men who are prepared to sexually assault adult female strangers. These offenders, Amir went on, are dismissed by criminologists and sociologists as being *'psychiatric entity'*, implying their offences are indicative of mental pathology. However, as we will see in Chapter 5, this assumption does not always apply, but it nonetheless illustrates how five decades ago, men who raped women outside of circumstances that could lend themselves to misinterpretation were regarded. Another clue left by Amir is the fact that when exploring the relational dynamics of what he termed *'victim-precipitated'* (VP) rapes, he found that most *'VP rapes'* were characterised by close relationships between the offender and victim, whereas this was so in only a minority of *'non-VP'* cases (1971, p. 275). The implication here is that in most cases where no close relationship existed between the offender and victim (i.e., strangers), the victim's behaviour was not a contributory factor. This finding is important as it illustrates a crucial feature that differentiates stranger from non-stranger sexual violence, which links to the definitions proposed earlier and the argument that relationships and the absence of them matter. This relates to the fact that at the material time there was little or no reasonable possibility of consensual sexual relations occurring between the offender and victim and little or no reasonable possibility of a prior dispute existing between them that could explain the offender's desire to assault his victim (see Greenall, 2018). Put simply, the stranger sexual offender is not a man who has made an honest mistake about the presence of consent or who has betrayed a woman's trust. Rather, he is a man who is prepared to intentionally sexually victimise a woman who, this time yesterday, he either did not know at all or not in any meaningful way. And to begin to understand the psychology of these men, we need to explore the social circles that influence our lives and the subtle rules that govern them.

Understanding social circles

In their study of homicide, Silverman and Kennedy (1987) divided victim–offender relationships into four types based on their *'relational distance'* or level of interpersonal intimacy. The *'spouse/lover'* type includes relationships most likely to include romantic involvement and a large amount of intimate interaction, such as husbands, wives, estranged lovers, or those involved in a love triangle. The *'family members'* type includes parents, grandparents, nieces, nephews, uncles, aunts, and siblings. Although these are close relationships, they would not include any romantic involvement. The third and more distant type was *'friends/acquaintances'* which includes work colleagues, friendships, casual acquaintances, and other non-kinship relationships. The final and most distant type was *'strangers'*, defined narrowly as *"those offenders who had no known relationship with the victim"* (Silverman & Kennedy, 1987, p. 282).

The work of Silverman and Kennedy (1987) can help us understand how the norms of traditional male–female relationships are disregarded by stranger offenders. For example, women typically have lots of men in their social circle. These relationships are governed by different behaviours and expectations, with transgressions leading to censure. As these relationships develop, they may include various negative (e.g., disagreements, arguments, violence, etc.) and/or positive (e.g., socialising, affection, intimacy, etc.) interactions. All things being equal, women will use these interactions and their associated opinions of these men to decide what kind of *'distance'* they wish to keep them at. Similar to Silverman and Kennedy (1987), we would expect spouse/lovers to be at the centre of a woman's social circle, followed by other men they like and who have a positive impact on their lives, such as family members and close friends. By contrast, men who women

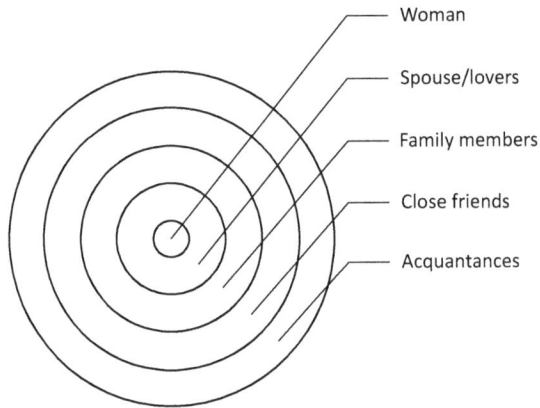

Figure 2.1 Hypothetical social circle

tolerate or dislike and who perhaps have a negative impact on their lives would typically be kept, as much as possible, on the periphery of their social circle (see Figure 2.1).

The key thing to understand here is that social circles are dynamic, and a man's position within a woman's social circle may change as their relationship and her opinion of him change. A man at the centre of a woman's social circle today may be relegated to the periphery tomorrow or even ejected from it altogether. Conversely, when a male stranger enters a woman's social circle she may evaluate him before deciding whether to allow him into her social circle, and/or how close she wants him to become. This decision may be made quickly, or it may take time for the woman to formulate her opinions of this male stranger. These social choices and the norms that underpin them are a fundamental feature of being an autonomous, thinking, feeling human being with our own needs, wants, and desires. However, whilst most men will abide by this social process, the male stranger intent on inflicting violence upon a woman will totally ignore it.

Canter *et al.* (2003) suggest that male-on-female stranger violence involves three sequential levels of violation: personal, physical, and sexual. When confronted by a male stranger intent on causing her harm, a woman faces a situation where none of the above social choices or norms are being observed or respected by him. Moreover, her right to decide to keep this man at a safe distance is totally ignored by him. The woman is not in the company of a man who is interested in taking time to get to know her and is mindful and respectful of her needs, wants, or desires. Rather, within a very short space of time, be it seconds, minutes, or hours after first encountering this male stranger, she finds herself facing the prospect of a personal, physical, and sexual violation and with little if any means of preventing it or influencing its outcome. This is the tactical disadvantage referred to by Scully (1994), and it illustrates why these assaults are so terrifying. But how the male stranger managed to break into a woman's social circle and come to be so close to her in the first place is the final consideration of this chapter. This will illustrate the available pathways that can lead some men into acts of stranger sexual violence.

Pathways to stranger violence

For stranger sexual violence to occur, a motivated offender must encounter a vulnerable victim in a suitable location. This simple idea from routine activity theory

(Cohen & Felson, 1979; Felson, 2017) helps us to consider how these two individuals came to be together at the same time and in the same location. To do this, we need to consider the scenarios in which men may encounter female strangers, how they may go about accessing female strangers, and the female stranger's intended role in the final encounter.

Scenarios for encountering strangers

Riedel (1993) suggests there are two types of stranger relationships, *'spontaneous'* and *'selective'*. Spontaneous relationships are unplanned, and each party can equally interact with the other. These encounters can occur in bars, at parties, or other places where people congregate, and conversations can involve trivial matters (e.g., the news or weather) or greetings and introductions. A woman approached by a male stranger in a bar may, for example, respond positively to his opening remarks or excuse herself to greet a fictitious friend if his advances are unwelcome. By contrast, selective relationships are one-sided and occur because one person correctly views the other as being approachable. Examples include people who work in shops, bars, or cafés, as they are routinely approached by strangers seeking their services. A man may, for example, attempt to ingratiate himself with a waitress who serves him, and she may accept or rebuff his advances. Riedel (1993) suggests these encounters can be exploited for deviant purposes or include confrontation. As shown in Table 2.1, exploitation may include lulling a woman into a false sense of security using a 'con' approach before attacking her, whilst confrontations may begin with a surprise or blitz attack.

Accessing female strangers

Whilst Riedel (1993) illustrates how men can meet female strangers in one of two scenarios, the work of MacCulloch *et al.* (1995) and Turvey (2014) helps us to understand how there are essentially three psychological pathways that men can follow to make this happen.

Premeditated precautionary pathway

This pathway is marked by premeditated violence coupled with precautions to help avoid detection. These men are aware they are going to attack someone beforehand,

Table 2.1 Methods of approach

The 'Con'	Offender engages his victim in an *'innocent'* conversation, e.g., offers of or requests for help. He may present as pleasant, friendly, or charming as his aim is to gain his victim's confidence and overcome any anxieties she may have. Once he feels this is achieved and he is in control, he attacks her.
Surprise Attack	Victim approached (perhaps from a hiding place) and with little or no warning, verbal threats and/or a weapon are used to subdue her. Victim may have been pre-selected, or the offender may not feel confident about using the 'con' approach or may not want to use a blitz approach.
Blitz Attack	Offender deploys immediate and serious violence, e.g., slaps, punches, blunt force with a weapon, strangulation, or suffocation. Victim has little or no opportunity to react as she is quickly subdued by the violence. This approach may indicate anger/hostility towards women.

Source: Adapted from Hazelwood and Burgess (2017)

and their assaults are driven by internal motivations (e.g., sexual fantasies), which they bring to the crime scene, along with weapons (e.g., hammers, knives, and bindings) to facilitate the attack and/or to help satisfy their subjective psychological needs. These men know the physical characteristics of their desired victim and have invested time searching in locations they themselves may not frequent, where they know these women can be found. They also know how to isolate their victims before the attack and the steps needed to reduce the chances of recognition and apprehension. These men therefore appear to have made a purposeful rational choice (Cornish & Clarke, 2014) to plan, seek out, and target female strangers to sexually assault.

Opportunistic convenience pathway

This pathway is marked by opportunistic, unpremeditated violence, carried out in a manner and location that indicate convenience. These men lack self-control, and their violence is not driven by internal motivation but triggered by situational events at the scene. These men, therefore, do not set out with violent intentions, but when faced with external circumstances which they consider provoking, they respond violently, especially if intoxicated, and they may improvise weapons obtained from the scene (e.g., stones, stockings, cutlery) to complete the assault. The opportunistic nature of these assaults means that victims are not specifically targeted. Rather, they are obtained due to opportunity and proximity, as the offender and victim both frequent the same locations, a factor which increases the chances of recognition and apprehension. It is during their routine activities (Cohen & Felson, 1979) that these men encounter female strangers, whom they subsequently decide to sexually assault.

Premeditated opportunist pathway

The final pathway, described by MacCulloch *et al.* (1995), is essentially a combination of, or at least draws key features from, the previous pathways. These men have intentions to commit violence, but the details of the attack, such as the victim, method, or location, are not predetermined. Rather, these men seek out opportunities to engage in sexual violence by walking around town, visiting bars, jogging in parks, or cruising in their cars. They may watch or follow women, contact them, or even strike up a conversation (i.e., the 'con' approach). If circumstances do not permit, violence will not occur, and they will return home disappointed but ready to try another day (for an example of this type of offender, see Greenall & Millington, 2021).

Victim's role

Having approached a female stranger in a spontaneous or selective manner after following one of the above pathways, Turvey (2014) suggests she may unknowingly become a man's primary or secondary target. Primary targets are of great importance to the offender, and accessing them will dictate the timing and location of the attack. Whilst premeditated precautionary offenders will travel to locations where their prior investigations suggest their preferred victims can be found (e.g., bars, parks, or student areas), opportunistic offenders will target women in their own immediate environment out of convenience. Secondary targets are of lesser importance to the offender, and accessing them will not dictate the timing or location of the attack, as their victimisation is due to their proximity to the primary target. Examples include a primary target's female friend who is also sexually assaulted or what Scully (1994) called *'added bonus'* rapes of an unexpected female occupant during a burglary.

Conclusion and implications for practice

Stranger sexual violence is comparatively rare, but criminal justice practitioners may still encounter these offences and the offenders responsible within their practice. The aim of this chapter has been to help criminal justice practitioners deal with these challenges by providing ideas upon which they can begin to formulate one or more hypotheses about the pre-crime phase (see Chapter 12) of a stranger sexual assault. Having considered the concept of stranger, this chapter has presented a working definition that criminal justice practitioners can apply. A crucial feature of stranger sexual violence this chapter has illustrated is how the offender disregards social norms and breaks into and through his victim's social circle to assault her. The way he achieves this, however, is not uniform, and criminal justice practitioners should give due consideration to the role the victim occupied before being assaulted and the pathway the offender followed to gain access to her.

Critical issues!

Although some ideas from the research have been presented about stranger violence and how strangers may gain access to potential victims, your job when next dealing with a case of stranger sexual violence is to keep an open mind. Use the ideas presented here to formulate hypotheses about how the offender you are investigating or working with sought out and succeeded in gaining access to his victim and how much effort or forethought he might have invested (or not) to achieve his aim. In the next chapter, we will draw upon some ideas from environmental criminology to explore this phase of the crime further.

3 A geographical perspective

The most objective and observable aspect of any crime is where it happens

(Canter, 2003, p. 6)

Introduction

In episode one of the hit TV series Breaking Bad, Jesse Pinkman explains to his former chemistry teacher and new partner in crime, Mr White, why they cannot manufacture Methamphetamine in Jesse's garage: *"this is my house; I don't shit where I eat"*. Their solution was to purchase a large campervan and drive out into the New Mexico countryside to conduct their criminal enterprise. Although a fictional story, the placing of some distance between one's home and the scene of one's criminal activity appears to be a sensible course of action aimed at reducing the chances of recognition and apprehension. Indeed, I can remember, as a child, the case of the Yorkshire Ripper, Peter Sutcliffe, and how he spread his attacks across large parts of Northern England (Kind, 2008). Even to a child's mind, the Yorkshire Ripper's actions appeared sensible. After all, if a man wants to kill women, then knowing that his actions will make him a national news story will surely mean he will do this as far away from home as possible, so no one will recognise him and report him to the police. However, my subsequent forensic work with offenders and a large body of research from the discipline of environmental criminology (Wortley & Townsley, 2017) show my childhood assumptions were wrong; offenders mostly carry out their offences close to where they live. Moreover, even the apparent sporadic locations of some offences, such as those of Peter Sutcliffe, are often related to other meaningful events within the offender's life. It is therefore crucial for every criminal justice practitioner to understand the geographical nature of stranger sexual violence.

Chapter aims

This chapter explores the geographical nature of criminal behaviour to enhance our understanding of how far some men travel to sexually assault adult female strangers. Additionally, this chapter aims to determine whether knowledge of the pre-offence journeys taken by offenders can assist our understanding of individual cases that we encounter within our practice. A key argument this chapter seeks to make is that unless we have a basic understanding of these factors, we will fail to develop a full understanding of the offences committed by offenders we encounter in our practice. To begin this process, we must return to the final section of Chapter 2.

DOI: 10.4324/9781003217763-4

Routine activity theory and the *'sexual assault triangle'*

As mentioned in Chapter 2, routine activity theory suggests that acts of interpersonal violence can occur when a motivated offender encounters a vulnerable victim in a suitable location (Cohen & Felson, 1979; Felson, 2017). In the context of stranger sexual violence, the motivated offender relates to a man who is prepared to sexually assault a female stranger, his motivations for doing this (see Chapter 4), his method of approach (see Chapter 2), and his familiarity with the area. The victim is a female stranger who fits the offender's desired victim profile and who is perceived by him as being vulnerable to being sexually assaulted and having a limited capacity to resist his assault. The location is made suitable due to the absence of factors that may dissuade the offender from assaulting his victim, such as an isolated or quiet area (e.g., a public park or a lonely pathway, alleyway, or street) with an absence of bystanders and/or surveillance. These three components come together in what is variously called the *'crime triangle'*, the *'problem analysis triangle'*, or more specifically for our purposes, the *'sexual assault triangle'* (see Figure 3.1). The idea that violence, including sexual violence, can only occur when all three components of the triangle are present has informed the concept of crime prevention. Just as the fire triangle we encounter in mandatory fire training shows that heat, fuel, and oxygen are required for a fire to occur, and the removal of one of them (e.g., oxygen with a fire extinguisher) kills the fire, addressing one of the three components within Figure 3.1 helps to prevent sexual violence (see https://popcenter.asu.edu/#).

Although there are several theories that seek to explain sexual violence (see Ward *et al.*, 2006), within my forensic/clinical practice, I have found that routine activity theory provides a useful framework for exploring how an offender and victim came to be in the same place at the same time and, where necessary, to explore the suitability of the location for the purposes of committing the offence in question. For an example of how this might work in your practice, see if the reflective exercise in Box 3.1 can help you think about the contexts and circumstances that may lead to acts of stranger sexually violence.

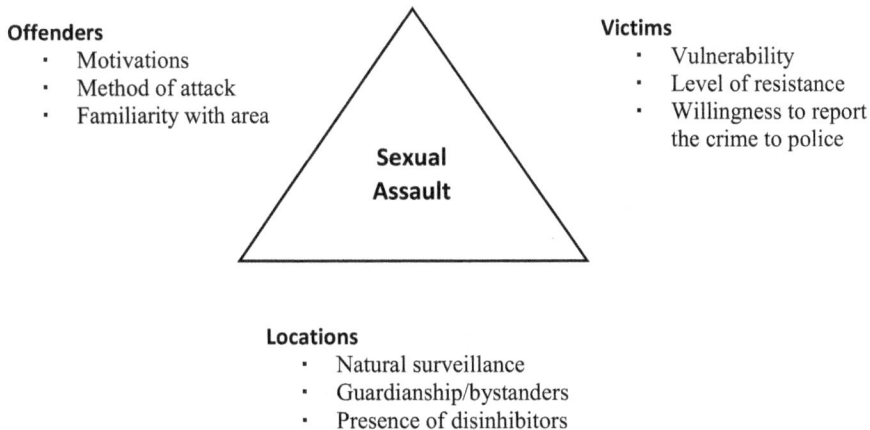

Offenders
- Motivations
- Method of attack
- Familiarity with area

Sexual Assault

Victims
- Vulnerability
- Level of resistance
- Willingness to report the crime to police

Locations
- Natural surveillance
- Guardianship/bystanders
- Presence of disinhibitors

Figure 3.1 Sexual assault triangle

Source: Adapted from Dedel, 2011 with permission from and thanks to Michael S. Scott, Clinical Director, https://popcenter.asu.edu/#

Box 3.1   Routine activity theory: Reflective exercise

When working with men with histories of sexual violence, I have found the challenge of trying to understand their offences can be aided by reflecting on our own experiences. Doing this can help us to ask some searching questions in our quest to understand the sexually violent actions of others.

Male readers

How many times have you been in a lonely, quiet, or isolated location, perhaps whilst walking your dog, riding your bike, or walking home from a bar at night, and found yourself in the proximity of an attractive woman, walking alone along the same path or quiet street? Given that two sides of the sexual offence triangle were present (vulnerable victim and suitable location), you had the perfect opportunity to sexually assault this woman, so why didn't you? Why didn't you drop your trousers and expose your erect penis to her (Chapter 8), sexually assault or rape her (Chapter 9), and perhaps to protect your identity, strangle her and hide her dead body (Chapter 10)?

Female readers

How many times have you found yourselves walking alone down a lonely, quiet path or street, only to discover a male stranger walking behind you? Did the prospect of being sexually assaulted cross your mind? Did you experience the fear that Scully (1994) and others have written about? Did you formulate a plan for what you would do if he got too close and started to make you feel uncomfortable? Again, with two sides of the sexual offence triangle present (vulnerable victim and suitable location), why didn't that male stranger sexually assault you in any of the ways asked of male readers above, when he had the perfect opportunity?

Key questions

1 Why do the vast majority of the above encounters end without incident?
2 Why is it that on some occasions, some men – *perhaps the man responsible for a sexual assault you are investigating as a police officer or an offender you are assessing as a criminal justice practitioner* – take advantage of similar opportunities and sexually assault women?

When reflecting on the encounters we experience in our own lives, the answer to question one might simply be that there was an absence of a motivated offender. Be that so, use that answer as a basis for considering possible answers to question two. Although some possible answers will be presented later in this book, for now, the hope is that this exercise illustrates how routine activity theory can help you to consider, investigate, and explore the actions of stranger sexual offenders. Moreover, these questions are designed to help you think about stranger sexual violence and stranger sexual offenders in a different way, i.e., by turning the age-old question about sexual violence from the traditional *'why do men do it?'* to *'why don't more men do it?'* And more importantly, for your own practice, consider the key question that lies at the heart of this book:

> Why and how did this man, commit this sexual offence, against this female stranger, at this time, and in this location?

Within the sexual assault triangle, location may appear as a passive component, as the offender and victim may encounter each other there by chance. Notwithstanding this, as the opening quote of this chapter suggests, the location is of great potential importance. For example, once a crime has occurred, the location becomes the *crime scene*. The importance of this is recognised within criminal investigations, as a structured forensic crime scene investigation can unearth crucial evidence about the offence and the offender (Osterburg *et al.*, 2019). However, the offence location can also aid a psychological understanding of the offence, as it represents a choice – *however fleeting* – made by the offender to commit a sexual offence there. For example, if a man sexually assaults a female stranger in an isolated location, one hypothesis could be that he gave some prior consideration to the suitability of that location in relation to the availability of suitable victims and the absence of bystanders (i.e., people or CCTV cameras) who may either witness the assault and/or intervene to prevent or terminate it. Alternatively, if a man sexually assaults female strangers in locations that do not appear suitable because they are neither isolated nor devoid of bystanders and/or surveillance, what might that tell us about his attitudes, beliefs, motivations, or thought processes, either at the material time or prior to the assaults? These questions are not the preserve of behavioural science experts called in to help the police (Bartol & Bartol, 2013). Rather, they can be asked by every criminal justice practitioner when trying to understand the actions of a stranger sexual offender they are seeking or working with. This point will become clearer as we progress through this chapter. Beforehand, however, we need to consider a simple, obvious, but important fact: before the offender can sexually assault a female stranger, he needs to arrive at and have travelled to the suitable location. It is this *'journey-to-crime'* (JTC) that we will now explore.

Journey-to-crime (JTC)

Within the ideas of routine activity theory, there is a concept alluded to in Chapter 2 that is fundamental to our understanding of violent crime. Namely, prior to sexually assaulting a female stranger, in many cases, the motivated offender would have travelled (on foot or by another means) from one place (e.g., his home, place of work, or recreation) to the suitable location where he selectively or spontaneously encounters and then assaults his victim. This journey may have been intentional (i.e., premeditated/precautionary) or not (i.e., opportunistic/convenience), but a journey, however long or short, would have occurred. The examination of JTCs undertaken by offenders has a long history within environmental criminology (Wortley & Townsley, 2017) and informs the contemporary criminal investigative strategy popularly known as *'geographic profiling'* (see, among others, Canter, 2003; Canter & Youngs, 2008a, 2008b; Rossmo, 1997, 2000; Rossmo &

Rombouts, 2017; Velarde, 2014). An important point to bear in mind is that rather than being a single unified entity, some researchers (e.g., Rengert, 2004) suggest the JTC comprises various elements, and it is important to recognise that each element is open to individual or situational influence.

- *Starting point:* This may be the offender's home, place of employment, worship, recreation, etc.
- *Direction of travel:* This may be influenced by the offender's routine activities (e.g., journey to work or to a place of recreation, etc.) or by a desire to visit locations where criminal opportunities may be found. For example, a burglar's direction of travel may be influenced by the expected availability of opportunities in places such as residential dwellings on specific housing estates or commercial properties in industrial areas or city centres (Putwain, 2012). For stranger sexual offenders, their directions of travel may be influenced by a desire to frequent places where women are found, either in numbers (e.g., bars or clubs, etc.) or in isolation (e.g., parks or quiet streets at night).
- *Location:* This may include single or multiple sites. Amir (1971), for example, referred to three potential sites: (1) the victim-offender meeting place; (2) the location of the assault; (3) the place where the offender and victim depart. In cases of sexual homicide, a fourth site may be utilised to dispose of the body (see Lundrigan & Canter, 2001a, 2001b).
- *Distance travelled:* It may be assumed that this relates to the distance between the offender's home and the offence location, which on some occasions will be correct. However, given that the location can include multiple sites and the JTC may not have originated from the offender's home, this assumption may not always be correct.

Whilst recognising the JTC has several elements, each open to potential influence, to further understand the JTCs that may be undertaken by stranger sexual offenders, we need to explore some key concepts in environmental criminology.

Key concepts in environmental criminology

Along with the ideas of offenders following one of the three pathways to access female strangers presented in Chapter 2, our understanding of the JTCs undertaken by stranger sexual offenders can be aided by considering some key concepts in environmental criminology. For example, from our everyday travels to and from work, shopping, recreational activities, etc., we develop knowledge of the routes taken and the general characteristics of the places we visit. These *'mental maps'* become cognitive representations of our environment and how we view and interact with it. Within our routine activities, the places we are familiar with and the routes we travel along and between them become our *'activity spaces'*. In addition to familiar locations, less familiar locations comprise our *'awareness space'*. This, however, is not a static process. If, for example, we start a new job located in another part of town or another city, then our travels to and from that new location will make us familiar with a new set of routes and locations. Over time, these will become incorporated into a broader mental map and a larger activity and awareness space. When a person decides to offend, they search through their awareness space for suitable criminal opportunities, the distribution of which within the environment is the *'target backcloth'* (Brantingham *et al.*, 2017; Velarde, 2014).

As mentioned in Chapter 2, for some offenders, the search through their awareness space for adult women to sexually assault may require minimal effort and result in opportunistic (unpremeditated) offending out of convenience. Others who are more precautionary may invest time and effort to find suitable female strangers before subjecting them to (premeditated) acts of sexual violence. However, whilst criminal opportunities may theoretically be distributed throughout an individual's environment, other factors relating to the offender, the victim, and circumstances need to be considered to understand the reality of individual cases. For example, as illustrated in cases such as Steve Wright, who was dubbed the *'Ipswich Ripper'* in 2006, if a man wants to (selectively) seek out prostitutes to engage in (premeditated/precautionary) sexual/physical violence up to and including murder, he will head for a red-light district, as he knows that is where these women are most likely to be found. Similarly, as illustrated in cases such as Pawel Relowicz, who raped and murdered student Libby Squire in Hull in 2019, if a man wants to (spontaneously) meet and pick up young, intoxicated women with a view to having (premeditated-opportunistic) sex with them, by force, if necessary, he will head for bars, clubs, or student areas of town, as that is where these women are more likely to be found. Alternatively, an intoxicated man walking home alone late in the evening after socialising with friends may (spontaneously) meet a lone woman, decide in an instant to have (opportunistic) sex with her out of convenience, and only use sufficient force to achieve his aim. Along with these individual factors, however, the distribution of offending is, in many cases, influenced by two more key concepts from environmental criminology, namely distance-decay and the buffer-zone.

Distance-decay

The concept of distance-decay suggests that as the distance from an offender's home increases, the chances of them offending decrease. Brantingham and Brantingham (1981) explain this by suggesting it takes time, money, and effort to travel distances and limitations in any of these factors, increasing the advantages of offending in more familiar locations closer to home. Moreover, whilst travelling from home, closer locations and the criminal opportunities they afford are encountered more frequently, and offenders will become more familiar with them compared to criminal opportunities in locations further afield. Additionally, factors such as routine activities, interpersonal networks, suitable triggers, and individual needs may influence criminal decision making (Brantingham *et al.*, 2017). So just as non-offenders generally favour travelling short distances to engage in non-criminal activities (e.g., employment, shopping, and recreation), offenders generally opt for the path of least resistance (Zipf, 1950) and travel shorter distances to offend.

So, whilst Jesse Pinkman's and Mr White's idea of placing some distance between one's home and the scene of one's criminal activity may appear to be a sensible course of action aimed at reducing the chances of recognition and apprehension, research supports the distance-decay hypothesis by finding this phenomenon applying to various types of crimes. These include criminal actions as diverse as burglary (e.g., Hammond & Youngs, 2011), robbery (e.g., Rhodes & Conly, 1981), and body disposal site location within serial homicide (e.g., Lundrigan & Canter, 2001b). Of particular relevance to our exploration and understanding of stranger sexual violence is the research by Beauregard *et al.* (2005). They reviewed a body of research spanning 1965–2000 and found the distance-decay hypothesis applies to sexual offenders, as most offences were committed relatively close to the offender's home. For example, in many studies reviewed by Beauregard *et al.* (2005), large numbers of offenders engaged in sexual violence within a mile or two or just a few blocks from their home. The consistency of these findings is evidenced by their replication in more recent studies into the geographic nature of sexual violence (e.g., Dern *et al.*, 2005; Lundrigan & Czarnomski, 2006; Rossmo, 2018; Rossmo *et al.*, 2004; Van Patten & Delhauer, 2007).

Buffer-zone

Whilst offending closer to home is less costly in terms of expenditure of personal resources, it coincides with an increased risk of recognition and detection as offenders are more likely to be known in such locations. To mitigate this risk, some offenders maintain an area or *'buffer-zone'* around their home where offending becomes less likely (Brantingham & Brantingham, 1981; Velarde, 2014). In many cases, according to Bartol and Bartol (2013), the buffer-zone may only be as little as a quarter of a mile around an offender's home. Canter and Larkin (1993) reported a similar finding in their study of serial stranger rapists, as their buffer-zone was at least 0.61 miles from home. However, Snook *et al.* (2005) suggest the buffer-zone can either indicate the average distance between an offender's home and their crime scenes or the distance between the offenders home and the scene of their closest crime. Regardless of how it is conceived, there appears to be one or two findings of note within the research in relation to the buffer-zone:

1   Contrary to the idea of a buffer-zone, in some cases, the smallest JTC unit of distance is the single most popular in terms of how many offences occur within that distance. For example, Rhodes and Conly (1981) found the 0–0.5 mile JTC unit of distance was the single most popular among robbers, burglars, and rapists. My research into stranger sexual homicide found the same result (Greenall, 2018).
2   In support of the idea of a buffer-zone, large percentages of offences occur beyond the smallest JTC unit of distance, and the percentages vary between offence types. For example, Rhodes and Conly (1981) found almost 50% of rapes, 70% of burglaries, and 75% of robberies occurred beyond the 0–0.5 mile JTC unit of distance. Again, my research into stranger sexual homicide concurs with this, as 69% occurred beyond the 0–0.5 mile JTC unit of distance (Greenall, 2018).

Whilst the concepts of distance decay and buffer-zone suggest that stranger sexual offences will mostly occur close to, but not too close to, the offender's home, this is not so for all sexual offenders. Beauregard *et al.* (2005), for example, found some sexual offenders travel several miles from home before offending, a finding supported by subsequent studies (e.g., Dern *et al.*, 2005; Lundrigan & Czarnomski, 2006; Martineau & Beauregard, 2016; Rossmo *et al.*, 2004; Van Patten & Delhauer, 2007), including my own into stranger sexual homicide (Greenall, 2018). This leads to consideration of another key concept in environmental criminology, namely the classification of pre-crime travelling patterns.

Pre-crime travelling patterns

At the end of Chapter 2, consideration was given to three potential pathways that sexual offenders may follow to access female strangers. Along with highlighting factors such as premeditation and impulsivity, these pathways suggest the JTCs taken by stranger sexual offenders may differ. Some offenders, for example, will set off with the intent of sexually assaulting a female stranger. The length and direction of their JTC will depend on where they live vis-à-vis suitable locations where female strangers can be found (e.g., bars, clubs, red-light areas, and public parks). By contrast, other offenders may not set off with criminal intent, but a chain of events leads them to (opportunistically) sexually assault a female stranger. Unlike the premeditated offenders whose JTCs originated from home, the JTCs of opportunistic offenders may originate from a location that they originally and innocently travelled to (e.g., bars, clubs, red-light areas, and public parks). The idea of there being different types of JTC undertaken by offenders has been explored and developed by several researchers, as illustrated by the following examples.

Canter's marauders and commuters classification

One of the most popular JTC classifications is Canter's marauder/commuter hypothesis (Canter & Gregory, 1994; Canter & Larkin, 1993). This views the offender's home as being central to his criminal activities, and two JTC patterns are proposed. The marauder travels from home to offend and returns home afterwards. Marauders travel in different directions from their homes to offend on different occasions. This led to what is called the *'circle hypothesis'* which involves identifying the two offences in a series that are furthest apart from each other, and the distance between them becomes the diameter a of a circle. In their studies of serial stranger rapists, Canter and colleagues (i.e., Canter & Gregory, 1994; Canter & Larkin, 1993) found that 87% of their sample lived within that circle. This suggests an overlap exists between the offenders' home and criminal ranges and supports the marauder and circle hypotheses. However, the finding that not all serial stranger rapists were marauders supports the alternative commuter hypothesis. In contrast to marauders, commuters travel from their homes to areas outside of their locality to offend. The reason for such journeys may relate to factors such as employment or wanting to find suitable victims if none are available within the offender's locality.

Rossmo's hunting typology

Another popular classification is Rossmo's hunting typology (Rossmo, 1997, 2000). This differentiates victim search methods between those who offend locally (i.e., hunter) and those who travel (i.e., poacher), and between those who opportunistically offend (i.e., trollers) and those who plan their offences (i.e., trappers). We can see similarities here with Canter's typology, as there appear to be overlaps between the marauder/hunter and the commuter/poacher types. Additionally, there are further similarities with some of the pathways presented at the end of Chapter 2, with overlaps between the trollers/opportunistic convenience offenders and the trappers/premeditated precautionary offenders. Rossmo also differentiated between different victim attack methods, such as those who attack their victim upon encountering them (i.e., raptor), those who follow their victim upon encountering them and then attack (i.e., stalker), and those who entice their victim into a location before attacking them (i.e., ambusher). Once again, we can see similarities here, but this time with the methods of approach in Chapter 2 (Table 2.1). The raptor, for example, deploys a blitz attack, the stalker a surprise attack, and the ambusher a con approach.

Geographical profiles

The idea of there being different types of JTC undertaken by offenders leads to a key question: can we formulate hypotheses about an unknown sexual offender's JTC based on reported aspects of him or his offence? Some researchers suggest the answer is yes. For example, Canter and Gregory (1994) found that among serial stranger rapists, age at arrest (older offenders), ethnicity (white offenders), offence location (outside attackers), and offence timing (weekends) were associated with longer JTCs. Davies and Dale (1995) also found that younger stranger rapists generally offend closer to home. These ideas were taken further by researchers in Canada, who suggested that sexual offenders are either geographically mobile or stable.

Beauregard's geographically mobile/stable classification

Building on the above and other studies, Beauregard *et al.* (2005) suggest the JTCs undertaken by sexual offenders can essentially be divided into two types: geographically mobile or geographically stable. These types do not simply describe victim search and attack methods like Canter's and Rossmo's above; rather, they also include personal characteristics of the offender. For example, geographically mobile offenders are described as:

> generally older, of above average intelligence, socially competent and with no criminal career or with one that reflects sexually related offenses. His offenses are planned, sophisticated and a great amount of time is invested in the pursuit of his fantasies. The geographically mobile offender tends to target a stranger victim and considerable precautions are taken against being caught. The crime scene reflects overall control with no weapon or evidence found. Spatially, this offender is mobile, operating outside his home range or even his home city. He may transport the victim's body to hide it and may travel throughout his criminal career to better avoid apprehension.
>
> (Beauregard *et al.*, 2005, p. 595)

By contrast, geographically stable offenders are described as being:

> younger, socially immature, of an average intelligence and is characterized by psychopathic personality traits. He usually lives alone and has a criminal career indicating his antisocial nature. His offenses are spontaneous, and he most often encounters his victims, who are usually known, during his routine activities. His crimes are unsophisticated and exhibit excessive force. The crime scene is most often random and sloppy, with the weapon or physical evidence present. The geographically stable offender commits his crimes over a smaller area and tends to live and/ or work near the crime scene. In most cases, the victim's body will be left at the death scene.
>
> (Beauregard *et al.*, 2005, pp. 595–597)

Although JTC research provides some insight into their potential pre-crime travelling patterns, two key points should be borne in mind. First, when considering the research into pre-offence travelling patterns, the idea is not to become too concerned with labels or try to classify an offender into one type or another. Rather, these ideas are useful to aid our understanding of the different types of JTCs that stranger sexual offenders may embark upon and complete, and how much thought and effort they may have invested before they encountered and sexually assaulted a female stranger. Second, we must not ignore what we may call the *'journey to victimisation'* (JTV) undertaken by victims. As Brantingham *et al.* (2017) argue, because the spatiotemporal movement patterns of victims are similar to those undertaken by offenders, just as offenders mostly offend near their own activity space, victims are frequently victimised near their own activity space. This point was supported by Amir (1971), who found that in the majority of rapes, the offenders lived in the same vicinity (i.e., five city blocks) as their victims and the location of the offence. Moreover, as we will see in more detail in Chapter 10, research into sexual homicide has found victims engaged in a range of normal routine activities prior to being attacked (Beauregard & Martineau, 2013). So, although this chapter has focused on the movements of offenders, as suggested in the exercise in Box 3.1, sometimes it is useful to consider the movements of victims to understand how they came to be a part of the sexual assault triangle.

Conclusion and implications for practice

Given that location *is* the most objective and observable aspect of any crime (Canter, 2003), the location or crime scene (or, in the case of a homicide, the body disposal site) becomes an anchor point for the consideration of the possible home area of a stranger sexual offender and the JTC travelled by him before he encountered and assaulted his victim. Contrary to what common sense might tell us, men who sexually assault female strangers can be expected to be very similar to other offenders when it comes to their pre-crime JTCs, as they will mostly offend close to their homes. On other occasions, however, the location of their offences may be associated with other anchor points, such as their place of employment or recreation, and so their homes may be further away. Consideration of the JTC and pre-crime travelling patterns draws upon some important concepts from environmental criminology, which can help criminal justice practitioners to consider how a motivated offender encountered a vulnerable victim in what he considered to be a suitable location to commit a sexual assault. These ideas can be used alongside the three pathways to access female strangers presented in Chapter 2 to formulate hypotheses about how a stranger sexual offender was able to gain access to his victim to carry out his sexual assault.

Critical issues

Just because the research tells us that most sexual offenders offend close to their home, it does not mean the next stranger sexual offender you encounter in your practice will have done so. In all probability, he may well have done so, but you need to keep an open mind and use the ideas presented in this chapter to formulate hypotheses about how and why the offender (and victim) came to be in that location at that time of day and how much effort or forethought he might have invested (or not) in order to have been there. In the next chapter, we will draw upon some ideas from clinical and investigative practice to help us understand the motivational and behavioural dynamics that can underpin individual acts of stranger sexual violence and which may have driven the offender to make the JTC in the first place.

4 The classification of sexual violence

One of the most basic observations one can make regarding men who rape is that not all such offenders are alike

(Groth & Birnbaum, 1979, p. 12)

Introduction

If one quote captures a key problem encountered when working with sexual offenders, it is the one above. Groth and colleagues realised from their clinical work that men with histories of sexual violence, even those who have committed the same kind of sexual offence, present as a diverse (or heterogeneous) group. Later, Grubin and Kennedy (1991) argued that sex offender heterogeneity was a fundamental problem that hinders our understanding of sexual violence, and without a reliable, practical, and valid classification system, it would be impossible to make any significant advances in the areas of understanding causality, individual prognosis (i.e., future risk), and treatment. Although these observations refer to forensic/clinical practice, the problem of sex offender heterogeneity is relevant to policing too, given their direct involvement in the investigation of sexual offences (National Policing Improvement Agency, 2010) and the community risk management of sexual offenders (National Police Chief's Council, 2017; Thomas, 2016). In response to these problems, various classification schemes have been developed. These have enhanced our understanding of sexual violence by illustrating the diverse motivational and interpersonal dynamics that underpin these crimes.

Chapter aims

This chapter introduces the problem of sex offender heterogeneity and how it has been tackled by various classification schemes. Although these schemes have enhanced our understanding in this area, this chapter is _not_ encouraging you to classify every sexual offender you encounter but to apply the ideas presented to individual cases within your practice. This is not only because we may have insufficient information to classify an offender, but perhaps, more importantly, when attempting to classify human behaviour, people do not always fit nicely into predetermined categories, and overlaps may occur.

Sex offender heterogeneity

The problem of sex offender heterogeneity is illustrated in Figure 4.1. This shows how the label _'sexual offender'_ includes those who target different victim types based on their age,

DOI: 10.4324/9781003217763-5

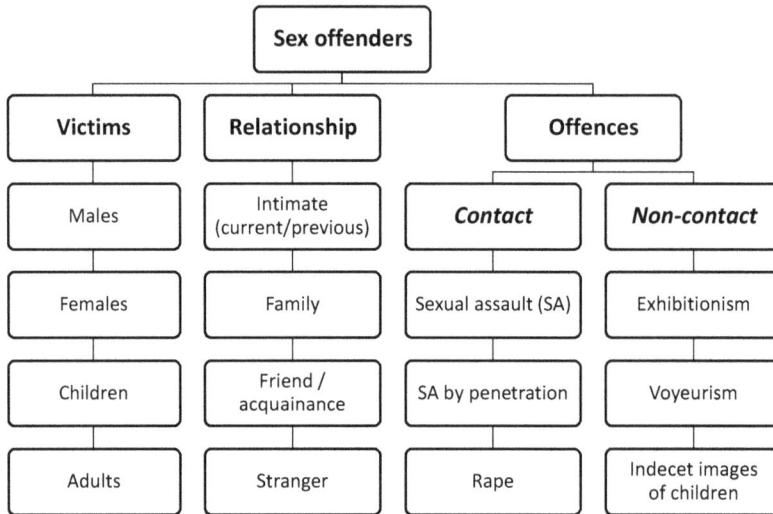

Figure 4.1 Sex offender heterogeneity

gender, and pre-existing relationship with their assailant. These factors are not always fixed, as sexual offenders can target males, females, or both; they can target children, adults, or both; and they can target victims they know and those they do not know. Differences also exist in relation to the type of sexual offences committed, as they can include contact or non-contact, penetrable or non-penetrable sexual acts, and/or any combination thereof. Additionally, whilst some sexual offenders may commit just one sexual offence, others may commit multiple sexual offences against different victims at different times and in different locations. An example of a repeat (serial) sexual offender was the London *'black cab rapist'* John Warboys, who drugged, raped, and assaulted numerous women in the early 2000s and whose potential release in 2018 caused much concern (The Psychologist, 2018a, 2018b). Along with these *'between group'* differences, as alluded to by Groth and colleagues above, *'within-group'* differences exist among the same type of sexual offender. Indeed, as we will see in later chapters, sex offender heterogeneity exists even among offenders who target female strangers, hence the need for this book!

Practical implications

The problem of sexual offender heterogeneity has practical implications. For example, almost two decades after Grubin and Kennedy (1991) highlighted this problem, Helfgott (2008) raised similar concerns. Sex offender heterogeneity, Helfgott (2008) argued, has made it difficult to draw conclusions necessary to deal with such offenders, as criminal investigations, correctional supervision, and treatment all depend on a clear understanding of who sexual offenders are, the nature of their offending, the factors and developmental pathways that shape their behaviour, and the propensity for future offending. The question of who sexual offenders are is noteworthy when viewed from a criminological perspective, because heterogeneity exists here too. For example, whilst some sexual offenders may only commit sexual offences and thereby be regarded as *'specialist offenders'*, others engage in various types of crimes and are regarded as *'generalist offenders'*

(Soothill *et al.*, 2000). The criminological diversity of men with histories of sexual violence means this criminally diverse group of offenders are known by the one thing they have in common, i.e., they have committed a sexual offence. In some cases, such as when police are investigating a stranger sexual assault, this point is crucial because, whilst they may reasonably conclude they are seeking a sexual offender, they may equally be seeking someone with a history of violence, burglary, theft, arson, criminal damage, and so on. Indeed, given the nature of criminal diversity among sexual offenders (Harris *et al.*, 2009), it is possible for the unknown sexual offender the police are seeking to have committed a non-sexual offence either before or after they committed the sexual offence in question. Similarly, prison officers based on a wing for sexual offenders or other forensic/clinical practitioners facilitating an intervention for sexual offenders within a secure or community setting will almost certainly be working with a criminally diverse group of offenders (e.g., see Beech *et al.*, 2005a). And again, some of them may have committed non-sexual offences before or after their sexual index offence.

Theoretical implications

The problem of sexual offender heterogeneity also has theoretical implications. For example, whilst several theories seek to explain sexual violence (see Ward *et al.*, 2006), how can any single theory explain the unlawful sexual conduct of such a diverse group of people? Indeed, just as Wilson (2012) argued that the complexity and diversity of murder make the idea of one grand explanatory theory illogical, the complexity and diversity of sexual violence and sexual offenders make the idea of one grand explanatory theory equally illogical. If that is so, how can we make sense of and understand acts of sexual violence and sexual offenders? One way the behavioural sciences have addressed this issue has been through the classification of criminal behaviour.

Classification of criminal behaviour

Classification is a means by which scientists make sense of the world, as it helps to illustrate the diversity of their subject material (e.g., animals, plans, and chemicals). Within the social sciences, classification seeks to identify homogeneous sub-groups among a heterogeneous sample and can be driven by pragmatism, theory, clinical opinion, or statistical analysis (Blackburn, 1993). Within the field of mental health, for example, classification systems such as DSM-5-TR (American Psychiatric Association, 2022) and ICD-11 (World Health Organization, 2022) classify a range of mental disorders and provide criteria to aid diagnosis, examples of which will be explored in later chapters. Similarly, within the field of criminology, the crime classification manual (Ressler *et al.*, 1992) differentiates offences into homicide, arson, rape, and sexual assault and provides offence descriptions to aid classification. Building on these ideas, a range of crimes have been classified into more homogeneous sub-groups (e.g., homicide – Brookman, 2005; arson – Canter & Fritzon, 1998; child abduction – Erikson & Friendship, 2002; parricide – Heide, 1992; and stalking – Sheridan & Boon, 2002) to aid our understanding of them.

In relation to sexual violence, statutes such as the Sexual Offences Act 2003 in England (and similar legislation in other countries) classify different types of sexual offences with labels such as exhibitionist, voyeur, and rapist. However, these labels have little investigative or clinical utility (see Beech, 2010). Consequently, our understanding of stranger sexual violence can be assisted by consideration of three key factors:

1 The role and function of physical violence within sexual offences,
2 The different motives for committing sexual offences,
3 The different behaviours exhibited by sexual offenders during their sexual assaults.

The role and function of physical violence

Research suggests that sexual violence is often accompanied by physical violence (Feist *et al.*, 2007; Stripe, 2021), including assaults by strangers (Astion, 2008; Jones *et al.*, 2004). Physical violence involves attempts to gain victim compliance by causing physical harm or fear of physical harm, using tactics such as threats to kill, the administration of noxious or stupefying agents, threats with or use of weapons, physical confinement, or severe physical assault (Boer *et al.*, 2017; Hart *et al.*, 2022). Within acts of sexual violence therefore, physical violence is not a single, unified entity, as it can have different manifestations and serve different purposes. A useful way to understand the role and function of physical violence is to consider the instrumental and expressive nature of the violence used by the offender. Originally proposed by Feshbach (1964), this classification is based on the goal(s) or reward(s) the offender anticipates from his use of physical violence.

Instrumental violence

Instrumental violence is used to achieve non-aggressive goals and involves hitting the victim to accomplish them. Examples include acquisitive offending, where only sufficient force is used to steal from an unwilling victim, or using sufficient violence during a violent confrontation to defend oneself. In cases of sexual violence, instrumental violence would be evidenced by the fact that the offender only used sufficient force to overcome victim resistance to complete the assault. A man may, for example, verbally threaten a woman; he may threaten her with a knife but not use it; he may slap her; or he may hold her down whilst kissing her or having sexual intercourse. The key point here is that whilst the woman may sustain scratches, cuts, or bruises, these will be minor injuries that only warrant limited if any medical attention (e.g., see Jones *et al.*, 2004).

Expressive violence

Expressive violence is used to cause injury to the victim, as the aim is not simply to *hit* them but to *hurt* them (Feshbach, 1964). Examples include assaults with high levels of violence resulting in serious injury (e.g., grievous bodily harm) or death. In cases of sexual violence, expressive violence would be evidenced by the fact that the attacker used a high level of violence over and above that required to overcome victim resistance, which resulted in serious injury or death. A man may, for example, not simply threaten but use a weapon; he may kick and punch the woman, leave her fearing for her life, and use unpleasant and derogatory profanity (e.g., bitch, slag, and whore). Two key notable factors here are: first, if they survive, victims will be left with serious physical injuries that warrant medical attention; and second, expressive violence is generally accompanied by high levels of emotional arousal (e.g., anger) and negative views (e.g., hatred) of the victim (Meloy, 2006).

Remembering the pathways to stranger violence in Chapter 2, we can think about how different types of violence may be used by such offenders. For example, a premediated precautionary offender may only use sufficient violence to obtain victim compliance to complete a sexual assault, or he may take weapons with him to inflict serious expressive violence as part of a predetermined offence script aimed at satisfying various psychological needs. Similarly, an opportunistic convenience offender may also only use sufficient violence to obtain victim compliance to complete an opportunistic sexual assault, or he may respond with expressive violence, perhaps with weapons obtained at the scene, if the victim responds in an unexpectedly negative way. The benefit of exploring the nature of physical violence within a sexual assault is that it can help us unlock an important feature of the crime, namely the motive that drove the offender to commit the sexual offence in the first place.

Motivational differences within sexual violence

In simple terms, motive relates to a reason for doing something. Within forensic/clinical practice, motivators make violence an attractive or rewarding option for the offender (Douglas *et al.*, 2013a). Examples include the expression of negative emotions such as anger or satisfying various sexual needs. Motive is an important consideration in the process of assessing and formulating sexual violence risk and is described as a *'driver'* within the 3Ds – *drivers, disinhibitors,* and *destabilisers* – formulation model (see Chapter 11). Within the realm of criminal investigations, motive has long been regarded as a key investigative question that needs answering (Adhami & Browne, 1996) and a main line of enquiry (Cook, 2019) that senior investigating officers want information on from behavioural scientists helping with their enquiries (Cole & Brown, 2011). The importance of motive is such that without an understanding of it, we will have no idea what rewards the offender was seeking by offending, what drove him to offend, and under what circumstances, if any, he may re-offend in the future (Copson *et al.*, 1997). An excellent starting place considering the possible motivational differences within sexual violence is to explore the motivational drives that can underpin such offences. Here, the work of Schlesinger (2004a, 2004b) is useful as his motivational spectrum illustrates how violence, be it physical or sexual, can be motivated by external or internal drives.

Schlesinger's motivational spectrum

Schlesinger's starting point is that the crime itself forms the basis of criminal classification because *"what offenders do …[as opposed to what they say]… is most important in understanding the motivational dynamics of their behavior"* (2004a, p. 196). Essentially, when seeking to understand criminal motivation, crime scene actions speak louder than post-conviction words. Schlesinger's (2004a, 2004b) motivational spectrum helps us to understand how violence can be motivated by external (social) or internal (psychological) drives. Of note, however, external/internal drives are best viewed as being almost mutually exclusive. So, violence driven by external factors has low levels of internal drive, and vice versa. For example, as shown in Table 4.1, environmentally driven violence has the highest level of external drive and the lowest level of internal drive, whilst compulsive

Table 4.1 Motivational spectrum

Driver	Motivation	Offence details
External	Environmental	Occur in a social context, e.g., rapes during wars, gang rapes, or a man being encouraged to rape by his friends.
	Situational	Behavioural reactions to stressful circumstances, e.g., sexual violence, occur in the context of an argument or dispute, perhaps at the end of an evening consuming alcohol, the man expects sex, but the woman refuses, so he rapes her.
	Impulsive	Usually unplanned and part of a general antisocial lifestyle, e.g., a man unexpectedly encountering a lone woman at night whilst walking home, and he commits an opportunistic sexual assault – the classic scenario feared by many women.
	Catathymic	Usually unprovoked as the offender's thinking changes because of emotionally charged inner conflicts over sexual inadequacy, e.g., sexual violence occurs in response to a perceived slight or other incident which triggers the assault and resolves his inner emotional conflict.
Internal	Compulsive	Compelling and having a high likelihood of repetition, e.g., sexual/physical violence, is gratifying to the offender and may include deviant sexual acts and/or satisfy other psychological needs, such as anger or misogyny.

violence has the highest level of internal drive and the lowest level of external drive. It was the recognition that sexual violence can be driven by various factors that inspired the development of clinical classification schemes, two of the most important we shall now consider.

Clinical classifications

Clinical classification schemes are essentially attempts by clinical practitioners and/or researchers to identify the differing motivations for committing the same type of crime. The process relies on knowledge of the offence '*and*' the offender, and the idea is that the identification of the motive will lead to an understanding of potential therapeutic interventions to reduce the chances of further sexual violence. Two of the most well-known classifications of sexual violence come from the work of Groth and colleagues and researchers from the Massachusetts treatment centre (MTC). As we briefly explore each of these, some common themes will emerge, and some themes from earlier chapters will also be apparent.

Groth's classification of rapists

Although several rapist typologies existed prior to Groth's (for a review, see Wilson & Alison, 2005), it was his work (Groth & Birnbaum, 1979; Groth *et al.*, 1977) that produced one of the most important classifications of sexual violence. Although the opening quote at the start of this chapter provided a flavour of the problem of rapist heterogeneity, the explanation that followed provided the details. As Groth and Birnbaum (1979) suggested, rapists do not always act in the same way for the same reasons. Some actions (e.g., fellatio) can serve different needs, and different actions (e.g., anal and vaginal penetration) can serve similar needs.

Groth *et al.* (1977) categorised rape into two broad types – *power and anger* – with each divided into two sub-types. In power rapes, the offender seeks power and control over his victim, using actual or threatened physical violence to overpower and subdue her and facilitate sexual intercourse. Assaults are premeditated and based on prior fantasy and may become compulsive and repetitive. The *'power-assertive'* rapist views rape as an expression of his virility, mastery, and dominance, and he feels entitled to sex as his dominance keeps women under control. The *'power-reassurance'* rapist offends to resolve self-doubts about his sexual adequacy and masculinity, which he achieves by placing women in helpless positions. In anger rapes, the offender expresses anger, rage, and hatred for his victim, whom he beats, sexually assaults, and forces them to perform degrading acts. Sudden expressive violence and profane language are used to subdue his victim, with violence directed at all parts of her body. The *'anger-retaliation'* rapist offends to express his hostility and rage towards women and is motivated by revenge. The *'anger-excitation'* rapist derives sadistic sexual pleasure from his assault and his victim's suffering. Groth and Birnbaum (1979) later refined this classification, and when discussing the possibility of victim resistance, they powerfully captured the importance of motive and how this can influence offender responses to such resistance:

> different motives operate in different offenders, and, therefore, what might be successful in dissuading one type of assailant might, in fact, only aggravate the situation with a different type of offender. Physical resistance will discourage one type of rapist but excite another type. If his victim screams, one assailant will flee, but another will cut her throat.
>
> (ibid, p. 8)

In their refined classification, Groth and Birnbaum (1979) suggested that the interaction of physical and sexual violence resulted in three patterns of rape being distinguishable:

- *Anger* rapes are the result of pent-up anger and rage. These assaults include expressive violence and profanity aimed at hurting and debasing the victim, who may be forced to perform sexual acts that he considers degrading (e.g., fellatio, anal intercourse, ejaculating onto the victim). These assaults are not linked to pre-offence sexual fantasies and are typically impulsive. The offender's "*weapon is sex, and his motive is revenge*" (ibid., p.17).
- *Power* rapes are sexual conquests that compensate for feelings of insecurity and inadequacy, with instrumental violence used to achieve this aim. Offences may be related to pre-offence masturbatory fantasies, where the victim initially resists but, once overpowered, becomes aroused and responds positively. Such offences may be premeditated or opportunistic, and a failure to achieve sexual satisfaction leads to compulsive offending.
- *Sadistic* rapes involve the fusion of sex and aggression. Although levels of expressive violence are similar to anger rapes, the violence is not aimed at discharging negative emotions, but satisfying the offender's deviant sexual appetite. Such offences are planned and may include bondage, torture, or forcing the victim to behave or dress in a certain way. Their compulsive nature means further offences are likely.

The success of Groth's work is evidenced by its subsequent application to other areas (e.g., criminal investigations – Hazelwood, 2017; Holmes & Holmes, 2009) and other kinds of sexual violence (e.g., sexual murder – Keppel & Walter, 1999). Notwithstanding this, researchers from Massachusetts developed what became an even more successful and widely used classification of sexual violence.

Massachusetts treatment centre rapist typology

The MTC rapist typology programme (Knight & Prentky, 1990a) took the classification of sexual violence to a new level of development and sophistication. Version three of this typology (MTC:R3) is a valid (Knight, 1999) and widely used typology of rapists (Fisher & Mair, 1998), which has been used in a large body of research (e.g., Barbaree *et al.*, 1994; Brown & Forth, 1997; Greenall & West, 2007, 2008; Polaschek, 1997; Smith, 2000a). Along with its usage in clinical and research settings, the MTC:R3 has been found to have investigative potential too (Knight *et al.*, 1998). The MTC:R3 proposes four primary motivations for rape, with classification based on a detailed knowledge of the offence and the offender's history:

1 *Opportunistic* rapes are impulsive, unplanned predatory acts, influenced by immediate contextual factors rather than sexual fantasy. Such assaults constitute another instance of poor impulse control generally, as indicated by a history of repeated antisocial behaviour. Although these offenders are indifferent to their victim, no evidence of gratuitous violence or anger is present, as only sufficient force is used to obtain sexual gratification.
2 *Pervasively Angry* rapes indicate undifferentiated anger, which is equally directed at men or women. These men have extensive histories of impulsive, antisocial behaviour in several domains. Gratuitous violence occurs with or without victim resistance and can result in the victim's death. However, the violence is not eroticised.
3 *Sexual* rapes are marked by the presence of a protracted sexual or sadistic fantasy or preoccupations that motivate the assault and influence the way it is committed. Here, two sub-groups are differentiated by the absence or presence of sadism.

   a *Sadistic assaults* include eroticised violence and acts of humiliation if overtly expressed or muted if present but not acted out.
   b *Non-sadistic assaults* have low levels of expressive aggression, and offenders tend to be concerned with factors such as masculinity, sexuality, and dominance.

4 *Vindictive* rapes are indicative of anger directed exclusively at women. Sexual assaults are marked by behaviours intended to physically harm, degrade, and humiliate them. Unlike pervasively angry rapists, these men display little or no undifferentiated anger. Their rage can range from verbal abuse to murder, but despite a sexual component to their assaults, violence is not eroticised, and sadistic fantasy is absent.

The key thing to note from clinical classifications is that, as shown in Table 4.2, despite the differing labels used, similar themes arise suggesting that serious acts of sexual violence, such as rape, essentially reflect various motivations that generally divide into sexual and non-sexual (i.e., angry/violent) types (Barbaree *et al.*, 1994). However, rather than focusing on motivation, other researchers have approached the problem of sex offender heterogeneity from another perspective, namely exploring behavioural differences within sexual assaults.

Table 4.2 Rapist motivational types

	Sexual types	*Sadistic types*	*Angry/violent types*
Groth *et al.* (1977)	Power-assertive Power-reassurance	Anger-excitation	Anger-retaliation
Groth and Birnbaum (1979)	Power rapes	Sadistic rapes	Angry rapes
Knight and Prentky (1990)	Opportunistic Sexual (non-sadistic)	Sexual (sadistic)	Pervasively angry Vindictive

Offence behavioural differences within sexual violence

Whilst clinical classifications aim to identify the motive that drives a sexual assault, other researchers, such as Canter (2003), have questioned the utility of trying to establish motive, as they view it as a *'slippery notion'* which will not necessarily assist criminal investigations. Additionally, in criticising the very idea of classifying offenders and their offences, Canter (2000) suggested the complexity of criminal behaviour means that any attempt to assign offenders or their offences to one of a limited number of *'types'* will always be an oversimplification. Following his ground-breaking work assisting police with a series of stranger sexual assaults in London committed by the *'railway rapist'* (see Canter, 1994), Canter and Heritage posed a fundamental question about the utility of classification systems and their applicability to cases of stranger sexual violence:

> typologies undoubtedly contribute to the understanding of the motivations of rapists and this can help to indicate why certain sorts of rapist will perform certain types of offence. Yet there remains the primary question of what variations in offence behaviour can be reliably identified without any knowledge of the person who committed them.
>
> (1990, p. 188)

Essentially, Canter and Heritage were interested in whether meaningful hypotheses could be formulated about an unknown sexual offender and his offence(s), without pigeonholing him into a particular classificatory type. It was this avenue of research that led to the development by Canter of what became known as investigative psychology

Canter's investigative psychology

An adequate summary of investigative psychology is beyond the scope of this chapter, and you are therefore advised to consult some key texts and resources (e.g., Canter, 1994; Canter & Youngs, 2009; Youngs, 2013; and also https://www.davidcanter.com/investigative-psychology/). For the purposes of addressing the problem of sex offender heterogeneity, a key contribution of investigative psychology relates to how the above question by Canter and Heritage (1990) was answered. One of the most important ways this was achieved was by examining the behaviours exhibited by samples of offenders during their sexual assaults. Using official information (e.g., victim statements) supplied by the police, Canter and Heritage (1990) analysed 66 stranger sexual assaults committed by 27 offenders, meaning some were repeat/serial offenders. Most of the crime scene actions of these men were captured by 33 offence variables, relating to method of approach (e.g., surprise attack), violent actions (e.g., threats), sexual actions (e.g., vaginal penetration), and other actions (e.g., stealing from the victim) (ibid., pp. 204–210). This analysis revealed that these offence behaviours were not random occurrences. Rather, various relationships existed between them, such that Canter and Heritage (1990) were able to hypothesise fives offence behavioural themes or *'modes of interaction'* between the offender and his victim during offences of stranger rape:

1 *Attempted intimacy*: Some offenders were attempting to engineer some form of personal relationship with their victim, indicating a lack of ability to form intimate relationships with women in their normal lives.
2 *Sexual behaviour*: Some offenders used sexual violence as a means of engaging in different sorts of sexual behaviour, indicating considerable earlier sexual experiences or a great interest in such behaviours as revealed through a collection of pornography.
3 *Overt violence and aggression*: Some offenders used sexual violence to inflict physical violence and aggression on their victims, and their relationship to a prior history of aggression would be worthy of consideration.
4 *Impersonal interaction*: Some offenders treated their victims as an object or entity entirely there for their own use, indicating a callous disinterest and disregard for their welfare. This would be anticipated to reflect an approach to women generally.
5 *Criminal behaviour and intent*: Some offenders evidenced actions within their offences that were more criminal than sexual (e.g., wearing a disguise and stealing from the victim), indicative of extensive criminal (but non-sexual) histories.

Although this study was later refined by Canter *et al.* (2003) and replicated by others (e.g., Alison & Stein, 2001; Canter, 1994; Canter *et al.*, 2003; Darjee & Baron, 2018; Gerard *et al.*, 2007; Godwin, 2001; Greenall & West, 2007, 2008; Greenall & Wright, 2020; Häkkänen *et al.*, 2004; House, 1997; Kocsis *et al.*, 2002a, 2002b; Lehmann *et al.*, 2013; Lundrigan, 2009; Salfati & Taylor, 2006), the 1990 study made two crucial contributions to our understanding of stranger sexual violence. First, in answer to Canter and Heritage's (1990) question above, it showed that variations in offence behaviours *'can'* be reliably identified without any knowledge of the offender who committed them. Second, along with confirming from a different perspective that sexual violence was related to sex and aggression, the study hypothesised that stranger sexual violence can also involve attempted intimacy, an impersonal interaction style, and include other offences such as theft.

Conclusion and implications for practice

Decades after the problem was highlighted by Groth and others, sex offender heterogeneity remains a fundamental problem that hinders our understanding of sexual violence and sexual offenders. Whilst this remains a key challenge for criminal justice practitioners who work with sexual offenders in secure or community settings, police officers are not immune to this problem. Indeed, when commenting on the role police officers play in the community management of sexual offenders, Deputy Chief Constable Michelle Skeer, the National Police Chiefs' Council lead for the management of sexual and violent offenders, stated:

> It is important to remember that people will be on the sex offenders register for a range of crimes – it could be from downloading indecent images to contact offending. There are also a wide range of factors that impact on the likelihood of an

individual reoffending. This means we need to take a tailored approach rather than following a one-size-fits-all model.

(National Police Chief's Council, 2017)

In understanding the diversity of sexual violence, this chapter has shown that a useful starting point is the exploration of the role and function of physical violence. This can help us to start asking some relevant questions, the answers to which can in turn be used in conjunction with the pathways discussed in Chapter 2 and the JTCs in Chapter 3, to develop evidence-based hypotheses about individual cases of stranger sexual violence. For example:

1 If an assault includes instrumental violence with no weapons, might this suggest it was an opportunistic sexual assault carried out by a man who spontaneously encountered his victim whilst travelling between two important anchor points within his life, e.g., a place of recreation and his home?
2 If a weapon such as a knife was brandished, might this indicate premeditation and the weapon being on his person for this specific purpose, or might it suggest this was an opportunistic assault carried out by an individual in the habit of carrying weapons as part of his antisocial lifestyle?
3 If an assault includes expressive violence with no weapons (e.g., punching and slapping), does this suggest the assault was carried out by an individual who wanted to satisfy more than just his sexual needs?
4 If physical violence was evident within the assault, did it appear to enhance the offender's sexual arousal, indicating the potential presence of sadism (see Chapter 6)?

Similarly, drawing on the work of Schlesinger (2004a, 2004b) allows us to consider what drove an individual to sexually assault a female stranger and to question the circumstances in which the assault occurred. For example:

1 Was the offender with a group, and if so, did the group dynamic play a part?
2 If the offender was alone, had he spent time with his victim beforehand, and did the assault occur in the situational context of a dispute between them?
3 If there was no prior contact, was this an opportunistic convenience assault that occurred by chance, or was it a purposeful, premeditated precautionary assault?
4 If the assault included physical violence, what was the offender's emotional state, i.e., did he appear to be experiencing emotional distress or anger, and may he have been discharging these emotions onto his victim?
5 Did the assault include any deviant sexual acts (see Chapter 6), which may be of a compulsive nature and drive the offender to offend in this way again?

Critical issues!

As Amir argued, "*rape has many motives but only one intent*" (1971, p. 131). Although the various methods of classification have succeeded in enhancing our understanding of what may motivate acts of stranger sexual violence and the interpersonal dynamics between the offender and his victim, they are not without their limitations.

Whilst clinical classification helps us to focus on the offender we are dealing with, a great deal of information about the offender is required to achieve this. Examples include family background, medical history, educational development, interpersonal development, occupational history, criminal history, and a range of behavioural, observational, and psychometric information obtained during a clinical assessment (see Chapter 5 in Groth & Birnbaum, 1979). Whilst this information may be available to forensic/clinical practitioners working with a known offender in community or secure settings, police officers involved in the investigation of a stranger sexual offence will have no such opportunities to access this information. Additionally, when classification is based on a set of defining criteria, requiring all criteria to be satisfied will be too rigid and lead to '*near-misses*' being excluded. However, when classification requires only some of the defining criteria to be satisfied, this can lead to within-group differences, which defeats the object of classification (Blackburn, 1993).

Mindful of these problems, Investigative Psychologists have sought to develop ways in which meaningful hypotheses can be formulated about unknown sexual offenders based on research into the crime scene behaviours of similar offenders. In doing this, Investigative Psychology has illustrated the importance of conducting a detailed analysis of crime scene actions (see Chapter 12). Despite this, however, this approach is not without its limitations. For example, although several researchers have replicated Canter and Heritage's (1990) seminal study using similar samples of offenders (e.g., Alison & Stein, 2001; Canter, 1994; Canter *et al.*, 2003; Greenall & West, 2007, 2008; Häkkänen *et al.*, 2004; House, 1997; Kocsis *et al.*, 2002b; Lehmann *et al.*, 2013; McCabe & Wauchope, 2005; Salfati & Taylor, 2006), the fact that they have found several offence behavioural themes that have been given different labels can cause confusion. Mindful of this, some researchers have suggested that offence behavioural themes within rape essentially divide into sexual and violent themes (Greenall & West, 2007, 2008), and possibly a third theme relating to criminality, where sexual violence is part of a varied criminal repertoire (Lehmann *et al.*, 2013). A final limitation of the Investigative Psychology approach relates to the problems discussed in Chapter 1, namely applying group-based research to an individual (Hart & Cooke, 2013; Hart *et al.*, 2007). The big question, therefore, is: can we combine the strengths of these two approaches whilst simultaneously dispensing with their weaknesses? If so, what might such an arrangement look like, and how would police officers and clinical practitioners be able to apply this to their practice? This question and a potential answer will be the focus of Volume 3.

5 The psychology of the offender

If the situation was right, why not?

(Scully, 1994, p. 142)

Introduction

As alluded to in Chapter 3 (Box 3.1), there are many occasions when men find themselves in the company of a female stranger, whom they could easily sexually assault. At such times, they may also feel sexually aroused and experience a range of positive or negative emotions. However, as Marvin suggests in Box 5.1, whilst most men let the opportunity pass, others think *'why not'* and take advantage of the situation. Bearing in mind that men who sexually assault female strangers will not have been forced to do this at the point of a gun, regardless of how premeditated or impulsive their sexual violence was, it follows that their actions were the result of a choice they made to sexually assault their victim. But are these *'rational choices'* (Pedneault, 2018) made by men of sound mind, or are they made by men whose minds are under the influence of factors such as intoxicants or some form of mental or sexual pathology? Given that all choices are made in the mind, this and the following chapter explores factors that can influence this decision-making process and lead some men to conclude that sexually assaulting a female stranger is acceptable, if not desirable.

Box 5.1   Marvin's account

A normal guy driving down the street sees a pretty girl. He might look at her and whistle, and just keep on going. After a few minutes, she doesn't even register. He can go home to his wife, hug his kids, and not think twice about that woman.

A sex offender who sees her, won't whistle at her. He wants to follow her. He wants to drive around the block and park quickly and run up behind her and follow her. He may even follow her home, all the while fantasising.

If I see a pretty girl, it would be hard for me to have a fantasy about normal lovemaking. My fantasy would be about holding a knife to her, forcing her to do this act. I always knew I had a choice. Would I have stopped? No, this was a sexual release.

(abridged from Bonnycastle, 2012, pp. 162–163)

DOI: 10.4324/9781003217763-6

Chapter aims

As shown throughout this book, several factors need to be considered when trying to understand stranger sexual violence. In Chapter 3, routine activity theory (Cohen & Felson, 1979; Felson, 2017) was used to highlight the importance of the JTCs that can lead an offender to a suitable location and the dynamics that may motivate him to offend. The aim of this chapter is to explore some of the factors that can contribute to someone becoming a motivated offender in the first place. This can occur because they feel disinhibited, their decision-making process becomes destabilised, or perhaps their early life experiences have predisposed them to engage in varied criminality, including sexual violence. This chapter will focus on some key factors that can contribute to this process, namely an individual's core values and beliefs, the presence of a mental disorder, and intoxication. This is not an exhaustive list of factors that can contribute to sexual violence, but from my experience, they are some of the main factors encountered when working with men with histories of sexual violence. Consequently, the importance of these factors is such that those who work with sexual offenders in whatever capacity will periodically encounter them and will therefore need to understand how they may have contributed to the stranger's sexual assault.

Psychological assumption

The heterogeneity of sexual offenders highlighted in Chapter 4 means there is no such thing as a typical sexual offender. When it comes to stranger sexual offenders, Chapter 1 shows that we do know one thing about them, which is their sexual violence is intentional and the result of them following a pre-offence decision chain. In trying to understand the behaviour of stranger sexual offenders, a basic psychological assumption will be made about human behaviour, which is people engage in voluntary conduct because they want to. Moreover, as Thorndike's (1898) *'law of effect'* suggests, behaviours that lead to a positive outcome are more likely to be repeated. As the reflective exercise in Chapter 3 (Box 3.1) illustrated, regardless of the opportunities presented, most men will never sexually assault a female stranger, because we do not want to, as we consider such behaviour wrong. However, clearly, other men take a different view, but why?

One potential answer comes from the fact that what are known as adverse childhood experiences (Felitti *et al.*, 1998) are common in samples of sexual offenders (see Craissati, 2009; Craissati & Blundell, 2013; Kahn *et al.*, 2021; Marshall & Marshall, 2000; Scully, 1994). Such early life experiences can, according to Marshall and Barbaree (1990), leave individuals with various psychological deficits, such as antisocial attitudes, impulsive tendencies, low self-esteem, and poor interpersonal skills. These deficits render these individuals more vulnerable to criminal behaviour in adulthood, including sexual violence. Essentially, therefore, the research suggests that in our work with sexual offenders, we are mostly dealing with people whose adverse childhood experiences have resulted in them holding attitudes, core values, and beliefs in their adult lives that are very different from our own and which can result in them viewing and interacting with the world around them in a very different way.

Core values and beliefs

An individual's core values and beliefs are relevant if they involve thoughts or fantasies of harming others and encouraging, excusing, justifying, minimising or denying engaging in sexual violence (Boer *et al.*, 2017; Hart *et al.*, 2022). The importance of such core values and beliefs is evidenced by the attention given to them by previous researchers.

For example, Scully (1994) illustrated how sexual offenders justify their offences with beliefs such as women are seductresses, they mean 'yes' when they say 'no', women being raped eventually relax and enjoy it, and nice girls don't get raped. Similarly, Groth and Birnbaum (1979) referred to *'myths'* that exist in relation to the offender (e.g., rapists are oversexed), the victim (e.g., she got what she asked for), and the solution (e.g., legalise prostitution). The idea of what became known as *'rape myths'* has been explored by researchers, who have developed scales to assess such values and beliefs. An example of one is presented in Table 5.1 and illustrates the nature of this problem.

From the perspective of mathematical probability, we can hypothesise that men who agree with statements such as those in Table 5.1 would be more likely to engage in sexual violence than men who do not. Indeed, research supports this by finding a correlation between acceptance of rape myths and committing sexual violence (Yapp & Quayle, 2018). Moreover, official guidance is provided to prosecutors in England to make them aware of the importance of various rape myths (see Annex A – Crown Prosecution Service, 2021). However, rape myths may not necessarily be the preserve of sexual offenders because research has found such beliefs may be held widely within society (Fenton, 2017). The difference is that whilst most men do not act on them, others do.

Table 5.1 Rape myths acceptance scale (sample questions)

Rape myths
When girls go to parties wearing slutty clothes, they are asking for trouble.
If a girl acts like a slut, eventually she is going to get into trouble.
It shouldn't be considered rape if a guy is drunk and didn't realise what he was doing.
If a girl doesn't physically fight back, you can't really say it was rape.
A rape probably didn't happen if the girl has no bruises or marks.
A lot of times, girls who say they were raped often led the guy on and then had regrets.
A lot of times, girls who claim they were raped just have emotional problems.

Source: Taken from McMahon & Farmer (2011)

Box 5.2 Stranger rapists excusing, rationalising, and justifying sexual violence

"It was about being there to make this person take part in my deviant behaviour..." (p. 159)

"Sexual assault is having something that you couldn't have if you were trying to have it the right way..." (p. 165)

"Why do women wear tight skirts? It's not because they're comfortable. And that's what I wanted beaten. When you attack that, you eliminate her power..." (p. 167)

"Didn't give two hoots about anything or anybody as long as my needs were met..." (p. 172)

"She was drunk. I thought, there's an easy target right there..." (p. 173).

"You are taking what she is not giving, and you feel powerful..." (p. 190)

"I didn't have a single thought about her, how it would hurt her, or how she would be affected..." (p. 191)

Source: Taken from Bonnycastle (2012)

Cognitive distortions, schemas, and implicit theories

If an individual subscribes to such myths, he may also engage in other cognitive processes (see Box 5.2), often referred to as *'cognitive distortions'*. These are believed to precede the onset of sexual offending and offer inaccurate and self-serving interpretations of the offence (Ward *et al.*, 2006). Ward (2000) suggests that cognitive distortions emerge from underlying schemas or *'implicit theories'* that operate at the automatic level outside an individual's consciousness and influence how they process information from their external world. Schemas or implicit theories can include core beliefs about oneself drawn from early (positive or negative) developmental experiences and/or inherent traits reinforced over the years, or they can relate to how the individual views himself in relation to their world (Young *et al.*, 2003). Schemas, or implicit theories, are not the preserve of offenders, as we all possess them (e.g., the world is a fair and just place), and they influence the choices we make and the goals we pursue. Among offender samples however, studies have found five schemas or implicit theories that are related to serious acts of sexual violence, including rape (Polaschek & Gannon, 2004) and sexual homicide (Beech, Fisher *et al.*, 2005; Fisher & Beech, 2007).

1 *Women are unknowable:* Women are fundamentally different from men, and men cannot understand how their minds work. Sexual encounters are adversarial as women know their desires are incompatible with men, whom they seek to deceive about their intentions.
2 *Women as sex objects:* Women are sexually receptive to men's needs but are not always aware of this fact. Their body language says more than their words when displaying their sexual receptiveness, and women cannot be injured by sex unless they are physically injured.
3 *Male sex drive is uncontrollable:* Men's sexual energy can escalate to dangerous levels if women do not make themselves sexually available. Once men have become sexually aroused, it is hard for them to control themselves if women do not help them experience an orgasm.
4 *Entitlement:* Men's sexual needs should be satisfied on demand by women. Men can have sex when they want and can use rape when women are not subservient to their sexual needs.
5 *Dangerous world:* The world is a hostile and threatening place, and men must be mindful of being exploited. They must be ready to fight back and achieve dominance and control over people, including inflicting punishment (e.g., sexual violence) on those (i.e., women) who seek to harm them.

Implicit theories do not exist in isolation, as they are similar to some of the motivational and interpersonal dynamics mentioned in Chapter 4. For example, some of the angry, violent, and misogynistic dynamics from Chapter 4 are similar to implicit theories one, four, and five, which view sexual encounters between men and women as being adversarial, confrontational, and violent. Similarly, some of the sexual and intimate dynamics from Chapter 4 are similar to implicit theories two and three, which view women as sex objects who are there to satisfy men's needs. As stated above, for some people, their pro-offending core values and beliefs may be a defining feature of their outward presentation and be associated with negative early childhood experiences and subjective antisocial cultural norms (Marshall & Barbaree, 1990). For others, however, such core values and beliefs may also be related to, or be a manifestation of, one or more mental disorders.

Mental disorder

Mental disorder is a term applied to a range of clinical conditions that are generally characterised by significant disturbances in an individual's cognition, emotion regulation, or behaviour and are usually associated with significant distress or disability in social, occupational, or other important activities (American Psychiatric Association, 2022). Mental disorders can be experienced by non-offending members of the public living in the community, as well as offenders within prisons, secure hospitals, and community settings. Indeed, the fact that mental disorders can co-exist with criminal behaviour is the reason why forensic mental health services and clinical disciplines like forensic psychiatry and forensic psychology exist (Greenall, 2023). In relation to sexual offenders, research suggests these individuals present with the full range of mental disorders (e.g., see Ahlmeyer *et al.*, 2003; Booth, 2010; Chen *et al.*, 2016; McElroy *et al.*, 1999). Two of the most important factors that can influence offender decision-making and are risk factors for sexual violence are personality disorder (PD) and mental illness (Boer *et al.*, 2017; Hart *et al.*, 2022).

Personality disorder (PD)

Whilst only some people hold pro-offending core values and beliefs, we '*all*' have a personality. Although a complex topic, personality is defined within most abnormal psychology textbooks. Hooley *et al.* (2017), for example, refer to characteristic traits, coping styles, and ways of interacting in the social environment. These factors emerge during childhood, crystalise into established patterns by the end of adolescence or early adulthood, and constitute the individual's personality. An individual with a healthy personality can engage successfully in various social, educational, and occupational tasks in accordance with societal norms and expectations. However, when, perhaps due to interactions between biologically based vulnerabilities, early trauma involving significant others, and the role of social factors (see the biopsychosocial model in Craissati *et al.*, 2020), an individual's personality is more unusual or extreme, causes suffering to self or others and hinders their social, educational, and occupational functioning, they may have a PD.

Although PD is another complex topic, excellent guides are available for those who work with these individuals (e.g., see Bolton *et al.*, 2014; Craissati *et al.*, 2020). One of these guides provides a definition of PD that can be used by specialists and non-specialists alike. For an individual to be regarded as having PD, Craissati *et al.* (2020) suggest that not only must their personality present as more unusual or extreme (see Table 5.2), but their personality difficulties must evidence the following '*3Ps*'.

1 *Problematic*: i.e., unusual and causing distress to self or others.
6 *Persistent*: i.e., starting in adolescence and continuing into adulthood.
7 *Pervasive*: i.e., affecting several different areas of the person's life.

Table 5.2 Spectrum of personality functioning

	Personality difficulty	*Mild personality disorder*	*Moderate personality disorder*	*Severe personality disorder*
Healthy personality with no evidence of dysfunction.	Dysfunction in discreate settings.	Persistent dysfunction but integrated life present.	More severe problems with risk to self or others.	Very severe breakdown of functioning.
No personality disorder		Personality disorder		

Source: Adapted from Tyrer & Mulder, 2022, who state we are all on this spectrum somewhere

The importance of PD to sexual violence is illustrated by the fact that whilst community-based studies suggest less than 5% of adults have a PD (McManus *et al.*, 2007; 2016; Singleton *et al.*, 2001), rates of PD among sexual offenders are around 52%–74% (Chen *et al.*, 2016; Craissati & Blundell, 2013; Kingston *et al.*, 2015; McElroy *et al.*, 1999; Singleton *et al.*, 1998). This large difference has clear implications for criminal justice practitioners who work with sexual offenders, as it means they '*will'* encounter sexual offenders with a PD. Therefore, it is crucial to have a basic grounding of this disorder and how it can interact with sexual violence. However, simply referring to PD as implying it is a singular concept is incorrect, as we should be referring to '*the PDs'* because, as we shall now see, there is not just one PD but several.

Which PD?

Two conceptualisations of PD exist in parallel, one provided by DSM-5-TR (American Psychiatric Association, 2022) and another by ICD-11 (World Health Organization, 2022). Although similarities have existed between these two systems over the years as they both differentiated several types of PD, ICD-11 has changed things. DSM-5-TR classifies 10 PDs into three clusters: A: odd or eccentric; B: dramatic, emotional, or erratic; and C: anxious or fearful (see Table 5.3). ICD-11 has dispensed with categories of PD and replaced them with a general description. This can be specified as mild, moderate, or severe, similar to Table 5.2, and an individual's behaviour can be described using one or more of five personality trait domains: negative affectivity (i.e., mood state), dissociality (i.e., antisocial), anankastia (i.e., obsessive-compulsive), detachment, and disinhibition. Clinicians may also specify a borderline pattern (i.e., similar to borderline PD in Table 5.3) qualifier (World Health Organization, 2022). Due to the popularity of the existing DSM approach, both in clinical and research settings, criminal justice practitioners should have a working knowledge of the DSM PDs and how they are associated with the individual having different views of himself and his world and how he is experienced by and relates to others. However, interested readers are advised to keep an eye on future developments in this area, because the similarity between the ICD-11 approach and DSM-5-TR's alternative model of PD (see Mulder, 2021) may result in future convergence between the two.

The existence of several PDs highlights an important point. Individuals with a PD may not always present with only one PD, as it has long been recognised that some individuals present with combinations of '*co-morbid'* PDs (Blackburn, 2000). These co-morbid presentations can involve two or more PDs from the same DSM cluster or from two or more

Table 5.3 DSM-5-TR personality disorders

Cluster	PD type	Key features	Core self-beliefs	World view	Experienced by others as:	Relates to others as:
A	Paranoid	Distrusting and suspicious interpretation of others' motives.	Right/noble	Malicious	Defensive	Suspicious or provocative
	Schizoid	Social detachment, restricted emotional expression.	Self-sufficient	Intrusive or unimportant	Impassive	Isolated or unengaged
	Schizotypal	Social discomfort, cognitive distortions, and eccentric behaviours.	Estranged	Varies	Eccentric	Secretive
B	Antisocial	Disregard for and violation of the rights of others.	Strong/alone	Dog eats dog	Impulsive	Deceive or manipulate
	Borderline	Unstable relationships, self-image, affects, and impulsivity.	Bad or vulnerable	Dangerous	Spasmodic	Attach or attack
	Histrionic	Excessive emotionality and attention seeking.	Inadequate	Seducible	Dramatic	Charm or seek attention
	Narcissistic	Grandiosity, need for admiration, lack of empathy.	Admirable	Threatening	Haughty	Compete or exploit
C	Avoidant	Socially inhibited feelings of inadequacy, and hypersensitivity to negative evaluation.	Worthless	Critical	Fretful	Avoid
	Dependent	Submissive behaviour needs to be taken care of.	Helpless	Overwhelming	Incompetent	Submit
	Obsessive-compulsive	Preoccupation with orderliness, perfectionism, and control.	Competent or conscientious	Needs order	Disciplined	Control or respectful

Source: Adapted from American Psychiatric Association (2022)

clusters. One such PD combination should be of particular concern to every criminal justice practitioner. Craissati *et al.* (2020) suggest this involves an extreme and co-morbid combination of antisocial and narcissistic PDs, the result of which is called psychopathy.

Psychopathy

Psychopathy is a serious PD that has the potential to impact the work of every criminal justice practitioner at some point in their career. The reason for this is illustrated by Craissati et al., who describe psychopathy as *"a particularly important personality type in offender services as it is linked to very high levels of re-offending, violence, and failure to comply with statutory supervision"* (2020, p. 11). Other research illustrates the importance of psychopathy to sexual violence, as in contrast to around 1% of community samples being psychopathic (Coid *et al.*, 2009), rates of psychopathy have been found to be much higher among rapists (35.9%) and those who victimise adults and children (66%) (Porter *et al.*, 2000). The best way to illustrate and understand the concept of psychopathy and why it is so important to criminal justice practice is to consult the *'Psychopathy Checklist'* (Hare, 2003). This is a popular assessment protocol used in clinical and research settings. Although a detailed summary of this tool is beyond the scope of this chapter, the items within it (see Table 5.4) describe the key characteristics of individuals with a psychopathic personality. Essentially, as described by Hare (e.g., Hare, 1993; Hare *et al.*, 2012), these individuals charm, manipulate, and exploit others, and their lack of conscience and feelings for others means they can do this without any sense of guilt or regret.

A way to understand where psychopathy may sit along the personality continuum within Table 5.2 is to consider that if PD is a more unusual or extreme presentation of normal personality, then psychopathy is an even more unusual or extreme presentation. This is illustrated by DeLisi (2019a), who describes three groups of people in society (see Table 5.5). Although the highly compliant would not be expected to engage in criminality, the moderately compliant (who may possess one or more PDs from Table 5.3) may periodically commit crimes such as drunk driving or acquisitive offences if it serves their purpose. Be that so, they may also engage in impulsive sexual violence if that too serves their purpose. However, the chronically non-compliant are those with more extreme behavioural and interpersonal presentations and are therefore regarded as having a psychopathic personality.

Table 5.4 Characteristics of psychopathy

Items	
Glibness/superficial charm	*Promiscuous sexual behaviour*
Grandiose sense of self-worth	*Early behavioural problems*
Need for stimulation/proneness to boredom	*Lack of realistic, long-term goals*
Pathological lying	*Impulsivity*
Conning/manipulative	*Irresponsibility*
Lack of remorse or guilt	*Failure to accept responsibility for one's actions*
Shallow affect	*Many short-term marital relationships*
Callous/lack of empathy	*Juvenile delinquency*
Parasitic lifestyle	*Revocation of conditional release*
Poor behavioural controls	*Criminal versatility*

Source: Adapted from Hare (2003)

Table 5.5 Behavioural functioning of three groups in society

Highly compliant and highly self-regulated	Moderately compliant and generally well-regulated	Chronically non-compliant and difficult
Easy to get along with, highly conscientious and agreeable, successful in social, educational, and occupational areas. Selfless moderation and control of thoughts and behaviours, impulses, and emotions, and lead crime-free lives.	Able to get along with others most of the time and can regulate their conduct in most situations according to social norms. Occasionally prioritises themselves over others and periodically engage in selfish, self-centred acts that violate social norms.	Have difficulty regulating their conduct and face many hardships due to their unwillingness and incapacity to get along with others. Severe self-regulation problems lead to frequent and diverse offending.

Source: Adapted from DeLisi (2019a)

Whilst there will always be exceptions to every general statement about how others present, from my experience, offenders with a PD would, to paraphrase an old legal concept (i.e., the McNaughton Rules, see West & Walk, 1977), know the nature and quality of the criminal act they committed and would have known it was wrong, but they chose to do it regardless. Indeed, when talking about psychopathic violence, Hare similarly suggested their offending *"results not from a deranged mind but from a cold, calculating rationality combined with a chilling inability to treat others as thinking, feeling human beings"* (1993, p. 5). However, this description may not apply to offenders who present with a mental illness.

Mental illness

The term mental illness covers a variety of often long-standing psychological disorders that, like PD, hinder an individual's social, educational, and occupational functioning. These disorders can generally be divided into neurotic and psychotic disorders. Neurotic disorders include a range of normal emotions that are manifested in more extreme ways. Examples include anxiety, mood disorders, and phobias. A key feature of neurotic disorders is that the individual is generally aware of their condition and the negative impact it has on their life, but they cannot help themselves (Hooley *et al.*, 2017). Psychotic disorders are not related to normal emotions. Rather, they are a collection of symptoms that result in the individual experiencing their world in a different way. As such, they may, for example, smell, hear, feel, or see things that others cannot (i.e., hallucinations); they may have strange thoughts or beliefs that can make them feel they are being persecuted or controlled (i.e., delusions); they may have confused or blocked thinking (i.e., thought disorder); and unlike neurotic disorders, they may experience a loss of reality and be unaware they are mentally unwell (Mind, 2020). An example of a well-known psychotic disorder is schizophrenia, which is characterised by delusions, hallucinations, disorganised speech, disorganised behaviour, and diminished emotional expression (American Psychiatric Association, 2022).

The importance of mental illness to sexual violence is illustrated by the fact that whilst community-based studies suggest less than 1% have a mental illness (McManus *et al.*, 2007; 2016; Singleton *et al.*, 2001), rates among sexual offenders are around 4%–11%

(Lewis & Dwyer, 2018; Singleton *et al.*, 1998; Stinson & Becker, 2011). These lower rates compared to PD mean that mentally ill sexual offenders are a distinctive group that many criminal justice practitioners may never encounter. However, those who work within forensic mental health services will encounter these individuals. As with PD, the issue of individuals presenting with co-morbid disorders is relevant here, as it has long been recognised that some individuals present with different types of mental illness (e.g., anxiety, depression, and psychosis) and/or with a mental illness and one or more PDs (Blackburn *et al.*, 2003; Tyrer & Mulder, 2022).

Having introduced these two mental disorders and found them to be more common among sexual offenders than among adults in the community, we need to explore their link with sexual violence.

Mental disorder and sexual violence

Although research suggests that rates of PD and mental illness are higher among sexual offenders than adults within community samples, this finding only tells half the story. To obtain the full story, we need to consider how a mental disorder may contribute to acts of sexual violence.

Personality disorder and sexual violence

The relevance of PD to sexual violence can be understood when we remember that individuals with PD view themselves, their world, and their place within it differently than most others. Consequently, their interactions with and expectations of others differ. In relation to how the DSM PDs may influence an individual's sexual interactions, the work of Vaknin (2018) offers some ideas that can help us to understand how a PD may contribute to sexual violence.

Cluster A PDs

This is the least common cluster among sexual offenders with a PD (Chen *et al.*, 2016; McElroy *et al.*, 1999). Vaknin (2018) suggests the idea of intimate relationships is problematic for these people. For example, sex can be depersonalised and the partner dehumanised (paranoid), and a preference for solitary activities means relationships are avoided (schizoid) because they cause acute discomfort and a fear of oddities and eccentricities being exposed (schizotypal). For these individuals, we can hypothesise that sexual violence may be their only means of securing sexual access to women, as establishing and maintaining traditional sexual relationships with them may be beyond their means.

Custer B PDs

This is the most common cluster among sexual offenders with a PD (Chen *et al.*, 2016; McElroy *et al.*, 1999). For those within this cluster, Vaknin (2018) suggests that sex can be a means of satisfying subjective needs at the expense of others. This can include gaining attention and increasing self-esteem and self-worth (histrionic), whilst cold and calculating individuals (narcissistic and antisocial) essentially use others for masturbatory purposes, as they are not viewed as sexual playmates but sexual playthings. For these individuals, we can hypothesise that sexual violence may be a result of their proneness to take advantage of others and/or is part of a wider antisocial, impulsive lifestyle, which may manifest itself in other related activities such as general criminality. We can further hypothesise that these tendencies will be even stronger among those with a psychopathic personality. As illustrated in Table 5.4, psychopathic individuals will present as quite different to most people, and again would be more prone to take advantage of others to satisfy their own needs. They would also be more likely to engage in serious interpersonal violence and not experience guilt or remorse afterwards. Indeed, a body of research (e.g., Chapters 21–27 in DeLisi, 2019b) suggests that sexual violence committed by psychopathic individuals is more impersonal, deceptive, and exploitative; includes higher levels of gratuitous (or expressive) violence; and is more sadistic. Although not every psychopath will present with a co-morbid deviant sexual preference such as sadism (see Chapter 6), when these factors do co-occur, the resulting presentation has been described as a "*deadly combination*" (Hare, 1999, p. 189) and these individuals being "*a potentially very dangerous type of offender*" (Jones & Chan, 2019, p. 407).

Other PD presentations

Finally, for some other PD presentations, Vaknin (2018) suggests their associated difficulties within interpersonal relations are evident in the sexual area. For example, some individuals will remain aloof and reclusive to conceal their self-perceived shortcomings due to a fear of rejection and criticism (avoidant). Others will use sex to reward or punish others as part of their unstable relations and impulsive presentation (borderline), whilst others will still use sex to enslave and condition their partner to secure their relationship (dependent). For these individuals, we can hypothesise that for some (e.g., avoidant), sexual violence may be their only means of securing sexual access to women, whilst for others, it may be a manifestation of their anxieties relating to interpersonal relations and/or their impulsive behavioural style.

Mental illness and sexual violence

The relevance of mental illness to sexual violence can be understood when we remember that individuals with this disorder perceive or interpret reality differently from others, and some may have lost touch with reality (Mind, 2020). Despite this, however, the sexual offences committed by these men are very similar to those committed by men without a mental illness, as bizarre or odd behaviours are largely absent (Smith, 2000b). Consequently, upon arrest, most will be taken into custody rather than to a hospital (Craissati & Hodes, 1992). Whilst mentally ill sexual offenders may not necessarily '*give themselves away*' by acting strangely, some aspects of their offences may reveal the possible presence of a mental illness. This can be illustrated by two avenues of research that have explored how sexual violence can be driven by the symptoms of mental illness and the impact this disorder has on the individual.

Symptoms of mental illness

The symptom approach to how mental illness can influence sexual violence is based on the idea that the symptoms of this disorder, such as delusions and/or hallucinations, can '*drive*' some offenders to engage in sexual violence. The idea that an individual can be driven to violence by delusions is as old as forensic psychiatry itself, as illustrated by the case of James Hadfield, who, in a deluded state, tried to assassinate King George III in 1800 (Moran, 1985). A more recent example of this was the Yorkshire Ripper, Peter Sutcliffe, who was assessed as being driven by a paranoid delusion that he was doing God's work by ridding the world of *'filthy prostitutes'* (MacCulloch, 1993). In relation to sexual violence, Smith and Taylor (1999) found that hallucinations and delusions can be directly or indirectly related. When directly related, the hallucinations and delusions contain a sexual element that is clearly linked to a sexual assault. Examples include the attack being carried out as part of a mission, as with Peter Sutcliffe, or an offender hearing voices instructing him to carry out a sexual assault. When indirectly related, the hallucinations and delusions contained a sexual component that was not directly linked to a sexual assault. Examples include an offender believing he is famous and admired by women, hearing voices discussing sexual matters, or feeling the sensation of being touched in the genitals (see appendix in Smith & Taylor, 1999). The idea that some men will engage in sexual violence in response to voices in their heads was supported by earlier research by Jones *et al.* (1992). They found that some offenders engage in sexual violence in direct response to auditory or *'command hallucinations'* instructing them to sexually assault someone. Examples include voices *"telling him that he should rape a girl to cure himself of all his ills"* (ibid., p. 47) and voices saying, *"go on, she wants it"* (ibid., p. 48). Indeed, a colleague and I have previously presented an example of such a case, involving a man with a mental illness who:

> *sat in a car armed with knives waiting for a particular type of woman to rape and murder. He had been acting like this for several weeks. This behaviour was apparently driven by voices in his head that instructed him to find rape and kill a woman. The thought of this excited him and had become incorporated into his sexual fantasies.*
>
> (see case 7 in Greenall & Jellicoe-Jones, 2007, p. 330)

Jones *et al.* (1992) suggest the idea of command hallucinations must be taken very seriously because some offenders obey these voices. This was supported by other research, which found large numbers of mentally ill offenders were driven to offend by symptoms of their illness (Taylor *et al.*, 1998) and that individuals experiencing command hallucinations were more likely to be violent (McNiel *et al.*, 2000). However, studies of sexual offenders suggest this occurs only in a minority of cases (Chesterman & Sahota, 1998; Hodelet, 2001; Phillips *et al.*, 1999; Smith & Taylor, 1999). This leads us to another possible way that mental illness can influence sexual violence, which is through the impact it has on the individual.

Impact of mental illness

In relation to how the impact of a mental illness may result in sexual violence, a seminal study was conducted by Craissati and Hodes (1992). They highlighted how mental illness can breakdown the normal inhibitory controls that most men have. Sexual offences were impulsively executed with little thought given to potential capture, and they were primarily triggered by feelings of sexual disinhibition. The concept of sexual disinhibition induced by mental illness was supported by Phillips *et al.* (1999), who found this was an important feature in the sexual offences committed by their sample.

Typology of mentally ill sex offenders

In an attempt to capture the different ways in which mental illness and sexual violence can co-occur, researchers from Australia (i.e., Drake & Pathé, 2004) developed a typology of mentally ill sexual offenders. This divides these individuals into four groups:

1 Those with a deviant sexual preference (see Chapter 6) that predates the onset of their mental illness. Their mental illness may exacerbate pre-existing sexually deviant behaviour through disinhibition or the influence of delusions or hallucinations.
2 Those for whom sexual violence arose in the context of a mental illness. This may be, for example, due to them experiencing hallucinations, delusions, disinhibition, or an increase in impulsivity.
3 Those for whom sexual violence is a manifestation of more generalised antisocial behaviour, which involves a co-morbid presentation of mental illness and antisocial personality traits.
4 Those whose sexual violence was related to other factors.

An example of how this typology can prove useful is provided by a case example from my forensic/clinical practice (see Box 5.3). When considering the case of '*Barry*', we can understand his assault in terms of him being an example of Drake and Pathé's (2004) type two presentation. This is because his offence postdated his illness and therefore arose in the context of that illness, a major aspect of which was disinhibition and failing to give due consideration to the aftermath (Craissati & Hodes, 1992).

Box 5.3   Case example: The role of mental illness

This case is taken from my clinical practice in a forensic medium secure unit

Barry is in his 40s, single, and has never been married or had a sexual relationship. One day he followed a young woman (a stranger) into a park, where he grabbed her from behind and tried to pull her shorts down. She screamed, and he ran off, and he was quickly identified and arrested. He later claimed he was sexually frustrated. His only sexual outlet was pornography; he wanted to see what a real woman looked like, and she looked nice. He was disinhibited by his mental illness, and this stopped him from considering the consequences of his actions.

Other presenting features

Although PD and mental illness are important presentations, studies of sexual offenders suggest they can present with other types of mental disorders (e.g., see Ahlmeyer *et al.*, 2003; Booth, 2010; Chen *et al.*, 2016; McElroy *et al.*, 1999). Examples include mood disorders (e.g., major depressive disorder, and bipolar disorder), anxiety disorders (e.g., social phobia, generalised anxiety disorder, and post-traumatic stress disorder), and Asperger's disorder. In considering the link between these disorders and sexual violence, Schug and Fradella (2015) make several important points. First, in relation to mood and anxiety disorders, although several studies have shown high rates of these disorders among sexual offenders, the link between them and sexual violence remains uncertain. For example, in relation to mood disorders, Schug and Fradella (2015) argue that there is no way of knowing whether high rates of mood disorders among sexual offenders are due to the characteristics of these disorders, such as hypersexuality, aggression, agitation, or impulsivity. Similarly, in relation to anxiety disorders, Schug and Fradella (2015) argue that more work is required to determine how this disorder may contribute to sexual violence. Second, Schug and Fradella (2015) suggest that more is known about the link between Asperger's disorder and sexual violence, as these assaults may be related to social skills deficits, which may lead to some men having poor relations with women and having limited knowledge of how to engage with them. In such circumstances, an individual who is ill-equipped to deal with relations with women may approach and touch a woman he desires, especially if he experiences a state of sexual arousal. Essentially, in these cases, we can hypothesise that an individual with a mood, anxiety, or Asperger's disorder may, like their PD and mentally ill counterparts, experience a sense of disinhibition and/or a destabilisation of their decision-making, which in turn may contribute to them engaging in sexual violence in certain circumstances. However, regardless of which mental disorder may be present, it will only ever be one of several contributory factors, some of which will be more stable or changeable than others.

Stable and dynamic factors

An individual's core values, beliefs, and mental state are potentially changeable but relatively stable features of their presentation. Consequently, if a stranger sexual offender presents with pro-criminal core values and beliefs and/or a mental disorder, we can reasonably hypothesise that these features may have contributed to his offending and were present on the day of his offence and in the days, weeks, months, and possibly years beforehand. However, other aspects of a stranger sexual offender's presentation are more dynamic and subject to rapid change, one of which is intoxication.

Intoxication from alcohol or drugs

One factor that can change rapidly in an individual is intoxication. Like PD, the usage of intoxicants such as alcohol or drugs exists on a continuum, with recreational usage at one end and usage that hinders an individual's social, educational, and occupational functioning at the other (American Psychiatric Association, 2022). However, whilst only some people may possess pro-criminal core values and beliefs and have a mental disorder, many more will have experienced the effects of intoxication and be aware of its potential to influence our decision-making and behaviours. Indeed, the chances are everyone reading this book has, at one time or another, said or done something when intoxicated that was the cause of regret the next morning. But if intoxication can make sensible people say or do silly things, can it also contribute to an individual's decision to engage in sexual violence?

On the one hand, the answer is yes. Research suggests that many sexual offenders have histories of abusing substances (Abracen *et al.*, 2000; Ahlmeyer *et al.*, 2003; Chen *et al.*, 2016; Craissati & Blundell, 2013; Grubin & Gunn, 1990; McElroy *et al.*, 1999), and a history of abusing substances is a risk factor for future sexual violence (Boer *et al.*, 2017; Hart *et al.*, 2022). Indeed, as we shall see in later chapters, intoxication may contribute to acts of stranger sexual violence in many cases, given the timings and locations in which some attacks occur. On the other hand, although many sexual offenders have histories of abusing substances, intoxication appears to be present in only a minority of cases, and the importance of its role may be viewed differently by different parties. For example, whilst Groth and Birnbaum (1979) argued the use of alcohol was insufficient to account for sexual violence, Scully (1994) found that intoxication can be used by sexual offenders to account for their offences. The key thing to bear in mind is that just because a stranger sexual offender has a history of substance abuse, it does not follow that he was intoxicated at the time of their offence. Likewise, just because a stranger sexual offender does not have a history of substance abuse, it does not follow that he was sober at the time of the offence. As ever, each case needs to be assessed, and the role (if any) of intoxicants, and indeed any other potential factor, needs to be considered on its merits.

Conclusions and Implications for practice

To help us to further understand the sexually violent actions of men who target female strangers, this chapter has explored factors that can influence their pre-offence decision-making and aspects of the offence itself. Consideration of these factors can help us to further develop an evidence-based formulation of how/why an offender came to conclude that sexually assaulting a female stranger was acceptable.

Perhaps one reason why some men sexually assault female strangers is because they have core values and beliefs that include thoughts or fantasies of harming others and which lead them to encourage, excuse, justify, minimise sexual violence, and/or deny engaging in sexual violence all together. Whilst these core values and beliefs may have their origins in adverse childhood experiences, Feminist writers argue they are part of a male-dominated society in which sexual violence is used by men to keep women in a state of fear (Brownmiller, 1975). Whether or not such core values and beliefs are a feature of our society, the important thing is that such values and beliefs only appear to be held, or at least acted upon, by some men. Indeed, as Herman argued, "*the unanswered question posed by feminists is not why some men rape, but why most men do not*" (1990, p. 178).

Perhaps another reason why some men sexually assault female strangers is because they have a mental disorder. Certainly, this idea will carry favour in some quarters, such as the media, where ideas of stranger sexual violence being related to some form of mental pathology are evidenced by these offenders being portrayed as '*sex fiends who prey on lone women*' (e.g., Knox, 2020). Moreover, research does suggest that rates of mental disorders are higher among offenders than the general population. Indeed, such is the mental health needs of offenders that in 2007, an official report found 80% of prisons in England and Wales had multidisciplinary mental health in-reach teams imbedded within them (HM Inspectorate of Prisons, 2007). However, in most cases, the nature, degree, and severity of their presenting mental disorder are such that they do not require detention under the Mental Health Act 1983 within secure forensic mental health services. In relation to sexual offenders, the rates of mental disorders appear similar to their non-sexual offender counterparts, and most end up in prison, as only a minority of those detained in secure forensic mental health services have index offences for sexual violence (Kasmi *et al.*, 2020; Völlm *et al.*, 2018). Consequently, whilst ideas of stranger sexual offenders being '*mad*' may serve to separate '*them from us*', research does not support this idea. Notwithstanding this fact, consideration of the potential role of a mental disorder within cases of stranger sexual violence has several important practice-based implications, not only for those working with known offenders but also for police officers who must apprehend them (Kelly, 2023b):

1 The fact that most sexual offenders will present with a PD means that criminal justice practitioners who work with sexual offenders 'will' encounter those with a PD from time to time. Therefore, some knowledge and understanding of PD and how it can contribute to offending is essential for their practice (Craissati *et al.*, 2020).

2 The fact that only a minority of sexual offenders will present with a mental illness means many criminal justice practitioners may only rarely, if ever, encounter these offenders. However, practitioners who work with sexual offenders may still encounter those with mental illnesses, especially if they work within forensic mental health services. Once again, therefore, some knowledge and understanding of mental illness and how it can contribute to sexual offending is essential for their practice (Drake & Pathé, 2004).

3 Although sexual offenders with a mental disorder may be a particular type of offenders, like all sexual offenders, they are a heterogeneous group. This not only extends to how their mental disorder may contribute to their acts of sexual violence, but as we shall see in more detail in volume two, even mentally disordered sexual offenders, including those who target strangers, offend for a variety of reasons beside their mental disorder (see Greenall & West, 2007, 2008).

4 Mentally disordered offenders often present with a combination of co-morbid mental disorders. Indeed, it has long been recognised that co-morbid presentations of multiple mental disorders may be the rule rather than the exception (Blackburn, 2000). Accordingly, criminal justice practitioners who work with sexual offenders will encounter those with other psychological presentations in addition to a PD and a mental illness (e.g., mood, anxiety, or Asperger's disorder). These disorders may also have contributed to their offending by disinhibiting them or by destabilising their decision-making at the material time.

This leads us to one final reason why some men sexually assault female strangers, which is perhaps they were intoxicated. Although this idea may be used by some to justify or excuse their offences, when considering the role of intoxication, we need to remember two important points. First, although intoxication may disinhibit some individuals and thereby contribute to their acts of sexual violence, this will not always be the case. As alluded to in Box 3.1, many men may find themselves in the company of female strangers when one or both are intoxicated, and even though these women may be an *"easy target"* (see Box 5.2), most of these encounters end without incident. Second, although intoxication may be a contributory factor in an opportunistic convenience assault of a female stranger encountered during or at the end of an evening socialising in a bar or club, this may not be the case in premeditated precautionary or premeditated opportunistic sexual assaults, as a clearer head may be required to carry out these assaults. Whether or not any of the factors considered within this chapter are relevant to the particular case you are dealing with, there is another important fact which can influence an offender's pre-offence decision-making and aspects of the offence itself, namely sexual deviancy. That is the focus of the next chapter.

6 The sexually deviant offender

We tend to see sex as a fundamental aspect of who we are as human beings. A person's sexuality is regarded as a vital aspect of their identity

(Barker, 2018, p. 13)

Introduction

The previous chapters have shown that stranger sexual violence is an intentional crime committed by men who attack female strangers to satisfy various psycho-sexual needs with some men going to some lengths to achieve this. On a behavioural level, many actions exhibited by stranger sexual offenders during their assaults, such as kissing, fondling, and sexual intercourse, are, under normal circumstances, traditional sexual interactions between men and women. However, as alluded to in Cchapter 4 when considering how some sexual offences are classified as sadistic, on some occasions, the needs a sexual offender seeks to satisfy by his offending are of a sexually deviant nature. This raises an important issue that every single criminal justice practitioner who works with sexual offenders should be mindful of: some sexual offenders are motivated by a desire to satisfy deviant sexual needs, and they target female strangers and invest some effort to achieve this. As with many topics within this book, sexual deviancy is not a uniform construct, as it presents itself in several different ways. Ironically, perhaps the best known sexually deviant presentation, paedophilia, is not relevant here as that involves the victimisation of children. However, several other sexually deviant presentations are relevant to the sexual victimisation of adult women by male strangers, and therefore, every single criminal justice practitioner who works with sexual offenders should have a basic understanding of this phenomenon.

Chapter aims

In the previous chapter, we explored factors that operate at a psychological level and influence offender decision-making, some of which amount to a mental disorder. Here we will continue with this theme by exploring the concept of sexual deviancy and how it too can influence offender decision-making, be evident within acts of stranger sexual violence, and amount to a mental disorder. Although sexually deviant behaviours are defined within DSM-5-TR (American Psychiatric Association, 2022) and ICD-11 (World Health Organization, 2022), this book will focus on the DSM approach, as that is perhaps more popular within academic and applied circles. This chapter will define

DOI: 10.4324/9781003217763-7

the concept of sexual deviancy and illustrate what we know about its development and prevalence in community and offender samples. Then, whilst chapters in volume two will focus on other sexually deviant presentations, this chapter will end with a focus on sadism. Doing this will (1) enhance our understanding of the importance of sadism to the classification of sexual violence, (2) provide a basis for understanding how sadism is evident in specific offences explored in volume two, and (3) allow us to consider one or two critical concepts in this area, which every single criminal justice practitioner whose role involves working with sexual offenders should be aware of.

Definition: *Sexual deviancy, paraphilias, and paraphilic disorders*

Definitions of sexual deviancy are influenced by prevailing societal norms, as illustrated by the changing status of homosexuality, which was once regarded as a treatable condition (Feldman & MacCulloch, 1971) and a mental disorder in earlier editions of the DSM (Moser & Kleinplatz, 2020). Sexual deviancy has been a contentious issue since biblical times (Aggrawal, 2009c) and has received attention from mental health (De Block & Adriaens, 2013), legal (Modern Propensities, 1791), and literary (Tarr, 2016) fields. One early famous contributor to this area was Austrian Psychiatrist Von Krafft-Ebing, who in the nineteenth century described the male sex drive as:

> "a natural instinct which, with all-conquering force and might, demands fulfilment" …[and]… "in the lustful impulse to satisfy this natural instinct, man stands on a level with the animal".
>
> (1894, p. 1)

Although from a bygone age, these sentiments raise a fundamental question that is relevant today. Whilst a sexual force like this has evolutionary benefits when directed at the process of procreation to ensure human survival, what happens when it is directed towards deviant sexual behaviours that victimise others?

Paraphilias

For many years, mental health professionals and laymen viewed deviant sexual behaviour as *'perverse'* or *'kinky'*. The potential danger of these behaviours was highlighted by another famous Austrian, Sigmund Freud, who cautioned that *"perversions are forms of incomplete maturity of sexual object and aim, which prevent full union of any kind with another individual"* (Stafford-Clark, 1965, p. 119). Today, such behaviour is labelled *'paraphilia'*. This term derives from Greek and illustrates that the deviation (*'para'*) relates to the source of erotic attraction (*'philia'*) (Moser & Kleinplatz, 2020). DSM-5-TR defines paraphilia as *"any intense and persistent sexual interest other than sexual interest in genital stimulation or preparatory fondling with phonotypical normal, physically mature, consenting human partners"* (American Psychiatric Association, 2022, p. 779). Essentially, DSM-5-TR is referring to atypical sexual behaviours that individuals can engage in alone and/or with others (see Table 6.1). On some occasions, paraphilias involve harmless activities conducted in private, such as a man cross-dressing and masturbating, or sadomasochistic sexual behaviour (e.g., spanking or bondage) between consenting partners. On other occasions, paraphilias can result in harm to the individual or others. For example, a man may accidentally kill himself whilst engaging in a masochistic sexual act called autoerotic asphyxia (see Sauvageau & Racette, 2006), or sadomasochistic sexual behaviour may result in the infliction of unlawful bodily harm (see R vs. Brown [1994] 1 AC 212). On other occasions, paraphilias can lead to the victimisation of non-consenting individuals and be incorporated into acts of stranger sexual violence (e.g., sadism) or constitute an act of stranger sexual violence itself (e.g., exhibitionism).

Earlier editions of the DSM regarded all paraphilias as a clinical condition, based on the assumption that acting on them would have negative consequences. Whilst this may be so in those cases that involve harm to self (e.g., autoerotic asphyxia) or others (e.g., exhibitionism), it may not be so in those harmless cases that are practiced alone. For example, a man with a long history of cross-dressing may be perfectly happy with this aspect of his life, and indulging in it may never have caused him any negative consequences. Despite this, earlier editions of the DSM would have classified his behaviour as a mental disorder. DSM-5-TR recognises this anomaly, and harmless deviant sexual interests such as indulging a rubber fetish, cross-dressing, or consenting to sadomasochism are classified as paraphilia, which *"does not necessarily justify or require clinical intervention"* (American Psychiatric Association, 2022, p. 780). However, as we shall see below and in more detail in volume two, the words *'not necessarily'* in that quote are very important, as the way some men indulge in what in most cases is harmless paraphilia is a matter of serious concern that requires more than simply *'clinical intervention'*.

Paraphilic disorders

When paraphilia causes distress or impairment to the individual or satisfaction entails personal harm or risk of harm to others, DSM-5-TR classifies this as a clinical condition (and a mental disorder) called a *'paraphilic disorder'*. DSM-5-TR provides diagnostic criteria for eight paraphilic disorders (see Table 6.1). For an individual to be classified as having a paraphilic disorder, their abnormal sexual focus needs to have been present for at least six months, and acting on them will have caused clinically significant distress or impairment in social, occupational, or other important areas of functioning. The diverse nature of paraphilic disorders is such that the DSM-5-TR divides them into

Table 6.1 DSM-5-TR paraphilic disorders

Label	Behavioural focus	Prevalence
Courtship disorders		
Exhibitionism	Exposing the genitals	4.8%–32.6%
Frotteurism	Touching or rubbing against non-consenting individuals	3.8%–30%
Voyeurism	Spying on others in private activities	9.6%–50.3%
Pain & suffering		
Sadism	Inflicting humiliation, bondage, or suffering	2.2%–2.7%
Masochism	Undergoing humiliation, bondage, or suffering	2.2%
Specific people		
Paedophilia	Sexual focus on children	3%
Objects		
Fetishism	Non-living objects or non-genital body parts	–
Transvestism	Sexually arousing cross-dressing	3%

two groups based on the related activities and targets (American Psychiatric Association, 2022, p. 779).

1 *Anomalous (i.e., abnormal) activity preferences:* This group is subdivided into courtship disorders that resemble distorted components of human courtship behaviour (e.g., voyeurism, exhibitionism, and frotteurism) and algolagnic disorders, which involve pain and suffering (e.g., masochism and sadism).
2 *Anomalous (i.e., abnormal) target preferences:* This group includes sexual behaviours that are directed at specific people (e.g., paedophilia) or objects (e.g., fetishism and transvestism).

DSM-5-TR also lists but does not provide diagnostic criteria for '*other specified paraphilic disorder*'. This includes recurrent and intense sexual arousal involving telephone scatologia (obscene phone calls), necrophilia (corpses), zoophilia (animals), coprophilia (faeces), klismaphilia (enemas), and urophilia (urine). Once again, these disorders need to have been present for at least six months, and acting on them will have caused marked distress or impairment in social, occupational, or other important areas of functioning (American Psychiatric Association, 2022, p. 801). However, as you will discover by typing '*list of paraphilias*' into an internet search engine, the above is not an exhaustive list. Rather, there are numerous other paraphilias that cover the full range of human activities, many of which are related to violent, criminal, or antisocial behaviour (see Chapter 10). One crucial factor here is that, as with personality disorder, the existence of several paraphilic disorders raises the possibility of some individuals presenting with combinations of co-morbid paraphilias. Indeed, as shown in Table 6.2, DSM-5-TR recognises that individuals with one paraphilia may present not only with another paraphilia but also with one or more other mental disorders. An example of this was provided by Blanchard and Hucker (1991), who found multiple paraphilias (e.g., bondage, cross-dressing) and other sexual behaviours (e.g., anal self-stimulation, self-observation with mirrors or cameras) coexisted in fatal cases of autoerotic asphyxia.

Origins of paraphilias

As alluded to above, one way of understanding paraphilias is to view them as existing on a continuum of harm, with harmless behaviours (e.g., fetishism) at one end and

Table 6.2 Paraphilic co-morbidity

Label	Co-morbid disorders
Exhibitionism	*Depression, bipolar disorder, anxiety, substance abuse, hypersexuality, ADHD, other paraphilias, and antisocial PD.*
Frotteurism	*Hypersexuality, exhibitionism, voyeurism, conduct disorder, antisocial PD, depression, bipolar, anxiety, and substance abuse disorders.*
Voyeurism	*Hypersexuality, exhibitionism, depression, bipolar disorder, anxiety, substance abuse, ADHD, conduct disorder, and antisocial PD.*
Sadism	*Other paraphilias.*
Masochism	*Transvestism.*
Paedophilia	*Depression, bipolar, anxiety, substance use, APD, and other paraphilia.*
Fetishism	*Other paraphilias and hypersexuality.*
Transvestism	*Fetishism, masochism, and autoerotic asphyxia.*

the more harmful (e.g., exhibitionism), violent (e.g., sadism), and deadly paraphilias (e.g., erotophonophilia or sexual murder) at the other. To gain an understanding of men who engage in these behaviours, especially those who do so by victimising adult female strangers, some consideration of what may have contributed to their deviant sexual presentation is useful. In doing this, we must remember the caveat expressed in Chapter 4 when considering how sex offender heterogeneity renders the idea of one explanatory theory illogical, as the heterogeneity of paraphilias and those who engage in them suggests a similar argument applies here. Put simply, the reason why one man becomes a cross-dresser may not be the same as why another becomes a sadistic sexual offender. When faced with a stranger sexual offender who has evidenced sexual deviancy in their offending, the work of Healey (2006) can help criminal justice practitioners to understand the origins of this aspect of their offence. Healey (2006) suggests the origins of paraphilias can be understood in terms of two pathways that commenced in adolescence: one relates to the introduction of deviant stimuli and the other to experiencing trauma.

Introduction of deviant stimuli

Adolescence is a time of sexual development, and Healey (2006) suggests that some people may develop paraphilia because they are exposed to deviant stimuli during this time. For example, a boy raised in a normal loving household where he is exposed to several female influences (e.g., mothers and sisters) may develop a fetish for women's underwear due to a chance encounter with these garments. Mindful of the sexual connotation of these items, he may become aroused by handling them whilst, for example, searching through some laundry and subsequently masturbates. In time, he may obtain and hide items of women's underwear for masturbatory purposes. Through masturbation and orgasm, the boy becomes conditioned to find women's underwear sexually arousing, and his pathway to adult transvestism has begun (Healey, 2006). In my forensic/clinical practice, I worked with a sexual offender who matched Healey's account. With him, a chance encounter with a pair of girl's tights during a PE lesson (i.e., back in the days when we all got undressed in the classroom!) triggered an erotic response that was later reinforced through masturbation and led him into adult transvestism. Healey's explanation also echoes comments by Von Krafft-Ebing, who, over a century ago, cautioned parents and teachers to avoid spanking boys as it could lead to masochism: "*it sometimes happens that in boys the first excitation of the sexual instinct is caused by a spanking, and they are thus incited to masturbation*" (1894, p. 28).

Experience of psychological trauma

In contrast to what may be a chance encounter that leads to a harmless paraphilic sexual interest, Healey (2006) suggests that some paraphilias are, like personality disorders, the result of early trauma. These more harmful paraphilias are the result of the individual equating feelings of inadequacy, shame, guilt, fear, hatred, or aggression with sexuality. The trauma underpinning these negative feelings may have occurred in early childhood or during adolescence. And similar to how early negative experiences can contribute to the development of negative schemas and ultimately a personality disorder, here the impact of early trauma can influence an individual's thoughts and fantasies, which become sexualised. Healey (2006) suggests that certain paraphilias may be related to certain negative experiences. For example, telephone scatologia, frotteurism, voyeurism, and exhibitionism are indicative of inadequacy and being made to feel this way by an overbearing parent during adolescence. Sadism, erotophonophilia (i.e., sexual murder), and biastophilia (i.e., rape) relate to issues of control. These individuals may have been physically, sexually, or emotionally abused as children, and to regain control, they resort to victimising others. Again, like many who have worked with sexual offenders, I have previously encountered offenders who have experienced various types of trauma in their early years. And whilst these experiences may not have been singularly causal in terms of their later sexual behaviour, they were almost certainly contributory. This explains why the experience of childhood abuse/trauma is regarded as a risk factor for sexual violence (Boer *et al.*, 2017; Hart *et al.*, 2022) and a focus of therapy in forensic settings (Wright & Warner, 2020).

Prevalence

Having defined and considered the possible causes of paraphilias, a key question is: how many men engage in them? Answering this question is difficult because the secretive nature of paraphilias means the true prevalence of these activities is unknown. After all, would *you* voluntarily reveal *your* sexual secrets to others? Despite this, research provides some indication of how widespread these practices are among community and offender samples.

Paraphilias among community samples

Within community samples, the DSM-5-TR provides some indication of the prevalence of the eight main paraphilic disorders among adult men. As shown in Table 6.1, the rates vary from 2.2% for sadism and masochism up to 50% for voyeurism (American Psychiatric Association, 2022). Researchers from Canada (i.e., Joyal & Carpentier, 2017; Joyal *et al.*, 2015) found large numbers of men from a community sample fantasising about paraphilias. Relevant examples include dominating someone (59.6%), tying someone up (48.4%), watching someone undress without them knowing (63.4%), spanking or whipping someone (43.5%), having sex with a fetish object (27.8%), exposing themselves in public (23.2%), abusing a drunk, asleep, or unconscious person (22.6%), forcing someone to have sex (22%), and cross-dressing (10%). They also found that almost half expressed interest in at least one paraphilic sexual activity, and approximately one-third had experienced such a practice at least once in their lifetime. Relevant examples experienced by men included voyeurism (50.3%), exhibitionism (32.6%), fetishism (30.1%), and frotteurism (32.4%). In a study of Italian university students, Castellini *et al.* (2018) found that just over half (50.6%) of men reported engaging in one paraphilia. Relevant examples include voyeurism (28%), exhibitionism (9.5%), frotteurism (10.3%), and sadism (9.5%). Paraphilias were also the subject of men's sexual fantasies and masturbatory stimuli. In the Czech Republic, Bártová *et al.* (2021) found that just under one-third (31.3%) of men admitted to at least one paraphilic preference, and almost a quarter (23.3%) had engaged in a paraphilia at least ten times in their lifetime. In relation to sexual fantasies, 40.2% of men reported being highly excited by some paraphilic topics, and 20.4% had paraphilic fantasies each week.

The above studies suggest a large ,minority and in some cases, over half of men in community samples are fantasising about, have experienced, or are engaging in one or more paraphilias. However, the fact that Bártová *et al.* (2021) found the percentage of people with paraphilia who confided in a healthcare professional was very low indicates that most are not adversely effected by their sexual deviancy. Indeed, Castellini *et al.* (2018) found that only 3.6% of their participants declared impairment or distress, meaning their paraphilia did not amount to a paraphilic disorder. Moreover, in their study of male psychiatric inpatients, Marsh *et al.* (2010) found that only 13.4% were diagnosed with at least one lifetime paraphilia and only 6.3% were diagnosed with a current paraphilia. Of note was the fact that Marsh *et al.* (2010) found rates of some of the most relevant paraphilias (i.e., voyeurism at 8%, exhibitionism at 5.4%, fetishism at 0.9%, and frotteurism at 0.9%) were lower than the rates found in community samples.

Paraphilias among sexual offenders

If indulging one or more paraphilias does not cause distress to most men or lead to psychiatric hospitalisation, then why should this topic warrant any attention from criminal justice practitioners? As with mental illness and personality disorder, one way of considering this matter is to explore the prevalence of paraphilia among sexual offenders. In doing this, we might assume that, as with mental illness and personality disorder, rates of paraphilias will be higher among sexual offenders. After all, if we assume that sexual offenders are a deviant group by virtue of their unlawful sexual behaviour, can we also assume they are sexually deviant too? The research suggests that, in many cases, this assumption is wrong.

In a study of sexual killers, sexual offenders, and murderers, Langevin *et al.* (1988) found very similar rates (i.e., 12%–13%) of courtship disorder and transvestism across these groups. However, rates of voyeurism were higher among the sex killers (54%) than the sexual offenders (38%) and murderers (17%). And whilst rates of exhibitionism and frotteurism were zero among the murderers, among the sexual killers, the rates were 23% and 31%, respectively, and 31% for both disorders among the sexual offenders. A finding of note, however, was that whilst sadism was low among the murderers (8%) and absent among the sexual offenders (0%), a significantly higher rate (75%) was found among the sexual killers. The idea that rates of some paraphilias are higher among sexual killers was supported by Grubin (1994), who found paraphilias noted in 43% of sexual killers and 26% of rapists. Similarly, Proulx and Sauvêtre (2007) found that, apart from exhibitionism, rates of fetishism, masochism, transvestism, and voyeurism were higher among a sample of sexual killers (i.e., all 6.7%) than a sample of sexual aggressors (i.e., 3%, 1%, 0%, & 4%). Sadism was the most common paraphilia among both groups, with 16.7% of sexual killers and 7.9% of sexual aggressors. Similar results were found by Chan and Beauregard (2016), who found that sexual killers manifested more paraphilias than sexual offenders. In relation to some of the paraphilias from Table 6.1, rates of paraphilias among sexual killers ranged from 5.4% to 33.8% and 0% to 7.3% among sexual offenders. Once again, sadism was the most common paraphilia among both groups, with 45.9% of sexual killers and 35.4% of sexual offenders. Research suggests that differences also exist between serial and single sexual offenders. For example, Prentky *et al.* (1989) found rates of exhibitionism, voyeurism, fetishism and transvestism were higher among serial sexual killers (i.e., 25%, 75%, 71%, & 25% respectively) than single sexual killers (i.e., 7%, 43%, 33% & 0%, respectively). Similarly, Chan *et al.* (2015) found higher rates of exhibitionism, fetishism, masochism, sadism, and voyeurism among serial sexual killers (i.e., 30.8%, 30.8%, 61.5%, 30.8%, & 23.1%, respectively) than single sexual killers (i.e., 8.2%, 16.4%, 12.3%, 17.8%, & 1.4%). However, single sexual killers had higher rates of frotteurism than serial sexual killers (i.e., 13.7% vs. 7.7%, respectively).

Apart from finding very high rates (85%) of paraphilia among high-risk sexual offenders, a finding of note from Woodworth *et al.* (2013) relates to levels of paraphilic co-morbidity. The number of paraphilias among these offenders ranged from 0 to 8 (mean of 1.3), with 57% having one paraphilia, 17% having two paraphilias, and 11% having three or more paraphilias. These findings mirror previous research which has found paraphiliac co-morbidity existing among sexual offenders (e.g., Abel *et al.*, 1988). However, as indicated in Table 6.2, co-morbidity among sexual offenders will not just include multiple paraphilias or, as highlighted in the previous chapter, multiple mental disorders, as some sexual offenders will present with one or more co-morbid paraphilias and one or more mental disorders, such as a mental illness, personality disorder, or substance abuse disorder (e.g., Marshall, 2007). Indeed, when referring to how trauma can lead an individual to develop violent paraphilic interests, Healey (2006) suggested that an important factor that may contribute to this process and lead them to act out violent paraphilia is the presence of a co-morbid psychopathic personality. Given that, as suggested in the previous chapter, childhood trauma can also contribute to the development of personality disorder (Craissati *et al.*, 2020), it is not surprising that individuals who engage in violent paraphilias may also harbour personality difficulties.

Concluding comments on the prevalence of paraphilias

Research on the prevalence of paraphilias suggests that although rates of paraphilias are generally higher among some types of sexual offender (i.e., sexual killers), there does not appear to be the same noticeable difference between community and offender samples as we saw in relation to mental illness and personality disorder. Rather, the research suggests that rates of paraphilia among sexual offenders vary in a manner that is not strikingly dissimilar to their community counterparts. Moreover, paraphilic co-morbidity exists in community and offender samples. Notwithstanding these similarities, research suggests that sexual deviancy *is* a relevant factor when it comes to understanding sexual violence. To understand how and why this is so, as with mental illness and personality disorder, we need to consider how the former can contribute to the latter.

Sexual deviancy and sexual violence

When considering the relevance of sexual deviancy to stranger sexual violence, an important point to consider is that sex is, by its very pleasurable nature, a type of behaviour that most people are motivated to engage in repeatedly during their lives. In many cases, this is not problematic, as it will involve consenting partners engaging in harmless sexual activity, be it for pleasure, pro-creation, or both. This can occur between lovers, casual acquaintances, or strangers. However, as alluded to above when considering the comments from Von Krafft-Ebing (1894), this raises a fundamental question for criminal justice practitioners to consider: if Barker's (2018) quote at the start of this chapter is correct, and sex is a fundamental aspect of who we are and our sexuality is a vital aspect of our identity, then what happens if some or all of an individual's sexuality can only be satisfied by engaging in deviant sexual behaviours at the expense of others? The answer is simple: if an individual is motivated to behave in this way, their deviant sexual preference constitutes a sexual violence risk-enhancing factor. Moreover, by suggesting such behaviours have their origins in childhood, Healey (2006) suggests this will be a chronic feature of an individual's presentation and will remain so for some time.

Sexual deviancy and sexual violence risk

The idea that sexual deviancy is an important contributory factor when understanding sexual violence is supported by some key studies. For example, Hanson and Bussière (1998) found that one of the best predictors of sexual re-offending was sexual deviancy. This was confirmed by Hanson and Morton-Bourgon (2004), who found deviant sexual interests were an important predictor of sexual recidivism, and "*individuals with identifiable interests in deviant sexual activities were among those most likely to continue sexual offending*" (ibid., p. 15). This is not to say that sexual deviancy was the only contributory factor, as Hanson and colleagues found general criminality (i.e., prior non-sexual offending, antisocial personality disorder, etc.) or an antisocial orientation (e.g., unstable lifestyle, history of rule violation) were equally important (Hanson & Bussière, 1998; Hanson & Morton-Bourgon, 2004). Nonetheless, findings such as these have resulted in sexual deviancy, often indicated by a diagnosis of paraphilia, being regarded as an important risk factor for future sexual violence and one that should be considered in all individualised formulations of sexual violence risk (see Chapter 11). However, although sexual deviancy is included in some of the most widely used risk assessment protocols (see Table 6.3), this leaves another important question for criminal justice practitioners to consider: are all paraphilic sexual preferences at equal risk?

An equal risk?

Although the widely used protocols within Table 6.3 define sexual deviancy, they do not provide guidance as to whether some paraphilias are more important or '*risky*' than others. Put simply, if one sexual offender has a history of sadism and another is cross-dressing, both would be regarded as having a deviant sexual preference, but should this aspect of their presentation receive equal weight in considerations of future risk? In considering this question, research by Baur *et al.* (2016) is relevant. On the one hand, they found 21.1% of paraphiliacs had engaged in sexual violence, compared to only 6.2% of non-paraphiliacs. However, although they found associations between exhibitionism, masochism, sadism, voyeurism, and sexual violence were moderate to strong, the percentages of each group who had sexually offended varied, i.e., exhibitionists (33.9%), masochists (16.6), sadists (27%), and voyeurs (25.9%). So, whilst the presence of a paraphilia may increase sexual violence risk, rates vary between individual paraphilic

Table 6.3 RSVP-V2 and SVR-20v2 definitions of sexual deviancy

Risk for Sexual Violence Protocol (RSVP-V2)	Sexual Violence Risk-20v2 (SVR-20v2)
"*a relatively stable abnormality in the focus of the person's sexual appetite that motivates or incites sexual violence*"	"*a relatively stable pattern of sexual arousal to inappropriate stimuli (e.g., age-inappropriate or nonconsenting people, animals or inanimate objects) that causes serious distress or social dysfunction*"

Source: Taken from Boer *et al.* (2017), Hart *et al.* (2022)

presentations. If a deviant sexual preference is a feature of an individual's presentation, a key consideration is whether it is '*relevant*' to his history or future risk of sexual violence (see Chapter 11). To help determine this, we need to understand how important this feature is to their overall sexual presentation.

The importance of sexual deviancy to the individual

Whilst many people may indulge their paraphilic sexual interests, the importance it has to their sexual presentation will differ between individuals. One factor that will influence this is the legal status of the activity. Indeed, Joyal and Carpentier (2021) found paraphiliacs were more likely to engage in legal paraphilias than illegal ones. Returning to Table 6.1, we can see that some paraphilias are clearly unlawful (e.g., exhibitionism, voyeurism, frotteurism, and paedophilia), and if, despite this fact, a man remains motivated to engage in these behaviours, then this aspect of his sexual presentation will clearly be a matter of concern. However, in other cases, the legal status of some paraphilias is a bit more complex, as although they are not unlawful in and of themselves, they can become unlawful under certain circumstances. For example, although sadomasochism is lawful, as stated above, this will not be the case if it results in the infliction of unlawful bodily harm (see R vs. Brown [1994] 1 AC 212). Similarly, although fetishism and transvestism are lawful, this will not be the case if an individual obtains the object of his sexual desires (e.g., women's underwear) through acquisitive offending (see Chapter 7). In such cases, if a man remains motivated to engage in unlawful variants of these behaviours, then this aspect of their sexual presentation becomes a matter of concern.

Another factor that will influence some peoples' decisions to indulge their paraphilic sexual interests is the importance they place on the activity in question and whether it can co-exist with other sexual behaviours. This is illustrated by Gavin (2019), who suggests paraphilias can be divided into three groups based on whether the activity in question is an optional, preferred, or exclusive feature of an individual's sexual presentation:

1 *Optional paraphilia:* This is where a paraphilic activity serves as an alternative or additional route to sexual arousal. For example, a man with otherwise unremarkable sexual interests '*sometimes*' enhances his sexual arousal by wearing women's underwear whilst masturbating or during sex with his partner, or he engages in consensual sadomasochistic behaviour with his partner.
2 *Preferred paraphilia:* This is where a man prefers to engage in a paraphilic activity but nonetheless also engages in conventional sexual activities. For example, a man may '*prefer*' to wear women's underwear or engage in consensual sadomasochistic behaviour during sex with his partner whenever possible.
3 *Exclusive paraphilia:* This is where a man experiences an inability to become sexually aroused without engaging in a paraphilic activity. For example, a man *must* wear women's underwear or engage in sadomasochistic behaviour to become sexually aroused. This description captures the man referred to earlier who had a chance encounter with a pair of girl's tights during a school PE lesson. Now middle-aged and married, he admitted to being obsessed with female underwear and being unable to become sexually aroused or to have sex with his wife unless he was wearing it. Indeed, he admitted that if he saw a beautiful woman dressed in sexy lingerie, he would be more interested in her underwear than in her!

Gavin (2019) suggests that optional paraphilias are more common than preferred paraphilias, which are more common than exclusive paraphilias. If so, one hypothesis could be that men whose stranger sexual violence involves one or more paraphilias that victimise others will more likely be preferential or exclusive paraphiliacs, as offending may be their best/only means of satisfying their paraphilic sexual needs. The idea of preference or exclusivity links into the work of Schlesinger (2004a, 2004b), cited in Chapter 4. Drawing on his work, we can further hypothesise that these preferential or exclusive behaviours lie at the compulsive end of Schlesinger's motivational spectrum and, therefore, have a high likelihood of repetition. This point is perhaps especially relevant to police officers investigating a stranger sexual offence, because if they can determine whether it included one or more paraphilias, the idea of similar offences occurring before or indeed after the incident in question becomes a reasonable investigative hypothesis.

Sexual sadism

As illustrated in Chapter 4, one paraphilia that may be evident in cases of stranger sexual violence is sadism. Of the paraphilic disorders mentioned above, sadism stands out as having the potential to result in serious physical harm to others, up to and including death. Von Krafft-Ebing defined sadism as the *"association of active cruelty and violence with lust"* and noted *"that lust and cruelty frequently occur together is a fact that has long been recognised and not infrequently observed"* (1894, p. 57). Today, the concept of sexual sadism disorder is defined by the DSM-5-TR as being part of an individual's sexual presentation when the following criteria are satisfied:

a *"Over a period of at least six months, recurrent and intense sexual arousal from the physical or psychological suffering of another person, as manifested by fantasies, urges, or behaviours"*.
b *"The individual has acted on these sexual urges with a nonconsenting person, or the sexual urges or fantasies cause clinically significant distress or impairment in social, occupational, or other important areas of functioning"* (American Psychiatric Association, 2022, p. 790).

As the above criteria suggest, sexual sadism is not a uniform construct, as it can have different manifestations. Some people may only fantasise about engaging in sadistic sexual acts; others may engage in consensual sadistic sexual acts with partners or prostitutes, whilst others may engage in sadistic sexual acts at the expense of non-consenting others, including strangers. It is the last group that we are concerned about here. As noted in Chapter 4, sadism appears in several classification systems. For example, Groth and Birnbaum (1979) described the sadistic rapist as someone who derives sexual gratification from the intentional mistreatment of his victim and who takes pleasure in her torment, anguish, distress, helplessness, and suffering. Within such assaults, sexual areas of the victim's body (i.e., breasts, genitals, and bottom) are targeted, and along with the offender sexually penetrating his victim, he may also use foreign objects, such as a stick or bottle, to penetrate her sexually. A key consideration here is the relationship between sex and violence and how one can almost feed off the other. Groth highlighted this when describing the sadistic rapist: *"the more aggressive they are, the more powerful they feel; and in turn, the more powerful they feel, the more excited they become"* (1979, p. 46). Understanding this link is crucial, because, as we saw in Chapter 4, some sexual assaults can be violent, but the violence is not a source of sexual pleasure for the offender. This factor was used by Groth and Birnbaum (1979) to differentiate between angry (violence not eroticised) and sadistic (violence eroticised) rapes and within the MTC:R3 (Knight & Prentky, 1990a) to differentiate between the pervasively angry and vindictive types (violence not eroticised) and the sexual sadistic types (violence eroticised). Indeed, when classifying offenders using the MTC:R3, the differentiating factor between angry/vindictive and sadistic rapes is:

> the violence either contributes to sexual arousal, or at least does not appear to inhibit sexual arousal. There should be no evidence that the offender lost his erection or failed to ejaculate while he was assaulting the victim.
>
> (Knight & Prentky, 1990b)

On a behavioural level, Dietz *et al.* (1990) found that sexual sadists mostly approach their victims using a 'con' approach (90%). Victims are mostly strangers (83%), whom they torture (100%), tie up and gag (87%), and subject them to various sexual acts, including anal intercourse (73%), vaginal intercourse (57%), fellatio (71%), foreign object penetration (40%), and sexual bondage (77%). Despite this, many sadists (43.3%) experienced sexual dysfunction (e.g., problematic ejaculation). Of the victims who were killed, most were asphyxiated (61%), whilst others were stabbed (10%) or received blunt force trauma (3.1%). Finally, some sadists (40%) kept mementoes of their assault belonging to the victim (e.g., underwear or jewellery).

Identification of sadism

Having defined and considered the importance of sadism, a key consideration for criminal justice practitioners relates to how they can identify sadism within a sexual assault, including one involving a stranger. Whilst forensic/clinical practitioners have access to information about an offender and his offence(s) gained from records and clinical interviews, which they can use to assess whether an individual satisfies the criteria for sexual sadism disorder, other practitioners (e.g., police officers) are not so lucky. One possible means of identifying the presence of sadism within a sexual offence is to use a protocol specifically designed for this purpose (e.g., Longpré *et al.*, 2019; Mokros *et al.*, 2012). One such protocol is the severe sexual sadism scale (Mokros *et al.*, 2012). In recognising that sadism is not illegal unless legal boundaries regarding the level of harm inflicted are crossed, the severe sexual sadism scale is designed to capture "*the forensically relevant form of …[sadism]… in which someone else is being victimized against his or her own will*" (ibid., p. 764). As shown in Table 6.4, the scale consists of 11 dichotomous (yes = 1, no = 0) items that code behavioural indicators of severe sexual sadism within an offence. Whilst higher scores indicate higher levels of sadism, a cut-off score of four can distinguish between sadists and non-sadists (Nitschke & Marshall, 2018).

This scale has the potential to help criminal justice practitioners consider whether a stranger's sexual offence contained sadistic behaviours. In the case of police officers investigating a stranger sexual offence, for example, if the answer was yes, this could help them to formulate investigative hypotheses relating to motive and the potential for other offences occurring in the future, or linking a series of similar offences to this unknown offender (Davies & Woodhams, 2019; Woodhams & Tonkin, 2018). Moreover, understanding that a stranger's sexual offence included sadistic elements would help police

Table 6.4 Severe sexual sadism scale

Item
1. Offender is sexually aroused by the act.
2. Offender exercises power/control/domination over the victim.
3. Offender humiliates or degrades the victim.
4. Offender tortures the victim or engages in acts of cruelty towards the victim.
5. Offender mutilates sexual parts of the victim's body.
6. Offender engages in gratuitous violence towards the victim.
7. Offender keeps trophies of the victim.
8. Offender mutilates non-sexual parts of the victim's body.
9. Victim is abducted or confined.
10. Evidence of ritualism in the offense.
11. Insertion of objects into the victim's bodily orifices.

Source: Taken from Mokros *et al.* (2012)

officers and other criminal justice practitioners formulate hypotheses about the origins of the sexual offence(s) in question. This task is very important as it can help us to understand more about the offender and how/why he ended up committing a sadistic sexual offence.

The origins of sadistic sexual violence

The identification of sadism within a sexual offence allows for the formulation of hypotheses about how the assault came about. In relation to sadistic rapists, for example, Groth and Birnbaum (1979) observed that their assaults are deliberate, calculated, and pre-planned. The offender takes precautions, such as wearing a disguise or blindfolding his victim, who is targeted, sexually and violently assaulted, and sometimes murdered. These premeditated assaults differ from those of angry rapists, as they are not the result of a sudden explosion of anger. Similarly, within the MTC:R3, one of the differences between sadistic and pervasively angry rapists is the greater planning of the former's sexual assaults (Knight & Prentky, 1990a). Indeed, the idea that sadistic sexual violence is mostly planned was supported by Dietz *et al.* (1990), who found that 93.3% of such offences were carefully planned by the offender. Of course, it may not be the case that every sadistic sexual offender plans their offence beforehand. However, the idea that sadistic sexual assaults do not come out of nowhere leads us to consider how and where they do come from. A clue as to the origins of sadistic sexual violence comes from the DSM-5-TR definition above and its reference to fantasies. This suggests that sadistic sexual violence does not erupt out of nowhere but is the culmination of the offender having fantasised about such behaviour before deciding to and/or having the opportunity to enact it. The idea that sexual fantasy precedes sexual behaviour is not surprising and has probably been experienced by all of us during our lives. Equally therefore, we should not be too surprised to find that research suggests that deviant sexual fantasies precede sexual violence (e.g., see Bartels & Gannon, 2011).

Of particular relevance to our purposes is a seminal study by MacCulloch *et al.* (1983), who illustrated how deviant fantasies can escalate into acts of serious sadistic sexual violence. MacCulloch *et al.* (1983) examined a group of men from a high security hospital, most of whom had a personality disorder and whose offences had sexual connotations or were clearly sexual. In most cases, it was found that prior to and at the time of their

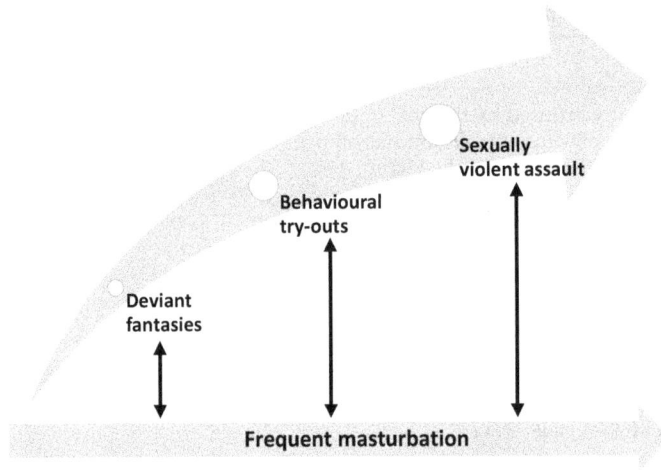

Figure 6.1 Escalation from fantasy to serious sadistic sexual violence

Source: Aadapted from MacCulloch *et al.* (1983)

offences, these men had been creating fantasies identical to all or part of their index offences. These fantasies included acts like rape, buggery, kidnapping, bondage, flagellation, anaesthesia, torture, and killing. These fantasies induced a state of sexual arousal in these men and were reinforced by masturbation. Over time, these fantasies escalated into real-life behavioural try-outs, whereby the offenders would leave home and try to enact part of the fantasy script, such as following a woman in a secluded location. These try-outs were required to maintain the effectiveness of the fantasies as a source of sexual arousal and were further reinforced by masturbation. This process escalated further and eventually culminated in the fantasised sexual assault occurring (see Figure 6.1).

Within my forensic/clinical practice, I previously worked with a young man who was on a fantasy-based offence trajectory similar to that shown in Figure 6.1. Although detention in the hospital between points two and three in Figure 6.1 put an end to his following of women, he simply transferred his deviant sexual attentions to female nurses, one of whom he wanted to rape and strangle (see Greenall & Millington, 2021). The key finding for criminal justice professionals from studies such as MacCulloch *et al.* (1983) is that the idea of sadistic sexual violence having its origins in deviant sexual fantasies is a reasonable hypothesis. Moreover, any pre-offence behavioural try-outs may have resulted in conviction for offences which, in retrospect, had a link with the sadistic sexual offence. Examples may include physical or sexual violence and acquisitive offences.

Conclusion and implications for practice

Carrying on with the theme of exploring the psychology of the stranger sexual offender, this chapter helps us to further understand the sexually violent actions of these men by considering the potential role and relevance of sexual deviancy. As with the previous chapter, consideration of this factor can help us to further develop an evidence-based formulation of how/why some offenders sexually assaulted female strangers in the way that they did. Although this chapter has focused on the concept of sexual deviancy, we cannot assume that all sexual offenders are sexually deviant or vice versa. Having said that, it would be wrong to ignore this concept. Whilst the research suggests that plenty of men are engaging in lawful deviant sexual behaviours, we cannot ignore the fact that sexual deviancy can involve unlawful behaviours committed at the expense of others. This explains why every single criminal justice practitioner whose role involves working with sexual offenders should have a basic understanding of the phenomenon of sexual deviancy. And depending on your role within the criminal justice system, to ask, as and when appropriate, a very important question:

1 *Police Officers:* Did the stranger sexual offence you are investigating evidence any sexually deviant acts?
2 *Other criminal justice practitioners:* Did the sexual offence(s) committed by the stranger sexual offender you are working with evidence any sexually deviant acts?

If the answer is no, then the concept of sexual deviancy is not relevant, and this chapter may only serve as some interesting background reading. However, if the answer is yes, then one or two other factors '*must*' be considered:

1 What kind of sexual deviancy was evident in the stranger sexual offence in question? Whilst this chapter has given some focus to sadism and provided a means by which this can be identified within an offence, other chapters later in this book will explore other sexually deviant presentations.
2 What might the sexually deviant behaviour exhibited by the stranger sexual offender tell us about the individual? By illustrating how the origins of deviant sexuality lie within an individual's adolescent years, this chapter has allowed us to formulate hypotheses about how and why a particular stranger sexual offender evidenced such behaviour within his offence. For example, is he enacting a deviant sexuality acquired through a chance encounter in his early years, or one that may be related to early trauma and perhaps be indicative of other dysfunctional presentations, such as a personality disorder?
3 How does the sexually deviant behaviour fit into the wider context of the offence? For example, if the offender took what might be regarded as unnecessary risks to commit the offence, this may suggest the deviant behaviour is of a preferential, exclusive, and even compulsive nature and therefore has a high likelihood of repetition.

By considering the contents of this chapter and by asking questions such as these, criminal justice practitioners can gain a better understanding of a stranger sexual offender and his offence(s), should they contain a deviant sexual element. Moreover, by exploring the link between sexual deviancy and sexual violence, we can understand how an individual's paraphilic sexual interest may exert different influences on their behaviour and potential sexual risk to others. For example, it is reasonable to view the occasional cross-dresser as presenting less of a sexual risk to others than the exclusive voyeur or exhibitionist, who in turn will present less of a risk than a preferential sadist, who enjoys combining serious violence and sex at the expense of others. In the next volume, we will explore individual presentations of stranger sexual violence. Some of them are well known, others will be of a deviant nature, and others will illustrate how an otherwise innocuous deviant sexual preference can have a devastating end.

Part 2

Stranger sexual violence

7 Acquisitive stranger sexual violence
Sexual burglaries and other thefts

Previously blameless in conduct, on the evening of July 5, 1876, he was detected taking stolen female under-garments from a place of concealment.

(case 82, Von Krafft-Ebing, 1894, p. 169)

Introduction

Acquisitive crime involves the invasion of personal space and the loss of private property. Burglary is perhaps the worst example of this, as that involves the invasion of one's home – a place where we are meant to be safe – and the loss of personal belongings. Although the number of burglaries in Britain has declined since the 1990s (Flatley, 2017), the nature of the problem is such that official guidelines exist to help police investigate burglaries (Association of Chief Police Officers, 2011) and to aid the courts when sentencing convicted burglars (Sentencing Council, 2022). These guidelines, however, view burglary as a crime that involves the unlawful acquisition of cash or valuables that can later be disposed of by the offender for financial gain. Although this view of burglary makes sense and, as we shall see, accounts for most cases, the danger is that other motives for burglary and its potential link with other types of crime will be missed by the police and the judiciary who follow these guidelines. The problem is that whilst most burglaries are financially motivated and, as the above guidelines recognise, may include other types of crime (e.g., threats/violence towards the occupant), as Von Krafft-Ebing (1894) recognised over a century ago, some burglaries have deeper psychological underpinnings and are aimed at satisfying the offender's deviant sexual desires. This raises an important issue that every single criminal justice practitioner should be mindful of: Some burglaries are sexually motivated and may be part of an escalating sexual offence trajectory (see Box 7.1).

Box 7.1 Sexual burglary: case examples

Colonel D Russell Williams (Canada)

A senior officer in the Canadian Airforce, at age 44 and with no previous convictions he commenced a series of sexual burglaries. During 2007–2010 he is believed to have committed around 82 sexual burglaries. They occurred during the hours of darkness, typically around midnight. Although valuables were often present, he never stole them. Rather his attentions were primarily focussed on women's underwear. During these burglaries he took almost 3,000 photographs of himself,

---

DOI: 10.4324/9781003217763-9

either wearing these garments and/or whilst displaying an erection or masturbating. Many victims were unaware they had been burgled and some were burgled more than once. Along with stealing sexual items, some offences included voyeurism. For example, on one occasion in July 2009, he disrobed and masturbated while watching an unsuspecting woman prepare to take a shower. He then entered her home through a window and stole her underwear. In September 2009 his offence trajectory escalated, as he physically and sexually assaulted the female occupants of two houses, blindfolding and tying them up and then photographing them. His offending then escalated further, first in November 2009 and then in January 2010, when he sexually murdered the female occupants of two houses, killing both by asphyxiation. He was identified by police because tyre tracks left at the second murder scene matched his distinctive car. After an intensive police interview in February 2010, he confessed his crimes. When asked why he committed them, he replied "*I don't know the answers, and I'm pretty sure the answers don't matter.*" He is now serving life in prison (source: Brankley et al., 2014; Watt, 2014).

Pawel Relowicz (Britain)

In 2021 26 year old Polish born Relowicz was convicted of the rape and murder of 21 year old university student Libby Squire in January 2019, after picking her up late one night after she had been out with friends. He had been driving round that night "*looking for a woman to have easy sex*". In the 18 months prior to this killing, he had committed a series of sexual offences in the student areas of Hull, that were later described in Court as a campaign of "*sexually deviant criminality*". These included acts of voyeurism, such as watching two students having sex through their bedroom window, observing one woman getting out of the shower and another in her underwear; acts of exhibitionism such as masturbating in front of women in public places, sometimes with his trousers round his ankles; and a string of burglaries during which he stole cash, sex toys (i.e., vibrators) and women's underwear. A used condom and a pair of knickers, described as his '*calling card*' by prosecutors, were left at more than one of his crime scenes. Due to him not having any previous convictions, his DNA was not on the police database, and so he was able to carry out these offences undetected. He is now serving life in prison (source: Various UK news reports).

Larry (USA)

At age 16 he was referred for a forensic assessment after being arrested for burglary. He had burgled five residences and stolen women's underwear; no cash, jewellery or other valuables were stolen. Each burglary took place at night after he was sure that no one was home. However, on one occasion he found a girl in bed, and he quickly left the house. Larry's attraction to women's underwear began at age 11. Although he denied using the underwear for sexual purposes, his attraction to women's underwear had expanded over a period of several years, leading up to the burglaries. He reported that he would sometimes steal women's underwear purely for the thrill of it.
Source: McCann (2000)

Chapter aims

This chapter introduces an unusual type of stranger sexual violence. These crimes mostly involve an offender entering someone's property with a view to stealing sexual items or engaging in sexual behaviours. On some occasions, there may be no contact between the offender and victim, who may not even be present when being victimised. On other occasions, contact between the offender and victim occurs with very serious and, in some cases, devastating consequences. This chapter explores how this type of stranger sexual violence may be defined, its prevalence, what typically happens within such offences and why, and what implications this type of sexual violence may have for future offending.

Definition: *What is this crime?*

To understand the concept of acquisitive sexual violence and the ways in which it can occur, we need to consider how the law may define this crime. This will show that once again, we are not dealing with a uniform construct but one that can be presented in various ways. Although acquisitive sexual violence is not defined under English Criminal Law, the two pieces of legislation most relevant are the Theft Act 1968 and the Sexual Offences Act 2003 (see Table 7.1).

Application: *Acquisitive sexual violence*

Based on the definitions within Table 7.1, we can appreciate that if a man enters a garden and steals women's underwear from her washing line, or if he steals these items from a public laundrette, he may have committed (sexual) theft. If he enters a house intent on stealing and/or damaging (i.e., tearing or ripping) women's underwear or other items of a sexual nature (e.g., sex toys), or if he sexually assaults a female occupant, he may have committed a (sexual) burglary. If he uses force against an occupant or puts them in fear

Table 7.1 Acquisitive sexual violence: relevant legislation

Theft Act 1968	Sexual Offences Act 2003
Theft (section 1): Involves the act of stealing or dishonestly obtaining property belonging to another person with the intention of permanently depriving them of it.	**Committing an offence with intent to commit a sexual offence (section 62):** Involves a man committing any offence with the intention of committing a relevant sexual offence.
Robbery (section 8): Involves the use of force or putting someone in fear of force whilst in the act of stealing.	**Trespass with intent to commit a sexual offence (section 63):** Involves trespassing on any premises with the intention to commit a sexual offence on the premises and the offender knows or is reckless as to whether he is a trespasser.
Burglary (section 9): Involves unlawfully entering a building or part of a building with the intention of stealing or attempting to steal something or inflicting or attempting to inflict harm on the occupant or damaging the building or its contents.	
Aggravated burglary (section 10): Involves committing burglary whilst carrying any type of weapon for this purpose.	

Source: Adapted from Macdonald (2018)

of force, he may have committed a (sexual) robbery. If he carries a weapon such as a knife, he may have committed a (sexual) aggravated burglary. Moreover, if he unlawfully entered the house intent on sexually assaulting the female occupant, he may also have committed one or both sexual offences. Having considered the various ways in which acquisitive sexual violence may be defined, a key question is: how often do they occur?

Prevalence: *How common is this crime?*

Acquisitive sexual violence is not recorded in the official criminal statistics. As such, the prevalence of such crimes is unknown. For example, although official statistics report 272,402 burglaries, 2.6 million thefts and 77,337 robberies occurring in England and Wales during the year ending June 2022, we have no way of knowing how many of them were of a sexual nature as that information is not provided (Stripe, 2023). What we do know from the research is that domestic burglary, for example, is a crime driven by a desire for financial gain. This is illustrated by Flatley (2017), who reports that the most frequently stolen items during domestic burglaries are purses, wallets, cash, jewellery, watches, computer equipment, and other electronic goods such as cameras. This reflects earlier research (e.g., Hearnden & Magill, 2004; Nee & Meenaghan, 2006), which found that along with cash, items targeted by burglars included jewellery and portable electronic goods, as they can be disposed of by the offender via second-hand shops or other similar outlets for financial gain, often to fund a drug habit (Hearnden & Magill, 2004). Although studies such as these provide an overview of domestic burglary, like the official guidelines in the opening paragraph, there is no mention of these crimes containing a sexual dynamic. The only finding of relevance for our purposes comes from Flatley (2017), who reports that around half of domestic burglaries are committed by strangers.

A very rare crime

The absence of any reference to acquisitive sexual violence within official reports suggests that such crimes are very rare. This is exactly what the limited research suggests. For example, in a study of 456 burglars, Vaughn *et al.* (2008) that found only 6.1% were of a sexual nature. These were labelled '*sexual predators*' as many of their burglaries were motivated by a desire to rape the household occupant. Harris *et al.* (2012) suggest one reason why sexual burglaries are rare is that many such cases end up being recorded as (or later plea bargained to) simple burglary. Be that so, whilst Vaughn *et al.* (2008) suggest that rates of sexual burglary are low among burglars, Harris *et al.* (2012) found that rates are higher among sexual offenders. In a study of 762 burglaries committed by sex offenders, Harris *et al.* (2012) found that just under a third (29%) were at least partially sexually motivated.

Media attention

When they do occur, acts of acquisitive sexual violence, even those that may be regarded as relatively minor, receive media attention. This point can be illustrated with reference to the crime of men stealing women's underwear from washing lines. Although undoubtedly annoying, such crimes are at the minor end of the stranger sexual violence continuum (see Chapter 1). However, as you will see if you type the words '*knicker thief*' into an internet search engine, there are many news stories relating to this type of acquisitive sexual violence available online, both in regional and national news media outlets. Greer (2003) suggests that several factors contribute to whether sexual violence is newsworthy, two of which may assist our understanding here. One is the *'novelty'* factor, and another is the *'shock'* factor. Drawing on these ideas, we can understand why a relatively minor form of sexual violence such as stealing women's underwear from washing lines becomes newsworthy, as it is a novel type of sexual violence that can happen to any woman the next time she hangs her underwear on her washing line. However, to further understand why these crimes may receive media attention, we need to understand what typically happens within them.

Offence details: What typically happens, when, and where?

To understand sexual burglary, we need to understand non-sexual burglary, because the former is a sub-type of the latter. Having established earlier that most domestic burglaries are financially motivated, the circumstances in which these crimes occur also need to be considered. In his overview of burglary and other household theft, Flatley (2017) provides the following summary of domestic burglary: The methods of entry are mostly through doors (70%) and windows (30%). Around 70% occur during the week and around 30% during the weekend. Approximately two-fifths occur during the morning or afternoon (6am to 6pm) and three-fifths during the evening or night (6pm to 6am). In over half of incidents where an offender entered the dwelling, someone was at home at the time. Those more likely to be victimised include younger people living in single-parent households in urban areas. In relation to how far burglars travel to commit a burglary, as we saw in Chapter 3, research suggests that most burglaries occur close to where the burglar himself lives (Ackerman & Rossmo, 2015; Hammond & Youngs, 2011; Rhodes & Conly, 1981).

Profile of sexual burglaries

In a study of sexual burglaries that occurred in houses and apartments in the USA, Pedneault *et al.* (2015) largely paint a similar picture. For example, almost half (49.1%) of the sexual burglars gained entry by breaking and entering, with the rest tricking their way in (18.5%), entering via unlocked doors or windows (17.1%), or using threats/violence (15.3%). Most cases (74.7%) occurred during the week and 25.3% during the weekend, with 53.6% occurring at night and 46.4% during the day. Most cases (93.8%) occurred on the first or second floor of the building, and most (87.5%) occurred in residences that were occupied at the time. When someone else was present in addition to the victim, these were children (12.9%), an adult woman (8.9%), and an adult man (7.6%). Further details about what occurs in sexual burglaries were provided by Harris *et al.* (2012). Among the 29% of burglaries committed by sexual offenders that were at least partially sexually motivated, Harris *et al.* (2012) found three behavioural sub-groups of sexual burglars:

1 *Covertly sexual burglaries:* Comprised 5% of the total sample and occurred when a residence was burgled to satisfy the offender's voyeuristic or fetishistic desires. Most of these (60%) were committed by rapists, and the use of weapons or violence was very low. Moreover, if something was stolen, it was typically women's clothing, lingerie, or accessories (86.5%). The residence was occupied in 30% of cases, perhaps suggesting

that in addition to theft, the offender's motivation included voyeurism. In most cases (97.5%), the method of entry was breaking and entering.

2 *Overtly sexual burglaries:* Comprised 15.6% of the total sample and included a contact sexual offence committed, but nothing was stolen. Again, most of these (79.8%) were committed by rapists, and although the most common method of entry was breaking and entering (63.6%), almost a third of cases (27.1%) involved trickery to gain entry to the house. Over a third of these offenders used a weapon (37.0%), mostly a knife (72.0%), and violence was present in 42% of incidents.

3 *Combination burglary/rape:* Comprised 8.5% of the total sample and involved a burglary in which a contact sexual offence was committed and valuables were stolen. This was considered to be indicative of both sexual motivation and a desire for material gain, as the items stolen were mostly cash, jewellery, and other valuables. Once again, most of these (78.5%) were committed by rapists, and the most common method of entry was breaking and entering (58.7%), followed by the usage of trickery (25.4%) and violence, threats, or a weapon (15.9%). More than half of these cases involved a weapon (53.8%), with a knife being used in 70% of incidents.

Given that most burglars offend relatively close to where they live, can we hypothesise that this applies to sexual burglars too? From the very limited research in this area, it appears the answer is yes. For example, in their case study of Colonel Williams (see Box 7.1), Brankley et al. report that all of his sexual burglaries *"took place in close proximity (less than 2 km) to either his home in Orleans or his cottage in Tweed"* (2014, p. 117). Moreover, according to local news reports (e.g., Campbell & Corcoran, 2021), Pawel Relowicz committed his sexual burglaries close to where he lived, including one on his own street and another on an adjacent street. Having considered what typically happens in cases of sexual burglary, a key question is why do some men commit this offence?

Motivation: *Why do some men commit this offence?*

The definition of sexual violence used by some of the most popular protocols for the assessment and formulation of sexual violence risk includes violating property rights for sexual purposes, such as stealing fetish objects (Boer *et al.*, 2017). Regardless of the legal position, the importance of this cannot be overstated, as there are clear practice implications:

1 *Police Officers:* If you are investigating a theft, robbery, or burglary where the items stolen were of a sexual nature (e.g., women's underwear), you are not simply searching for a man who has committed an acquisitive offence, but a man who has committed an act of sexual violence.

2 *Other criminal justice practitioners:* If you are tasked with assessing or managing the risk presented by a man who has previously stolen items of a sexual nature (e.g., women's underwear), you are not simply working with a man with a history of acquisitive offending, but a man with a history of sexual violence.

In both cases, an understanding of how and why he came to commit such a sexual offence in the first place is required. This in turn requires an understanding of the context and circumstances in which sexual violence and acquisitive offending can co-occur and how each of these crimes has the potential to motivate and/or trigger the other. The idea that sexual violence and acquisitive offending can co-occur has long been recognised, and the research suggests this co-occurrence can have criminal or sexually deviant dynamics.

Criminal sexual burglaries

As we saw in Chapter 4, Canter and Heritage (1990) highlighted the co-occurrence of sexual violence and acquisitive offending when they identified a criminal theme within rape that included theft from the victim, a finding replicated by subsequent similar studies (e.g., Canter *et al.*, 2003; Häkkänen *et al.*, 2004; House, 1997). Warr (1988) had previously suggested an overlap exists between burglary and sexual violence because the same characteristics that make a dwelling attractive to a burglar are also likely to make it attractive to a sexual offender. Warr (1988) referred to the concept of '*home-intrusion rape*', which he defined as rapes committed after an unlawful entry into a residence. These rapes may or may not accompany burglaries and may involve strangers or known assailants. In either case, the key feature of these attacks is that the victim's home is the location of the rape, which the offender entered without consent. Warr's idea that home-intrusion rapes may or may not accompany burglary allows us to consider two variations of this type of sexual offender and their offending, namely sexual offenders who burgle and burglars who sexually offend.

Sexual offenders who burgle and burglars who sexually offend

Scully (1994) referred to the idea of rape being an '*added bonus*' that can sometimes occur during a burglary or robbery. Indeed, Scully (1994) reported that 39% of her sample of rapists had also been convicted of burglary or robbery committed in connection with their rapes. In some cases, the original intent was rape, and burglary or robbery was an afterthought. In her research, a surprising number of men reported that they decided to rape subsequent to their original intent to commit burglary or robbery. More specifically for our purposes, Scully (1994) found that in 27% of stranger rapes, burglary or robbery was their original intention. The decision to rape was made by these men once they realised they were in control of the new situation they found themselves in.

   The idea of women being sexually assaulted in their own homes by burglars has been found by other researchers. As stated above, the '*overtly sexual burglaries*' and the '*combination burglary/rape*' types found by Harris *et al.* (2012) are examples of this scenario. One difference between them is the absence of any theft committed by the overtly sexual type, indicating more of a sexual motive than a desire for material gain. Similarly, of the three types of sexual burglary found by Pedneault *et al.* (2012), women at home were sexually assaulted in two of them. First, '*versatile contact burglaries*' primarily occur in occupied homes and involve contact sexual violence accompanied by physical violence, theft, and weapons frequently used. Second, '*sexually oriented contact burglaries*' occur during the night and include acts of contact sexual violence. However, in contrast to the versatile contact types, these had low probabilities of both physical violence and theft. Moreover, the probability of a weapon being used was very low. Finally, as stated above, the '*sexual predator*' burglars identified by Vaughn *et al.* (2008) involved men with high levels of rape and prostitution offences. They were a violent group, with previous convictions for violence and acquisitive offences, and many of their burglaries were motivated by a desire to rape the female occupant.

It may not be clear in cases such as these whether the original intention was acquisitive offending or sexual violence, and therefore whether the offender is a sexual offender who burgles or a burglar who sexually offends. However, these cases illustrate a type of sexual burglary that results in the female occupant being sexually assaulted by a man who breaks into her home. Such offenders can be hypothesised to have criminal intent, be it to steal valuables or to steal sex. Moreover, in support of Warr (1988), these men recognise that dwellings are good places where opportunities to steal and/or commit sexual violence can be found. In my forensic/clinical practice, I have encountered an example of this. The man in question was detained in a secure hospital and had a personality disorder. He had previously entered a staff residential block within the grounds of a general hospital, broken into one of the flats, raped a nurse, and stole from her. A few weeks later, he broke into the home of an elderly woman, whom he raped, murdered, and stole from.

Sexually deviant burglaries

The idea that some men are driven into acquisitive offending by a desire to satisfy their deviant sexual desires has long been recognised. For example, Revitch (1978) presented several case examples of sexual burglars. Some of them involved stealing, ripping, or wearing the female occupant's underwear, and in some cases, masturbating whilst doing so. Others involved a desire to look around the house, to inspect open drawers, and to see naked women. These ideas were explored further by Schlesinger and Revitch (1999), who differentiated between two types of sexual burglaries. First, *'fetish burglaries'* contain clear overt sexual dynamics and involve the theft or destruction of women's underwear. Popular examples of these cases include the *'knicker thief'* who steals women's underwear from washing lines or from their bedrooms, or the case examples presented in Box 7.1. On some occasions, the burglar may soil the premises, either by defecation, urination, or ejaculation. The key feature of these crimes is not financial gain but the burglar's sexual gratification, either at the scene or afterwards at home. Second, *'voyeuristic burglaries'* contain covert sexual dynamics, as the sexual aspect of these crimes is less obvious. In these cases, the burglar's voyeuristic impulses often drive the burglary. Many voyeuristic burglars express a strong urge to look around the home and inspect the occupant's drawers whilst entertaining the fantasy of seeing a naked woman. Schlesinger and Revitch (1999) suggest these burglars frequently steal something of minimal value to help them rationalise their actions, citing one man who reported, *"I'd feel stupid if I broke in and didn't take nothing"* (ibid., p. 232).

The idea of some burglaries being driven by sexual deviancy has been found by other researchers. As stated above, the *'covertly sexual burglaries'* found by Harris *et al.* (2012) are examples of this scenario. Similarly, of the three types of sexual burglary found by Pedneault *et al.* (2012), one of them was driven by sexual deviancy and was labelled *'fetishistic non-contact'* burglaries. These typically occur in unoccupied homes and do not include contact sexual violence. They do, however, include high probabilities of fetishism but very low levels of theft, violence, or weapons.

Sexually deviant dynamics

We can see from the examples of sexually deviant burglaries that some paraphilic disorders are relevant here. Voyeurism will be explored in chapter eight, so the focus here is transvestism and fetishism. As stated in Chapter 6, in both disorders, the fantasies, sexual urges, or behaviours cause the individual clinically significant distress or impairment in social, occupational, or other important areas of functioning. However, as per DSM-5-TR (American Psychiatric Association, 2022) criteria, they each have a different behavioural focus:

- **Transvestic disorder:** "*over a period of at least 6 months, recurrent and intense sexual arousal from cross dressing, as manifested by fantasies, urges, or behaviours*" (ibid., p. 798).
- *Fetishistic disorder:* "*over a period of at least 6 months, recurrent and intense sexual arousal from either the use of non-living objects or a highly specific focus on non-genital body part(s), as manifested by fantasies, urges, or behaviours ...[and]... The fetish objects are not limited to articles of clothing used in cross dressing (as in transvestic disorder) or devices specifically designed for the purpose of tactile genital stimulation (e.g., vibrator)*" (ibid., p. 796).

When considering these disorders and the case examples in Box 7.1, it is interesting to note that Colonel Williams' interest in women's underwear started in his 20s or 30s, but he had not acted on this for many years (Watt, 2014). Similarly, Larry's interest in women's underwear started when he was 11 years old, but he acted on it much sooner (McCann, 2000). Given that paraphilias generally commence in childhood (American Psychiatric Association, 2022), we can hypothesise that Pawel Relowicz harboured his deviant sexual interests for over a decade and Colonel Williams' interests predate his 20s or 30s. A key question here, however, is: why steal such items?

This is an important question because men who experience these paraphilias can of course obtain the object of their sexual desires lawfully, by, for example, purchasing women's underwear from clothing shops or fetish items from sex shops. However, in some cases, the desire to obtain these items unlawfully appears to be an important feature of their paraphilic presentation. In such cases, these men will break into gardens and/or houses to steal these items from washing lines or bedrooms, or perhaps, if the opportunity presents, from a public laundrette. The items stolen may not be limited to women's underwear but may also include scarfs and skirts (Öncü *et al.*, 2009), and on some occasions, items such as gloves have been stolen from the victim herself following a physical assault (Noguchi & Kato, 2010). It appears therefore that in some cases, rather than obtain new items and be the first and only person to wear them, some men want to own underwear, clothing, or shoes that belong to and have previously been worn by a woman. Indeed, as Lowenstein suggests, "*sometimes in a search for fetishist objects housebreaking occurs as the individual searches for women's used bras or panties*" (2002, p. 136). However, the word '*used*' may not equate to '*soiled*' as some men steal freshly washed women's underwear from washing lines.

Kleptomania

One final point to consider is that, whilst many sexual thefts contain a sexual dynamic, in some cases other factors may be relevant too. DSM-5-TR defines kleptomania as a recurrent failure to resist impulses to steal objects that are not needed for personal use or for their monetary value. The individual may experience an increasing sense of tension before committing the theft, then pleasure, gratification, or relief at the time of committing the theft, which is not committed to express anger or vengeance and is not in response to a delusion or a hallucination (American Psychiatric Association, 2022). In his case study of Larry, McCann (2000) reports that he was irritated or angry each time he committed a sexual burglary, and sometimes he stole women's underwear for the thrill of it. Moreover, as illustrated by Turvey (2016) and cases such as Colonel Williams (see Box 7.1), some men who steal women's underwear collect and store the items at home and end up owning hundreds of pairs of knickers and bras. DSM-5-TR recognises that some kleptomaniacs may hoard the stolen objects, so kleptomania might also (at least partially) explain it as acquisitive sexual violence (see Öncü *et al.*, 2009).

Future implications?

A key consideration in relation to the concept of sexual burglaries and other thefts is: why is this relevant, and what might this type of offending tell us about a possible future offending trajectory? To answer this question, we need to consider the presence and relevance of burglary in the criminal histories of sexual offenders and potential warning signs that may indicate an individual's offence pathway is on an upward trajectory.

The presence of burglary in the criminal histories of sexual offenders

Although research suggests a minority of sexual offenders have previous convictions for sexual violence, large numbers of them have previous convictions for burglary. For example, Scully (1994) found 39% of rapists had convictions for burglary or robbery. Soothill *et al.* (2000) found 21% of sex offenders had a history of burglary, with rates being highest among those who victimised females. In Massachusetts, Harris *et al.* (2012) found 34% of sex offenders had a previous history of burglary. Among stranger rapists, Davies *et al.* (1998) found 56% of a British sample had previous convictions for burglary, whilst Scott *et al.* (2006) found the rate was 76% among a New Zealand sample. Similar findings have been found among sexual homicide offenders. For example, Schlesinger and Revitch (1999) report that several notorious sexual murders had histories of burglary, and several studies cited by them found the incidence of burglary among sexual homicide offenders ranged from 31.5% to 45.5%. Moreover, in their own study of 52 sexual homicide offenders, Schlesinger and Revitch (1999) found 42% had a history of burglary. From these findings, Schlesinger and Revitch concluded that *"about 40% of sexual murderers have a history of burglary"* (ibid, p. 236).

The relevance of burglary in the criminal histories of sexual offenders

The relevance of burglary to sexual offending can be illustrated in two ways. Firstly Harris *et al.* (2012) suggest it can be an important *'stepping-stone'* in the development of a sexual criminal career, similar to how marijuana has been linked to serious drug taking. However, as Harris et al. continue *"although the progression from marijuana to cocaine makes intuitive sense, the link between burglary and a sexual offence (such as rape) seems much less understandable"* (2012, p. 1). However, given that burglary can provide opportunities for acquisitive offending and sexual violence (Warr, 1988), we can understand how burglary and sexual violence can be linked and how a desire for one can lead to the other. The second way burglary may be relevant to a sex offender's criminal history is its potential to reveal information about an unknown offender and their criminal history. For example, Schlesinger and Revitch (1999) found that among women who were sexually killed in their own homes, 77% were killed by men with a history of burglary. Similarly, other studies have found men who rape after gaining entry into their victim's home have a greater likelihood of having convictions for burglary (Davies *et al.*, 1998; Jackson *et al.*, 1997). Finally, men with convictions for burglary have been found to have longer criminal careers (Harris *et al.*, 2012). Indeed, the *'sexual predator'* burglars identified by Vaughn *et al.* (2008) had long criminal careers with an early age of onset. Given such findings, it is not surprising that the presence of burglary in an offender's criminal history has been viewed as a risk factor for future violence (Thornton *et al.*, 2003).

Warning signs of an upward offence trajectory

A final consideration is whether we can differentiate between those men whose acquisitive sexual violence may be part of an upward offence trajectory and those who are not. Although the research is limited here, it appears that three factors are relevant. First, the location of the offence is important. For example, some men who steal women's underwear from washing lines in a garden may simply take them home and use them for their own sexual pleasure. Moreover, like Larry in Box 7.1, they may flee the scene if they encounter a household occupant, as they have no desire to engage with them sexually or otherwise. Indeed, the opportunity to sexually assault a woman in her garden may be limited, given her ability to raise the alarm by screaming and shouting. However, as illustrated by cases such as Colonel Williams and Pawel Relowicz (see Box 7.1), some men are prepared to engage in more serious acquisitive conduct, such as breaking into homes to steal women's underwear or other sexual items. And some men are prepared to take advantage of the opportunities that breaking into houses provides by sexually assaulting, raping, and murdering female occupants if they encounter them. The importance of sexual burglary in the offence trajectory of sexual offenders was highlighted by Revitch (1978), who suggested that breaking and entering committed alone and in bizarre circumstances, stealing women's underwear, and the destruction of women's clothing have ominous significance. Moreover, Revitch (1978) suggested that such crimes may be a precursor to a violent attack on a woman, such that in cases of bizarre attacks on women, compulsive burglars with a history of violence towards women should be investigated by the police.

A second factor that may be relevant is the age of the offender. Within some actuarial sexual violence risk assessment protocols (see Chapter 11) youthful age is considered a risk factor (e.g., Thornton *et al.*, 2003). Put simply, younger offenders are considered more at risk of future violence than older offenders. A similar argument was made by McCann, who suggested that *"the sexual dynamics of burglary, particularly in adolescence, may represent the early manifestation of criminal behaviour that may become progressively more aggressive and violent"* (2000, p. 13). Having said that, Colonel Williams did not start his offending until his early 40s, but the point remains that if a young man is apprehended for sexual burglary, alarm bells should ring regarding where his offence trajectory may go, especially if, as McCann (2000) suggests, his sexual deviancy also presents with a co-morbid personality disorder.

Finally, other factors that may be difficult to pin down academically should also raise concerns. For example, one knicker thief in Bristol not only *"carried out a perverted act with a bra"*, but when police searched his car, they found *"several pairs of gloves, two torches, rope, a shovel, five rolls of tape and a misshapen coat hanger"* (Bennett, 2018). Whilst it is difficult to draw solid conclusions from limited information, a reasonable hypothesis would be that these items could be viewed as a means of facilitating more serious acts of sexual violence and that by carrying such items, the offender had contemplated such behaviour. Similarly, if a knicker thief engages verbally with his victims, that too may be cause for concern. For example, one man in Lancashire was reportedly banging on the doors of two houses in the early hours of the morning and shouting sexually suggestive comments at women through their letter boxes after they refused to open the door to him, before stealing knickers from one of the victim's washing lines (Connor & Jeffay, 2015). Again, whilst it is difficult to draw solid conclusions from limited information, a reasonable hypothesis would be that these are more than the actions of a man intent on stealing women's underwear for his own sexual pleasure, as he is drawing attention to himself in a sexual manner and deriving excitement from his verbal comments.

Conclusions and implications for practice

This chapter has introduced an unusual type of stranger sexual violence, one which involves acquisitive offending but which can also include contact sexual violence. On some occasions, victims may not be present when they are victimised, and they may only feel irritation when they realise some of their underwear has gone missing from their washing line. On other occasions, victims can be physically and sexually victimised in very serious ways. Acquisitive sexual violence is not defined by law, and its prevalence is unknown. However, crimes such as sexual burglary are similar to non-sexual burglaries in many ways. Our understanding of sexual burglary can be aided by recognising that, essentially, there are three types: those committed by burglars who sexually offend, which involve a burglary that included an opportunistic sexual assault of a female occupant; those committed by sexual offenders who burgle, which are more driven by a desire to encounter an occupant to sexually assault; and those committed by men who are motivated by sexual deviancy. Whilst some of the latter cases may have no intent to engage with an occupant, as Colonel Williams illustrates, some men who offend in this way can follow an upward offence trajectory that leads them into more serious acts of sexual violence.

Whilst other chapters highlight several implications for criminal justice practice, this chapter highlights only one, but it is important for every single criminal justice practitioner to note: When working with an offender with a history of acquisitive offending, it is very important to know exactly what was stolen or damaged, or who was assaulted and how. This will help to highlight the difference between an individual with a history of acquisitive offending motivated by financial gain, perhaps to fund a drug habit, and an individual with a history of acquisitive offending motivated by a desire to satisfy his sexual desires, either by stealing sexual items or targeting women in their own homes. Although similar in that these offenders have histories of breaking into people's homes to get what they want, their presentations are fundamentally different in relation to their offence motivations and potential future risk.

8 Non-contact stranger sexual violence
Exhibitionism and voyeurism

Non-contact sexual offences involve a sexual offence, occurring in the absence of physical contact between perpetrator and victim

(Hocken & Thorne, 2012, p. 243)

Introduction

The popular profile of a woman being sexually assaulted by a stranger probably involves her being attacked by a man at night in an isolated, outdoor location, and along with being sexually assaulted, she sustains physical injuries. However, research suggests this situation only occurs in a minority of cases (Waterhouse *et al.*, 2016). Just as the previous chapter showed that some acts of stranger sexual violence (i.e., stealing women's underwear) do not fit this popular profile, this chapter continues with this theme by exploring two other atypical types of sexual violence that are important to our considerations, namely exhibitionism and voyeurism. These behaviours have been recognised since biblical times (Aggrawal, 2009b) and later caught the attention of scholars such as Von Krafft-Ebing, who expressed unflattering views about exhibitionism; *"the silly manner of this sexual activity, or really sexual demonstration, points to intellectual and moral weakness"* (1894, p. 383), and voyeurs being; *"so cynical that they seek to get sight of coitus in order to assist their virility"* (1894, pp. 396–397). Despite these negative observations, the fact that many people engage in similar activities during their lives suggests there is nothing intrinsically pathological or illegal about exhibitionistic and voyeuristic behaviours. However, the context and circumstances in which these behaviours occur mean they are acceptable, welcome, and legal in some situations, but unacceptable, unwelcome, and illegal in others. Therefore, every single criminal justice practitioner should have a basic understanding of these offences.

Chapter aims

This chapter introduces two more unusual types of sexual violence. Although they may not fit the popular profile of a sexual offence committed by a stranger, they warrant consideration by criminal justice practitioners for two reasons. First, the deviant nature of these offences means they can be regarded as a risk of further sexual violence (Boer *et al.*, 2017; Hart *et al.*, 2022). Second, as we saw in chapter seven in relation to voyeuristic burglaries and the behaviours of Colonel Williams and Pawel Relowicz (i.e., exhibitionism and voyeurism) and the examples presented in Box 8.1, in some cases these behaviours are a precursor to further similar offending or to more serious sexual violence.

DOI: 10.4324/9781003217763-10

This chapter, therefore, explores how this form of sexual violence is defined, its prevalence, what typically happens within such offences and why, and what implications these offences may have for future offending.

Definition: What is this crime?

Unlike acquisitive sexual violence presented in Chapter 7, the non-contact sexual offences are defined under English Criminal Law within the Sexual Offences Act 2003 (see Table 8.1). Along with legal definitions, these behaviours also amount to a paraphilic disorder (see Chapter 6), meaning they have both a legal and a clinical definition.

Legal definitions

Table 8.1 shows the definitions of these offences leaving little room for doubt as to what behaviours are being referred to. Moreover, we can see how the law can evolve to accommodate new variants of these offences. For example, voyeurism can be undertaken with electronic equipment (e.g., cameras) and include the new offence of *'up-skirting'*.

Clinical definitions

As stated in Chapter 6 exhibitionism and voyeurism may be indicative of a paraphilic disorder as per DSM-5-TR (American Psychiatric Association, 2022) and ICD-11 (World Health Organization, 2022). In both cases, the individual must have acted on their sexual urges with a nonconsenting person, or their sexual urges or fantasies cause clinically significant distress or impairment in social, occupational, or other important areas of functioning. However, whilst the requirement to have acted upon and been negatively impacted by these behaviours is the same in both cases, the behavioural focus is different (see Table 8.2).

In relation to exhibitionistic disorder, DSM-5-TR requires individual sexual preferences to be specified regarding whether the individual becomes aroused by exposing his genitals to children, adults, or both. In relation to voyeuristic disorder, the offender must be at least 18 years old (American Psychiatric Association, 2022). Acute stress reactions and uncomplicated bereavement are exclusionary criteria under ICD-11 (World Health Organization, 2022).

Table 8.1 Legal definitions of exhibitionism & voyeurism

Sexual Offences Act 2003
Exposure (section 66): A person commits an offence if he intentionally exposes his genitals, and he intends that someone will see them and be caused alarm or distress.
Voyeurism (section 67): A person commits an offence if for the purpose of obtaining sexual gratification, he observes another person doing a private act, and he knows that the other person does not consent to being observed for his sexual gratification.
Voyeurism additional offences (up-skirting, section 67A): A person commits an offence if he operates equipment beneath the clothing of another person, to observe their genitals or buttocks (whether exposed or covered with underwear), or the underwear covering their genitals or buttocks, in circumstances where the genitals, buttocks or underwear would not otherwise be visible, either to obtain sexual gratification or to humiliate, alarm or distress the other person.

Source: www.legislation.gov.uk

Table 8.2 Clinical definitions of exhibitionism & voyeurism

Exhibitionistic disorder	Voyeuristic disorder
Over a period of at least six months, recurrent and intense sexual arousal from the exposure of one's genitals to an unsuspecting person, as manifested by fantasies, urges, or behaviours (DSM-5-TR). Is characterised by a sustained, focused and intense pattern of sexual arousal – as manifested by persistent sexual thoughts, fantasies, urges, or behaviours – that involves exposing one's genitals to an unsuspecting individual in public places, usually without inviting or intending closer contact (ICD-11).	over a period of at least six months, recurrent and intense sexual arousal from observing an unsuspecting person who is naked, in the process of disrobing, or engaging in sexual activity, as manifested by fantasies, urges, or behaviours (DSM-5-TR). Is characterised by a sustained, focused, and intense pattern of sexual arousal – as manifested by persistent sexual thoughts, fantasies, urges, or behaviours – that involves observing an unsuspecting individual who is naked, in the process of disrobing, or engaging in sexual activity (ICD-11).

Box 8.1   Case examples of an exhibitionist and a voyeur

Robert

Robert is 45 years old, divorced, and has been exposing himself since his teens. He claims it began after he was arrested for urinating against a wall, but police reports state he was seen exposing his erect penis to women walking by. He received a caution for this, following which he started exposing himself for most weeks. His offence pattern followed a similar script. When out driving, if he saw a park or field, he would park up, enter the area, and walk around looking for women out walking. If he saw a woman, he would run ahead, hide behind some bushes or a tree, and wait for her. When she approached, he would jump out with his trousers and underwear around his ankles, expose his erect penis, and invite the woman to look at him, saying things like, *"hey what do you think of this?"*. He enjoyed some victim responses more than others. For example, he did not like it if they screamed and ran off or made derogatory comments about his behaviour or the size of his penis. However, he found it very exciting when some women, especially those who were with other women, responded by *'egging him on'* and laughing. After exposing himself, regardless of the response, he would masturbate either at the scene or when he got home. Although many of his exposures occurred in various locations on his way to and from work, on other occasions he would go out for a drive in the evening looking for opportunities to expose himself in parks or fields near where he lived. When asked to explain his actions, he stated he could not help himself as he received a great deal of sexual pleasure from exposing himself to female strangers and would often become sexually excited and masturbate simply from the thought of it. Although he was imprisoned twice for this behaviour, he felt he could not stop. A few months before his latest arrest, his offending escalated. In the space of a month, he drove up to girls in the street and offered them photographs of his erect penis, saying, *"hey, look at this!"* and he committed three contact sexual offences. All three of them began with his usual script. However, along with exposing himself, his first offence involved him grabbing his victim's breasts and bottom before running off. The second involved him grabbing and dragging a woman into a more secluded area, where he again grabbed her breasts and bottom before running off. The third offence was a further escalation, as he grabbed and dragged a woman into a more secluded area, where he raped her and ran off. Having left his semen at this third offence, he was identified through DNA evidence due to his previous convictions.

Dominic

Dominic is 30 years old and single. He has previous convictions for acquisitive, violent, and sexual offences. He has engaged in voyeurism since the age of 16. This has co-existed with what he called an obsession with women's feet, which he claims led to him peeping at women on buses and through their windows. Whilst looking through their windows, he would masturbate, ejaculate at the scene, and run away. He has never had a girlfriend, and he claimed he repeated his voyeurism after one or two women appeared to like being watched by him. After being placed on the sex offenders register, he managed his obsession for women's feet by using pornography. However, unable to control his urges, he started to walk and cycle around his area looking for voyeuristic opportunities (i.e., houses with female occupants) and would return later to secretly watch the women whilst he masturbated. On two occasions, he entered the woman's home through an open window because he wanted to touch their feet. However, the women woke up and startled him, and he ran off. Whilst in prison, he recognised he could easily return to voyeurism in the future, as he could not help himself.

Application: Non-contact sexual violence

The legal definitions in Table 8.1 would include the behaviours of Colonel Williams when he disrobed and masturbated (exhibitionism) while watching a woman prepare to take a shower (voyeurism). It would also include the behaviours of Pawel Relowicz when he masturbated in front of women in public places (exhibitionism), watched two students having sex through their bedroom window, observed one woman getting out of the shower, and another in her underwear (voyeurism). Additionally, Robert's behaviour amounted to the offence of exhibitionism, and Dominic was a voyeur, fetishist (i.e., women's feet) and sexual burglar. Although each is different, these cases illustrate how exhibitionism and voyeurism can present in real individuals. Moreover, Colonel Williams, Pawel Relowicz, and Dominic highlight the findings of Abel and Rouleau (1990) that individuals can often present with both of these disorders and/or with one of them plus other sexually deviant presentations (Abel *et al.*, 1988; Heil & Simons, 2008). Having considered the ways in which non-contact sexual violence is defined, a key question is: how often do these offences occur?

Prevalence: How common is this crime?

Official statistics (Elkin, 2023a: 2023b) do not provide data on voyeurism and exhibitionism. Whilst there is no mention of voyeurism, in an earlier overview of sexual offending, Matheson (2013) reported the majority of other (i.e., less serious) sexual offences recorded by the police in 2011/12 *"related to exposure or voyeurism (7,000)"* (ibid., p. 6). It is therefore difficult to gain an accurate picture of the prevalence of exhibitionism and voyeurism from official sources, as victims are less likely to report less serious offences such as these to the police (Matheson, 2013). This *'dark figure'* of unreported sexual violence is described as enormous by some researchers (e.g., DeLisi *et al.*, 2016) and means the true prevalence of these offences is unknown. By way of illustration, some researchers (e.g., Clark *et al.*, 2014; Szumski & Kasparek, 2020) report that fewer than 10% of women reported their exhibitionist victimisation to the police. Given the intended secretive nature of voyeurism, we can hypothesise that Matheson (2013) is correct and that most of those offences go unreported too. The difficulty with official figures means we must consult alternative sources to gain an understanding of the prevalence of these offences.

Media reports

Various regional media outlets provide some indication of the prevalence of exhibitionism and voyeurism, and a sample of these reports suggests these offences are widespread. For example, in 2020/21, more than 2,000 cases of exhibitionism and voyeurism were reported in London (Phillips, 2021), 321 cases in West Yorkshire (Clarke, 2022), 312 cases in the Thames Valley area (Young, 2022), 285 cases in Sussex (Green, 2022), almost 200 cases in Cambridgeshire (Ault, 2021), over 100 cases in North Wales (Nuttall, 2021), almost 100 cases in Hull (Ault & Kitching, 2021), and with 192 cases, Liverpool was described as a *'hotspot'* (Ault & Duffy, 2021). A national picture was provided by Channel Four News (see Fallon, 2021), which presented data obtained from 37 British police forces under the Freedom of Information Act 2000. They found 45,000 offences were recorded during 2015–20, a rise of 31%. One common factor in the regional news reports is that most cases go unsolved. Channel Four News also found the number of prosecutions had halved during 2014–2020. These findings are important because if only a minority of cases are reported to the police and if most of them do not result in conviction, then most exhibitionists and voyeurs are getting away with their offences, and the men we deal with within our practice are just the tip of the iceberg.

Academic research

A final way to consider the prevalence of these offences is to explore how common they are within various samples of men. As stated in Chapter 6 (Table 6.1), DSM-5-TR reports prevalence rates of 2%–4% for exhibitionistic disorder and 12% for voyeuristic disorder. These figures suggest two things. First, these disorders are relatively uncommon. Second, voyeurism is more common than exhibitionism. Both assumptions are supported by Långström and Seto (2006), who found the lifetime prevalence rates for exhibitionism and voyeurism in Swedish men were 4.1% and 11.5%, respectively. In Brazil, de Oliveira Júnior and Abdo (2010) found rates of exhibitionism and voyeurism were 9.3% and 13%, respectively, although not specified by gender. In Germany, Ahlers *et al.* (2011) found rates of voyeurism were higher than exhibitionism in relation to male fantasies (34.9% & 3.5%, respectively), masturbatory fantasies (24.5% & 3.3%, respectively), and actual behaviour (18% & 2.2%, respectively). Similarly, Marsh *et al.* (2010) found higher lifetime prevalence rates for voyeurism (8%) than for exhibitionism (5.4%) among voluntarily detained psychiatric patients. Subsequent research, however, suggests that whilst voyeurism remains more common than exhibitionism, both behaviours are more common than previously reported. For example, in Canada, Joyal and Carpentier (2017) found 60% of men had a desire to engage in voyeurism and 50.3% had done so, whilst 35% of men had a desire to engage in exhibitionism and 32.6% had done so. Similarly, in Italy, Castellini *et al.* (2018) found 64.6% of men had fantasies of voyeurism, 48.6% had these thoughts when masturbating, and 28% had engaged in voyeurism. In relation to exhibitionism, 21.4% of men had fantasised about this, 17.7% had these thoughts when masturbating, and 9.5% had engaged in exhibitionism.

When it comes to considering how common exhibitionism and voyeurism are, the available data paints a generally consistent picture. Whilst official statistics mask an unknown *'dark figure'* of these offences, research suggests that sizeable numbers of men fantasise about and/or engage in them. This is supported by media reports, which suggest that exhibitionism and voyeurism are widespread. However, the fact that media reports also suggest these offences have little chance of ending in the offender's conviction means that for most exhibitionists and voyeurs, these are low-risk, high-reward sexual crimes (Scully, 1994). This means many criminal justice practitioners may only have limited experience working with such offenders. Notwithstanding this, to investigate these offences and to assess and formulate these offenders, we need to understand what typically happens within this type of sexual violence.

Offence details: *What typically happens within these offences?*

As shown in Table 8.3, exhibitionism and voyeurism have similarities and differences. Although a victim is essential for both offences to occur, an absence of physical contact with the victim is intended by the offender. By virtue of it being more of an interactive offence with a woman who is aware she is being victimised, the exhibitionist must make his sexual desires and physical appearance known to his victim(s) and thereby risk identification, apprehension, and arrest. By contrast, the careful voyeur can avoid these dangers by ensuring his victim(s) and any passersby remain unaware of his activities.

Exhibitionism

The exhibitionist seeks to obtain the attention of others so he can subject them to a visual display of himself. Just like Robert in Box 8.1, we can hypothesise that such men search for suitable victims in a premeditated opportunistic manner (see Chapter 2) during daylight hours, either in their own areas or whilst travelling to and from other locations.

Table 8.3 Exhibitionism & voyeurism: Offence details

Offence Details	Exhibitionism	Voyeurism
Offender		
Physical contact with victim	No	No
Verbal contact with victim	Yes	No
Visual contact with victim	Yes	Yes
Victim		
Awareness of victimisation	Yes	No
Verbal contact with offender	Yes	No
Visual contact with offender	Yes	No

When opportunities present themselves, these men take advantage of them and expose themselves, hoping for a particular reaction from their victims. However, whilst the exhibitionist enjoys himself, the account below suggests victims do not:

> When I lived in London, I was walking through an underground tunnel to get to the underground station. As I turned around the corner, I saw a man who had a mask over his face and his penis in his hand, he was erect and masturbating. I was the only person in the tunnel with him, I was absolutely terrified. I kept my eyes on the ground and kept walking, luckily, he didn't hurt me.
>
> (Source: www.everydaysexism.com)

Szumski and Kasparek (2020) found 58.7% of women had been victims of exhibitionism. The average victim age was 15.9 years, with almost half (46.5%) no more than 15 years old and almost a quarter (24.8%) under 12 years old. About a fifth (21.1%) had encountered an exhibitionist once, 17.2% twice, and 21.7% three times. Almost half (49.8%) of the women encountered an exhibitionist in a big city. The most popular time of day was the afternoon or around noon (66.9%), with night-time being the least popular. The most common offence locations were parks and other similar leisure areas (40%). A fifth of victims (20.1%) encountered exhibitionists in streets, bridges, and underground passageways. Another fifth in places connected with public transport (e.g., bus stations), 11% encountered exhibitionists in housing areas, and 10% near educational institutions. In most cases (90.4%), the offenders were strangers, described as being of average height and build. Over half (56.1%) were estimated to be aged 31–50, around a fifth (21.1%) aged 18–30, and 13.7% over 50. In most cases (55.4%), the offender only made eye contact with his victim, with a third of victims (33.2%) reporting he verbally communicated with them. When verbal contact was made by the offender, it mostly involved requests to look at him (19%), to engage in sexual activity (16.4%), to ask for directions or the time (9.5%), to comment on his penis (7.8%), or other sexual comments (19%). In only a few cases did the offender appear intoxicated (2.6%) or offer an apology for his behaviour (1.7%). In most cases, the offender was touching his genitals (76%) and/or masturbating (56.7%) and did not follow the victim (79.1%). Over half of the victims were not alone at the time and did not attempt to attract the attention of others. Victim reactions to these incidents were mostly negative (81.5%) and included surprise (92.5%), disgust (82.5%), fear (63.6%), and anger (42.2%). Other victim reactions included shame (41.5%), amusement (27.4%), and feeling sorry for the offender (19.3%). In contrast to what some exhibitionists might think, only 1.3% reacted with contentment. Although most women (77.3%) told someone about the incident, this was mostly friends (55.5%), family (35.3%), and colleagues (17.1%), with only 7.1% reporting the incident to the authorities.

Similar results came from Clark *et al.* (2014), who found 40% of women had been exposed to. Most victims were around age 16 and mostly with someone at the time. Most exhibitionists were described as not well groomed (55.9%) and were masturbating at the time (52.6%). Although many exhibitionists did not show any reactions, the most common reactions that were shown were smiling/laughing (18.4%), moving away from the victim (13.6%), and remaining at the scene afterwards (73.5%). Victim reactions to these incidents mostly involved feeling violated/disgusted (61.7%), and although most victims reported the incident to someone (73.3%), these were mostly friends and family, as only 8.9% told the police.

Voyeurism

Observing someone without their consent means voyeurism is a secretive and predatory activity. Consider, for example, the actions of a man like Dominic who walks or cycles around his area in a premeditated, opportunistic manner (see Chapter 2), looking for opportunities to observe unsuspecting women who are getting undressed or engaging in sexual activity. If such opportunities are found, these men will take advantage of them and perhaps return to subject these women to *'repeat victimisation'* another time. As with exhibitionism, whilst the voyeur enjoys himself, the account below suggests victims do not:

> I was 14 and was showering in a public shower place and when I was showering, I heard a noise and looked up and saw someone peeping over at me whilst jerking off and I tried to grab a towel as quick as I could and when I did, he was not peeping over anymore. It was early and I thought I was the only one in there. So, I said "Hello?" and he'd already ran out, so I dried off and went back inside to the place I was staying at, and I still think to this day has he done this to other girls?
>
> (Source: www.everydaysexism.com)

In contrast to other types of sexual violence, research into voyeurism remains limited but is improving (e.g., see Duff, 2018). Whilst exhibitionism mostly occurs in outdoor locations, victims of voyeurism, by the very nature of their behaviour being secretly observed, will often be victimised within their own homes or that of a significant other within their life (e.g., boyfriend, etc.). Voyeurism is therefore unique as far as stranger sexual violence is concerned, as it can occur without the victim having any knowledge or awareness that she is being or has been sexually victimised (see Table 8.2). In a similar vein to the concept of the *'perfect crime'*, some researchers have suggested that acts of voyeurism that involve an absence of victim awareness and harm are examples of *'perfect voyeurism'* (Doyle, 2009). Although Duff (2018) rejects this idea, it does highlight the fact that we simply do not and cannot ever know how prevalent this type of stranger sexual violence is. Who knows, for example, how many women have been unaware of and unharmed by a male stranger who, having secretly and quietly observed them undressing or engaging in sexual activity, then secretly and quietly disappears into the night, only to repeat his covert operations against them or other women on an unknown number of occasions?

Motivation: Why do some men commit this offence?

When trying to understand why some men become exhibitionists or voyeurs, we can draw upon various bio-psycho-social theories (e.g., see DeFeo, 2020; Duff, 2018; Kaylor & Jeglic, 2019, 2021). However, perhaps a more useful starting point is to recognise that these behaviours are not limited to sexual offenders or sexual deviants. Rather, similar behaviours are engaged in by many people. For example, men who view pornography or who visit lap-dancing bars and the women who provide these services, are engaging in exhibitionistic and voyeuristic behaviours. Cuckolded husbands who enjoy watching their wives have sex with other men, who in turn enjoy being watched by their husbands whilst having sex with other men are engaging in exhibitionistic and voyeuristic behaviours. Even the simple act of dressing in a particular way to attract the attention of the opposite sex and a member of that sex noticing this and responding positively

Table 8.4 Classification of exhibitionism & voyeurism

Class	Exhibitionism	Voyeurism
1	*Fantasists:* Limit themselves to fantasies only.	*Pseudo:* Limit themselves to erotic fantasies involving watching others having sex.
2	*Pure:* Exhibit themselves and masturbate from a distance.	*Opportunistic:* Will take the opportunity to observe others engaging in private acts if it presents.
3	*Criminal:* Engage in other sexual offences too.	*Computer:* Fulfil their voyeuristic desire online.
4	*Exclusive:* Exhibitionism is the sole source of sexual gratification, as they cannot form relationships with women or engage in sexual intercourse with them.	*Video:* Use recording equipment to film and watch others engaging in private acts.
5	N/A	*Classical:* The true voyeurs described within DSM-5-TR or ICD-11.
6	N/A	*Criminal:* Engage in other sexual offences too.

Source: Adapted from Aggrawal (2009a)

are exhibitionistic and voyeuristic behaviours. The difference is that within these and many other situations, exhibitionistic and voyeuristic behaviours are expected, welcome (i.e., consented to), and lawful, whilst in the situations we are concerned with here, they are unexpected, unwelcome (i.e., not consented to), and unlawful.

Aggrawal (2009a) suggests that exhibitionism and voyeurism exist along a continuum from harmless fantasies to variants that are more dangerous when acted upon (see Table 8.4). Those that concern us are the pure, criminal, and exclusive exhibitionist, and the classical and criminal voyeur. A hypothesis we can formulate from this is that just as personality disorder is viewed not as something fundamentally different from normal personality but as a more extreme variant of normal personality (see Chapter 5), then perhaps exhibitionism and voyeurism should be viewed as more extreme variants of behaviours we all engage in during our encounters with those we find attractive and wish to establish sexual relations with. Having said that, the findings of Rye and Meaney (2007) suggest that in relation to voyeurism, large numbers of men would go further and secretly observe an attractive woman undressing or having sex if they thought they would not get caught. Such findings suggest that Forsyth may be correct that *"watching sex on a movie screen is not much different, nor does it have any more or less erotic quality than watching sex through someone's window"* (2001, p. 431). A theory we can draw upon to understand exhibitionism and voyeurism in terms of being more extreme variants of normal behaviour is courtship disorder, as this is how these (and other) deviant sexual presentations are viewed.

Courtship disorder

The concept of courtship disorder as proposed by Freud (Freund, 1990; Freund & Blanchard, 1986) is based on the idea of a four-stage human courtship process. This begins with non-contact interactions, such as searching for and finding a suitable partner, then looking at, smiling at, and talking with them. This is followed by contact interactions, such as touching and kissing, and finally sexual intercourse (see Table 8.5).

Table 8.5 Stages of human courtship

	Courtship phase	Normal behaviour	Deviant but lawful	Sexual violence
Non-contact stages of courtship	1 *Partner location*	Searching for and selecting a suitable partner	Frequenting lap dancing or strip bars	Voyeurism
	2 *Pre-tactile interaction*	Verbal and non-verbal interactions aimed at attracting a possible partner	Telephone sex lines Physically or verbally flirtatious behaviour	Telephone Scatalogia Exhibitionism
Contact stages of courtship (see Chapter 9)	3 *Tactile interaction*	Kissing, fondling	Casual sexual encounters with one-night stands or prostitutes	Frotteurism / Toucherism
	4 *Genital union*	Sexual intercourse		Preferential rape pattern

On some occasions, we pass through all four stages and reach a satisfactory conclusion. However, on many occasions, our progression through these stages is halted, as we do not always have sexual intercourse with every attractive person we meet. For most people, the process of courtship involves each of the four stages playing an equal part in the process. This ensures we can befriend, engage with, and enjoy sexual relations with members of the opposite sex. Moreover, even if one or two stages are the source of deviant desires, they can be satisfied in lawful ways. However, for some people, one or two of these stages are intensified, distorted, or exaggerated, whilst the remaining stages are entirely omitted or retained in a minimal form. This results in deviant and unlawful manifestations of normal courtship behaviours.

As shown in Table 8.5, the non-contact stages of courtship disorder include voyeurism and exhibitionism, which the DSM-5-TR describes as *"distorted components of human courtship behavior"* (American Psychiatric Association, 2022, p. 779). These are within stages one and two and are intensified, distorted, or exaggerated forms of the process of searching for and finding a suitable partner and looking at, smiling at, and talking with them. It is worth noting that verbal interactions within stage two can also involve telephone scatalogia or making obscene telephone calls, which is one of the *'other specified paraphilias'* within DSM-5-TR (American Psychiatric Association, 2022). Although the verbal nature of telephone scatalogia means it can be understood as a type of exhibitionism, Freund (1990) suggested it is an auditory variant of voyeurism. Indeed, we can imagine how a voyeur could use the telephone to secretly make contact with someone they have observed, with a view to engaging them in sexual conversations (Durkin, 2001).

Whilst the courtship disorder theory explains certain deviant and unlawful sexual behaviours, it arguably fails to explain how/why these behaviours develop in the first place. Often, there is no simple answer, as human behaviour is a complex multifactorial construct. This calls for an individualised consideration of the case in hand and whether factors such as a history of child abuse, substance abuse, poor parental attachment, and sexual dysfunction, as suggested by Seeman (2020), or early trauma leading the individual to equate feelings of inadequacy, shame, guilt, fear, hatred, or aggression with sexuality, as suggested by Healey (2006), are relevant. Regardless of how an individual's exhibitionistic and/or voyeuristic tendencies developed, one thing appears certain, namely they contain a strong sexual dynamic, which appears to motivate and drive these offenders.

Sexual dynamics

The sexually driven nature of exhibitionism and voyeurism is supported by Freund *et al.* (1988), who found almost half (49%) of exhibitionists had exposed their penis and almost a third (31%) had exposed their penis and bottom to a woman who was almost or totally a stranger. Additionally, 14.6% had masturbated to orgasm whilst exposing themselves, 8.5% had masturbated whilst fantasising about exposing themselves, and 40.6% had done both. Almost two-thirds (64.3%) of exhibitionists had engaged in public masturbation, including times when they thought no one was watching them. After exposing themselves, most exhibitionists (62.4%) wanted to intimately touch their victims and have sex with them (51.9%). However, only around a third (35%) wanted their victim's response to be wanting to have sex in return, as other desired victim reactions included showing him their private parts (15%), admiring him (14%), and any reaction (11.9%). Very few (0.5%) wanted their victim to experience fear. Freund *et al.* (1988) found similar results among a sample of voyeurs. Large numbers had masturbated whilst secretly watching people having sex or who were fully or partly undressed (70%). Large numbers had masturbated while observing or trying to observe a woman who was unaware of their presence (85%), and large numbers had spent a substantial amount of time trying to observe women who were nude or partly nude, urinating, having sex, or engaging in other private acts (85%).

Future implications?

As with acquisitive stranger sexual violence, a key consideration in relation to exhibitionism and voyeurism is their relevance and what they might indicate about a possible future offence trajectory. Put simply, will they do it again, and if so, will they commit the same type of sexual offence, or *'cross-over'* into contact sexual violence?

Will they do it again?

Although this may appear to be a simple question, it is not easy to answer as the available evidence is limited and contradictory. This is illustrated when we explore research on recidivism. This involves following up with offenders after release from prison, secure hospitals, or probation to determine whether they have re-offended during a specified timescale.

In relation to exhibitionists, McNally and Fremouw (2014) conducted a review of 12 peer-reviewed studies published since 1981. Over an average follow-up period of greater than five years, sexual offence recidivism rates ranged from 18.6% to 56.9%, whilst rates of *'cross-over'* into contact sexual violence ranged from 0.9% to 16.2%. The studies with the highest escalation and recidivism rates included offenders with prior histories of contact sexual violence, whilst the study with the lowest escalation rate included offenders receiving treatment to address their sexual offending. From these findings and consideration of methodological strengths and limitations, McNally and Fremouw (2014) estimated that approximately 25% of exhibitionists committed another exhibitionistic offence, whilst 5%–10% *'crossed-over'* into contact sexual violence. To put these findings another way, an estimated 75% of exhibitionists did not commit another exhibitionist offence, and 90%–95% did not *'cross-over'* into contact sexual violence. That said, some of the studies reviewed by McNally and Fremouw (2014) highlight other important factors regarding exhibitionists, namely their propensity to engage in other types of offending. For example, Firestone and colleagues (Firestone *et al.*, 2006; Rabinowitz Greenberg *et al.*, 2002) found that between 16.8% and 31.3% were subsequently convicted for violent offences, and between 32.7% and 38.9% were subsequently convicted for other types of offences. Similarly, Sugarman *et al.* (1994) found that 75% of exhibitionists were convicted for any offence other than exhibitionism. This suggests that many exhibitionists are generalists rather than specialist offenders (Soothill *et al.*, 2000). Indeed, when McNally and Fremouw (2014) tried to determine the risk factors that contributed to the process of escalation, they found the most supported risk factor was a general clustering of antisocial behaviour, including a history of sexual and nonsexual convictions. This accords with other research that found sexual deviancy and general criminality (or an antisocial orientation) are important considerations when it comes to the risk of further offending posed by sexual offenders (Hanson & Bussière, 1998; Hanson & Morton-Bourgon, 2004). Whilst research into exhibitionist re-offending is available, some notable researchers into voyeurism (e.g., Duff, 2018) have reported an absence of studies exploring re-offending by this group of offenders (Personal communication, Dr Simon Duff, University of Nottingham, September 25th, 2022). This therefore remains an outstanding area of research.

Will they 'cross-over' into contact sexual violence?

The above findings suggest that, in some cases, non-contact sexual violence is a precursor to more serious sexual violence. Although different studies report different prevalence rates, research into the histories of men convicted of serious sexual violence confirms this point. For example, in a study of sexual killers, sexual offenders, and non-sexual killers, Langevin *et al.* (1988) found rates of voyeurism among these three groups were 54%, 38%, and 17%, respectively, whilst rates of exhibitionism were 23%, 31%, and 0%, respectively. This follows earlier research cited above that voyeurism is more common than exhibitionism, but also that these disorders are more common in sexual offenders than in violent offenders. However, Proulx and Sauvêtre (2007) found lower rates in their study of sexual murderers and sexual offenders. Rates of voyeurism among these two groups were 6.7% and 4%, respectively, whilst rates of exhibitionism were 0% and 4%, respectively. In a study of serial and single sexual killers, Prentky *et al.* (1989) found rates of voyeurism among these two groups (i.e., 75% & 43%, respectively) were higher than rates of exhibitionism (i.e., 25% & 7%, respectively), whilst rates of exhibitionism and voyeurism were higher among serial offenders (i.e., 25% & 75%, respectively) than single offenders (i.e., 7% & 43%, respectively). However, although Chan *et al.* (2015) found rates of voyeurism were lower among serial (23.1%) and single (1.4%) sexual killers than rates of exhibitionism (i.e., 30.8% & 8.2%, respectively), as with Prentky *et al.* (1989), they found rates of exhibitionism and voyeurism were higher among serial offenders (i.e., 30.8% & 23.1%, respectively) than single offenders (i.e., 8.2% & 1.4%, respectively).

When considering research on sexual recidivism, we need to remember that the findings are limited by an enormous '*dark figure*' of unreported sexual violence (DeLisi *et al.*, 2016). Therefore, determining recidivism rates among exhibitionists and voyeurs will prove very difficult. In response to this problem, DeFeo suggests that, in relation to non-contact sexual offenders, "*more strategic research practices need to be employed to assist with determining recidivism rates*" (2020, p. 382). One option is to consider what can best be described as behavioural research, as that leads us to reach another conclusion about whether exhibitionists and voyeurs will do it again.

Behavioural research

Whilst recidivistic research suggests most exhibitionists (and perhaps, by implication, voyeurs) will not do it again, an alternative hypothesis is that most of them will. The reason for this is that, like all paraphilias, exhibitionism and voyeurism are driven by the internal (psychological) needs of the individual (see Table 4.1), who derives sexual gratification from his actions. Exhibitionism and voyeurism have their origins in adolescence (American Psychiatric Association, 2022; World Health Organization, 2022). Indeed, Abel and Rouleau (1990) found 50% of exhibitionists had an interest in that behaviour before age 18 and 50% of voyeurs had an interest in that behaviour before age 15. Robert began his exhibitionistic behaviour during his teens, and his explanation when first apprehended that he was urinating against a wall is, according to Hollender (1997), the most common cover story. Similarly, Dominic began his voyeuristic behaviour in his teens.

Given that these behaviours have an early onset and continue into adulthood, it appears reasonable to conclude that such behaviours are compulsive with a high likelihood of repetition. To understand this, consider your own sexual preferences and ask yourself whether you could stop indulging your sexual desires if you had to. The chances are you would find this very difficult, and the research suggests exhibitionists and voyeurs do too. For example, Abel and Rouleau (1990) found their sample of 142 exhibitionists had each committed an average of 504 acts of exhibitionism, whilst their sample of 62 voyeurs had each committed an average of 469 acts of voyeurism. These findings not only confirm that exhibitionism and voyeurism are compulsive presentations but also confirm that these are serial sexual offenders. Indeed, in my clinical sessions, Robert admitted that he had exposed himself countless times over the years but had only received a handful of convictions. Similarly, Dominic stated he had engaged in voyeuristic acts countless times over the years but had only received a handful of convictions. For large parts of their adult lives, therefore, Robert and Dominic were unable to resist their deviant sexual urges, and the criminal justice system was totally unaware of most of their indulgences. Robert and Dominic are therefore living proof of the enormous *'dark figure'* of unreported exhibitionistic and voyeuristic sexual violence, and had any recidivistic research included these two men, most of their offending would have been missed.

Conclusions and implications for practice

This chapter has introduced the concept of non-contact stranger sexual violence and has shown how these offences involve sexually deviant behaviours akin to paraphilic disorder. These behaviours, however, are not simply indicative of a deviant sexual presentation, as they are also unlawful and therefore a legal construct. As happens on many occasions when exploring deviant and/or unlawful sexual behaviours, the *'dark figure'* of unknown/unreported incidents means we have no idea how common these offences are. What we do know is that whilst some people limit their exhibitionistic and/or voyeuristic desires to the realm of fantasy, others indulge them in the real world (Baur *et al.*, 2016) and receive convictions as a result. Whilst exhibitionism is a very public offence that requires interaction between the offender and his victim, the voyeur operates under the radar with the aim of satisfying his needs without anyone knowing. Although non-contact sexual violence may be regarded as a nuisance offence (e.g., see Chapter 4 in Holmes & Holmes, 2009), its impact on victims is serious (Clark *et al.*, 2014; Grant, 2021), and they raise some important practice-based points to note and questions to consider:

1 Exhibitionism and voyeurism are compulsive offences that have a high likelihood of repetition.
2 Given that individuals often present with multiple paraphilic disorders, police officers investigating a case of exhibitionism or voyeurism might want to explore whether any reports of men engaging in other types of deviant or unlawful sexual behaviour have recently been made locally.
3 Whilst some exhibitionists and voyeurs can limit themselves to engaging in similar behaviours in the future, others will escalate their offending and *'cross-over'* into more serious sexual violence.
4 Those who *'cross-over'* appear to have more deviant and criminally orientated presentations and will have engaged in other types of offences.
5 Given that rates of exhibitionism and voyeurism are higher among serial sexual offenders than single sexual offenders, the compulsive and repetitive nature of these offences means they must not be regarded as simply nuisance behaviours but as offences that need to be taken seriously.
6 Although recidivism research suggests most exhibitionists and voyeurs do not re-offend, behavioural research suggests otherwise. Therefore, if you are a police officer investigating an exhibitionist or voyeur in your area or a probation officer managing a convicted exhibitionist or voyeur in the community and you are wondering whether he will do it again, from my experience, your best option is to assume the answer is yes, he will do it again until he is caught.

9 Contact stranger sexual violence
Rape and other sexual assaults

You have two options – you can give me what I want, and you tell nobody what has happened, or tonight is the night you die

(A stranger rapist to his victim, cited in Duell, 2014)

Introduction

Although the popular profile of a woman being sexually assaulted by a stranger, i.e., raped and physically assaulted by a man at night in an isolated outdoor location, only refers to a minority of sexual assaults (Waterhouse *et al.*, 2016), nonetheless, these types of assaults do occur. Moreover, as stated in Chapter 2, their unpredictability means they are feared by many women (Scott, 2003; Scully, 1994). Whilst rape may be the first offence that comes to mind when we consider contact sexual violence committed by strangers, the reality is that even here we are dealing with a construct which is not uniform. Rather, contact sexual violence exists on a continuum, with what might be regarded as *'minor'* non-penetrative sexual touching at one end and penetrative offences like rape at the other. Within this continuum, some of these offences may be indicative of a paraphilic disorder (see Chapter 6), not only in the sense that some may be carried out in a sadistic manner but also in the sense that the act itself may be indicative of a frotteuristic presentation. Consequently, whilst we may be inclined to view some of the *'minor'* offences as nuisance assaults, this may not always be so. Rather, as in the previous two chapters, such offences may be a precursor to further similar offending or to more serious sexual violence. Therefore, once again, every single criminal justice practitioner should have a basic understanding of these offences.

Chapter aims

This chapter introduces contact sexual offences such as rape, sexual assault by penetration, and sexual assault. Such offences are perhaps the epitome of what most people think stranger sexual violence involves, as along with hands-on sexual violence, physical violence often occurs. Although contact sexual assaults involving strangers are more likely to be reported to the police, meaning the *'dark figure'* of unreported cases (DeLisi *et al.*, 2016) may be smaller, the process of attrition means not all reported cases result in conviction. This chapter, therefore, explores how this form of sexual violence is defined, its prevalence, what typically happens within such offences, and why. Finally, this chapter will explore what implications contact sexual violence may have for future offending.

DOI: 10.4324/9781003217763-11

This is especially important in those cases that evidence sexual deviancy, as that is an important risk factor for further sexual violence (Boer *et al.*, 2017; Hart *et al.*, 2022).

Definition: *What is this crime?*

As with non-contact sexual offences, contact sexual offences are defined under English Law, within the Sexual Offences Act 2003 (see Table 9.1). Similarly, some sexual assaults may be indicative of a paraphilic disorder (see chapter 6), meaning they are both a legal and a clinical construct.

Legal definitions

Table 9.1 shows the three offences that constitute acts of contact sexual violence. Of note is the usage within these definitions of *'person A'* and *'person B'* to identify the offender and victim, respectively. This was aimed at making the Sexual Offences Act 2003 as gender neutral as possible in recognition of the fact that men and women can be victims or perpetrators of sexual violence. However, whilst that may be so in most cases, under English Law, rape remains a gender-specific crime. Whilst rape victims can be male or female, only males can commit rape as that involves penile penetration. Penetrating another person's vagina, anus, or mouth without their consent using something other than a penis is not rape under English Law but sexual assault by penetration. It is worth noting, however, that the situation is different under Scottish Law. Under Section 1(4) of the Sexual Offences (Scotland) Act 2009, a penis *"includes a surgically constructed penis if it forms part of A, having been created in the course of surgical treatment..."*. Therefore, under Scottish Law, a female-to-male transsexual can commit rape using their surgically constructed penis, but not under English Law.

Clinical definitions

Along with being an unlawful act, the desire to touch another person in a sexual manner without their consent may be indicative of a frotteuristic disorder, as per DSM-5-TR (American Psychiatric Association, 2022) and ICD-11 (World Health Organization,

Table 9.1 Legal definitions of contact sexual offences

Sexual Offences Act 2003

Rape (section 1):
Person A intentionally penetrates the vagina, anus, or mouth of person B with his penis.
  Person B does not consent to the penetration and person A does not reasonably believe that person B consents.

Sexual assault by penetration (section 2):
Person A intentionally penetrates the vagina or anus of person B with a part of his body or anything else.   The penetration is sexual and person B does not consent to the penetration and person A does not reasonably believe that person B consents.

Sexual assault (section 3):
Person A intentionally touches person B in a sexual manner when person B does not consent to the touching and person A does not reasonably believe that person B consents.

Source: www.legislation.gov.uk

Table 9.2 Clinical definition of sexual assault – frotteuristic disorder

DSM-5-TR	ICD-11
Over a period of at least six months, recurrent and intense sexual arousal from touching or rubbing against a nonconsenting person, as manifested by fantasies, urges, or behaviours.	Is characterised by a sustained, focused, and intense pattern of sexual arousal – as manifested by persistent sexual thoughts, fantasies, urges, or behaviours – that involves touching or rubbing against a non-consenting person in crowded public places.

2022). As with other paraphilic disorders, the individual must have acted on their sexual urges with a nonconsenting person, or their sexual urges or fantasies cause clinically significant distress or impairment in social, occupational, or other important areas of functioning. Essentially, individuals with this presentation engage in contact sexual behaviour(s), which in law would amount to a sexual assault (see Table 9.2).

Application: Contact sexual violence

Contact sexual violence involves criminal justice practitioners dealing with individuals who have committed more serious sexual offences, which by their very nature can have important psychological and physical consequences for victims. In cases of sexual assault, we are dealing with men who have touched or rubbed a female stranger's legs, bottom, breasts, or genitals. This may occur in crowded places like bars or tube trains, university campuses, or less crowded public places like parks (see Box 9.1). Whilst women who experience this type of victimisation may not necessarily feel they are in any real physical danger, they may still experience the fear we considered in Chapter 2. However, in those cases where sexual touching is a precursor to a more serious sexual assault, the situation is very different. In such cases, we are dealing with men who have inserted their fingers, a bottle, a broom handle, or another foreign object into a female stranger's vagina or anus, and/or raped the woman. As we shall see below, these assaults have the potential to leave women physically injured as well as sexually assaulted. The latter may include the offender ejaculating inside his victim, leaving her facing the prospect of sexually transmitted diseases and/or pregnancy.

Prevalence: *How common is this crime?*

Official figures for England and Wales (Elkin, 2023b) report that in the 12 months to March 2022, there were 46,114 rapes of women aged 16 or over and 51,420 sexual assaults of females aged 13 or over. Although the number of rapes and sexual assaults was relatively stable for several years after the Sexual Offences Act 2003 came into being, since 2014, the number of cases has risen sharply (see Figure 9.1). Although definitions and recording methods within Scotland differ, the picture there is very similar. For example, during 2021–2022, there were 2,498 rapes and attempted rapes and 2,545 sexual assaults of an adult (gender not specified) aged 16+. Although these smaller numbers reflect a smaller population, of note is the fact that, just like in England and Wales, the rates of these offences have risen sharply in recent years. For example, in comparison to the 2021–2022 figures cited, during 2012–2013 the number of rapes and attempted rapes

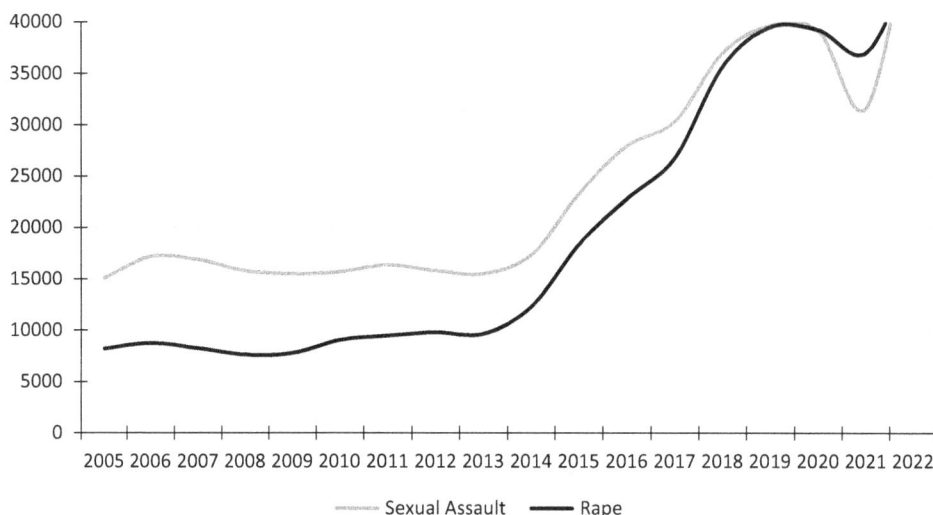

Figure 9.1 Rates of sexual assault and rape in England & Wales

Based on appendix table A4 in Elkin, 2023b

was 1,462, and 1,149 sexual assaults of an adult (gender not specified) aged 16+ (see supporting documents Table A4 in Scottish Government, 2022).

'Dark figure' of contact sexual violence

Although official statistics provide some indication of the prevalence of contact sexual violence, other research suggests the real prevalence of these offences is masked by a *'dark figure'* which is truly enormous (DeLisi *et al.*, 2016). For example, whilst official figures suggest 15,518 sexual assaults and 9,646 rapes occurred in England and Wales in the year ending March 2013, other reports suggest the numbers were much higher around that time. For example, Matheson (2013) found one in twenty adult women reported being a victim of serious sexual violence (i.e., rape or sexual assault by penetration) since the age of 16. This figure rose to one in five when less serious offences (i.e., sexual threats, unwanted touching, and indecent exposure) were included. From these figures, Matheson (2013) estimated that around 85,000 adult women are the victims of serious sexual violence each year. In line with Figure 9.1, this figure has risen sharply in recent years, as Elkin (2023a) found 798,000 women aged 16+ were victims of sexual assault (including attempts) in the year ending March 2022.

Attrition process

Another key problem that hinders our understanding of the prevalence of contact sexual violence is the process of *'attrition'*. This involves cases dropping out of the criminal justice system at various points and therefore not resulting in a conviction. For example, Harris and Grace (1999) found that only 6% of rapes originally recorded by the police resulted in convictions. Fourteen years later, Matheson (2013) found this problem persisted, as only around 1% of sexual assaults and less than 2% of rapes resulted in conviction. More recently, Wunsch *et al.* (2021) found only 1% of rapes in London resulted in conviction. These figures suggest Scully's (1994) description of rape as a low-risk, high-reward crime still applies.

Contact stranger sexual violence: Not as rare as we might originally have thought?

In relation to victim–offender relationship, Matheson (2013) found that strangers accounted for 10% of serious sexual assaults (i.e., rape or sexual assault by penetration) and 52% of less serious sexual assaults (i.e., sexual threats, unwanted touching, indecent exposure). Applying these percentages to the latest figures would suggest that in the year ending March 2020, 3,908 women aged 16 or over were raped by a stranger, and 20,331 women aged 13 or over were sexually assaulted by a stranger. These figures equate to almost 60 stranger rapes and 390 stranger sexual assaults each week in England and Wales alone. However, using Elkin's (2023a) figure of 798,000 would mean that between 79,800 (at 10%) and 414,960 (at 52%) women are sexually assaulted each year by a stranger, which equates to between 1,534 and 7,980 cases each week.

Whilst official figures report the prevalence of sexual assault, no reference is made as to whether these offences are indicative of a frotteuristic disorder. As stated in Chapter 6 (Table 6.1), the DSM-5-TR (American Psychiatric Association, 2022) reports that frotteurism may occur in 30% of adult men in the general population. Other community studies broadly support this figure. For example, in Germany, Ahlers *et al.* (2011) found that almost half (49%) of men fantasise about frotteurism, and around a quarter masturbate to (26%) or engage (34%) in frotteurism. In Canada, Joyal and Carpentier (2017) found 26.7% of men had a desire to engage in frotteurism, and 26.1% had done so. In Italy, Castellini *et al.* (2018) found 19.8% of men had fantasies of frotteurism, 17.7% masturbate to these fantasies, and 10.3% had engaged in frotteurism. Applying these figures to the UK illustrates the potential scale of this problem. For example, the UK population is now estimated to be almost 67 million. If, for arguments sake, we assume half of them (i.e., 33.5 million) are adult men, around a quarter of them are engaging in frotteurism, and if 52% of them are targeting strangers, then this means there are around four million frotteurs active in the UK targeting female strangers. If the above figures are correct, then contact stranger sexual violence is not as rare as we might originally have thought. Consequently, it is crucial for criminal justice practitioners to understand how and why these offences occur.

Offence details: *What typically happens, when, and where?*

Contact stranger sexual violence is an interactive encounter between a man and a woman and typically includes sexual acts that occur within consensual heterosexual relationships. These offences occur in various locations and often include physical violence. When understanding the psychology of these offences, we need to consider what I can call the stranger's sexual offender's dilemma, as this is a key feature of these assaults as far as his decision-making is concerned. On the one hand, he must engage with his victim in a close-up and personal manner to complete the sexual (and physical) aspect of the offence. On the other hand, the close-up and personal nature of these offences leaves the victim able to provide the police with a description of her assailant and his crime scene actions. In response, some stranger sexual offenders either do not consider this dilemma or, if they do, are prepared to take the risk. Others, however, are clearly aware of this dilemma, and they take various steps to address it. As we shall see in the next chapter, some of these steps are very efficient but deadly.

Sexual assault (non-penetrative)

These offences typically occur in pubs and clubs and involve (perhaps intoxicated) men impulsively groping women's' breasts or pinching or smacking their bottoms. As stated above, these offences are regarded as less serious; they are very common and often involve strangers (Matheson, 2013). Indeed, the frequency with which these offences occur is such that they are viewed by many women as being a normal feature of a night out in a pub or club (Brown, 2017). Whilst many such assaults are probably impulsive, others contain a sinister and premeditated dynamic. For example, to address the stranger sexual offender's dilemma, some men incapacitate their victims by administering a *'date rape'* drug, either by *'spiking'* the woman's drink or using a hypodermic needle to inject it into her (Loveridge-Greene, 2021). This leaves the woman highly vulnerable to sexual exploitation and unable to describe her assailant or the offence afterwards. The scale of these offences and the serious implications they can have for some women were evidenced by the fact that they were the focus of a parliamentary investigation (House of Commons, 2018). Moreover, in many parts of Britain, undercover police officers now operate in pubs and clubs to deter potential offenders (Morrison, 2021).

Sexual assaults in public locations

Whilst pubs and clubs provide a ready supply of women to sexually assault, plus a suitable location due to the hustle and bustle affording the offender some protection from the risk of identification, other sexual assaults occur in places where these factors are largely absent. Examples include university campuses, where the problem of sexual misconduct (some involving strangers) is so prevalent that the Office for Students recently launched an initiative to address it (Office for Students, 2022). Other examples include sexual assaults occurring in public locations in broad daylight (see Box 9.1). These assaults can perhaps be viewed as a *'step-up'* from exhibitionism because, just like the exhibitionist, these men engage in pre-meditated opportunistic behaviour, which involves looking for opportunities to sexually assault women. These men walk or cycle around public areas such as parks, and if they find a suitable woman, they approach her, assault, her then run or cycle away. A key point to bear in mind about non-penetrative sexual assaults is that, whilst in many cases they will be limited to sexual touching, in other cases, the sexual touching will be a precursor to a more serious sexual assault. This can occur either there and then or, as illustrated in the case of Robert (see Box 8.1), later as the offender's offence trajectory escalates.

Box 9.1 Case examples of sexual assault

Barry

Barry is 30 years old, unmarried, and successfully employed. He has a previous conviction for indecent exposure and another for sexual assault. He was being managed in the community, and the police wanted a better understanding of his presentation. The sexual assault occurred when he sat next to a woman in a café. She was wearing a skirt and tights, and on impulse, he touched her leg. He stated he was sexually excited by her appearance and "liked how her legs looked and wanted a feel". One year later, he was in a supermarket when he approached a woman and stroked her bottom. Although an argument ensued between them, the woman did not pursue the matter. He described this as an impulsive act which made him feel sexually excited. During subsequent clinical sessions, he self-reported that he had touched the bottoms of several women in public places (i.e., clubs, public transport, waiting at a pedestrian crossing, and shopping centres). These incidents involved random strangers and had not come to the attention of the police. He suggested his motivation for these acts was to relive stress and have an attraction towards the women. He described hoping something positive would come out of these incidents, e.g., a "one-night-stand or a fling". He stated there were several incidents of this nature. He found these incidents sexually exciting but denied masturbating to the ideas of them.

20-year-old man jailed for 20 counts of sexual assault by touching

A series of sexual assaults occurred between 1 and 7 March 2021, along the banks of the Bridgewater Canal, the River Mersey, and the Trans Pennine Trail in Greater Manchester. The man assaulted 19 women and a teenage girl across the seven-day period, including nine women in one day. His offences followed a similar pattern in that the women were all walking or running, often alone, when he would approach them from behind on a bicycle. As he approached and began to pass the women, he would then either grab or slap their bottoms and quickly flee the scene on his bike. Following one assault, his victim and a family member drove around the local area and spotted a male who she was confident was her assailant. She managed to take photographs of him, which she passed to the police. He was apprehended a few days later by plain-clothed police officers who were patrolling that area. (Source: www.gmp.police.uk/news).

18-year-old jailed a second time for smacking six women's bottoms

The assaults happened during February and March 2014 in Derbyshire. Just one month after being released from prison for smacking other women on the bottom the previous year, the man started to follow girls and women into secluded areas, where he would smack them on the bottom and then run off. His victims included schoolgirls, a mother pushing her child in a pram, and a woman aged 60. The accused admitted sexually assaulting six women but showed no remorse as he was sentenced to 25 months in a young offenders' institution.
(Source: https://www.dailymail.co.uk/news/article-2687190/Teenager-jailed-smacking-six-womens-bottoms-including-two-schoolgirls-mother-pram.html)

Rape (and sexual assault by penetration)

These offences are perhaps the epitome of what most women think about when imagining being sexually assaulted by a stranger. Because these are such interpersonal crimes, it is useful to explore the contexts and circumstances in which they occur.

Pre-crime phase

In a study of rapes committed by strangers, Greenall and West (2007, 2008) found most offences (52%) occurred in public locations (e.g., carparks, alleyways, parks, etc.), with the remainder (48%) occurring in private locations, mostly the victim's home. The latter finding builds on chapter seven by highlighting the importance of burglary to our understanding of stranger sexual violence. Pre-offence offender–victim interactions mostly involved a contact approach (55%), similar to Hazelwood and Burgess' (2017) 'con' (see Table 2.1). This aims to distract the woman prior to being sexually assaulted. Other offences (45%) commenced with a surprise attack involving immediate violence to overpower the woman.

Although Greenall and West (2007, 2008) did not report on the timing of when the stranger rapes occurred, Ruparel (2004) found 53% of stranger rapes in London occurred between Friday and Sunday, and the majority of all rapes (i.e., stranger and non-stranger) occurred between 9 pm and 4 am. Similarly, in Massachusetts, Astion (2008) found victims were more likely to be assaulted during the evening or early hours. These findings suggest that many stranger rapes are associated with socialisation and intoxication. Indeed, Greenall and West (2007, 2008) found that in 37% of cases, the rapist was reportedly intoxicated, and Ruparel (2004) found that just under half (49%) of all rapes where the victim consumed alcohol were perpetrated by strangers.

Crime phase

Building on the research of others (e.g., Groth & Birnbaum, 1979; Knight & Prentky, 1990a), Greenall and West (2007, 2008) found stranger rapes include a sexual and violent dynamic:

- *Sexual dynamic:* Involved behaviours such as sexual assault, vaginal intercourse, anal intercourse, sexual assault by penetration, and fellatio, with some women subjected to multiple sexual penetrations. Additionally, some women were forced to sexually engage with their assailant in various ways, such as hugging and kissing him, masturbating themselves or him, and *'talking dirty'* to him.
- *Violent dynamic:* Involved behaviours such as issuing verbal threats, pushing/wrestling the woman to the ground, punching/slapping the woman, pulling her hair, grabbing her by the throat, biting the woman, brandishing a weapon, and using restraints. Consequently, most women (56%) sustained injuries during these assaults.
- *Other behaviours:* Involved some offenders stealing items from their victims (24%) and appearing intoxicated at the material time (37%).

Post-crime phase

Following the assault, Greenall and West (2007, 2008) found that most offenders (64%) fled, but around a third (36%) spent time with their victims. These post-offence interactions included escorting the victim away from the crime scene, conversing with them, and even complimenting and/or apologising to the woman.

These findings largely mirror those of some classic studies into stranger sexual violence. For example, Bownes *et al.* (1991) found victims mostly encountered their assailant in an outdoor location; a large number were assaulted in public locations (47%) and had consumed alcohol prior to the attack (40%). Moreover, the assaults included a range of violent and sexual behaviours, and most (83%) were abandoned afterwards. Jones *et al.* (2004) found that whilst sexual assaults by strangers occurred in various locations, the single most popular location (43%) was the victim's home, which again highlights the importance of burglary to our understanding of stranger sexual violence. Jones *et al.* (2004) also found that these assaults involved weapons or physical violence and resulted in more non-genital injuries. Other research has similarly found stranger sexual assaults occur in the late evenings or early hours, involve one assailant, include force resulting in victim injuries, and are more likely to be reported to the police (Astion, 2008) and receive a forensic medical examination (Grossin *et al.*, 2003). The geographic nature of stranger sexual violence was explored by Davies and Dale (1995; 1996), who found most cases occurred within a few miles of the offender's home. They also found that younger men tend to rape strangers closer to home, as 79% of cases involving younger men (aged 26 or less) occurred within 1.8 miles of their home.

Motivation: *Why do some men commit this offence?*

As with non-contact offences, when trying to understand why some men engage in contact sexual offences, a useful starting point is to recognise that behaviours such as sexual touching and sexual intercourse are not limited to sexual offenders or sexual deviants. Rather, the same behaviours are engaged in by most people. Although the differentiating feature between lawful and unlawful sexual behaviour (i.e., lack of consent) has been highlighted many times by many people over the years, as Baroness Stern reported in her review of how rape cases are handled, *"rape is unique as it is an inherently lawful activity made illegal because of lack of consent"* (Stern, 2010, p. 45). What this quote illustrates is that whilst some stranger sexual offenders are mentally disordered (see Greenall & West, 2007, 2008), the pathological nature of stranger sexual violence lies not so much in the sexual behaviours themselves but in the context and circumstances in which these behaviours occur.

In the previous chapter, we drew upon the concept of courtship disorder (Freund, 1990; Freund & Blanchard, 1986). We saw how voyeurism and exhibitionism are distorted components of human courtship behaviour (American Psychiatric Association, 2022) within stages one (i.e., partner location) and two (i.e., pre-tactile interaction) of the four-stage human courtship process. Just as the process of courtship progresses into stages three and four with contact interactions (e.g., touching and kissing) and genital union (i.e., sexual intercourse), distorted variants of these involve frotteurism and a preferential rape pattern. Whilst the former is defined in Table 9.2, the latter involves a preference for rape over consenting sexual intercourse. Given that Freund suggested *"the preferential rapist virtually always chooses a woman who is a stranger or almost a stranger as his victim"* (1990, p. 198), understanding his actions is a necessity for every criminal justice practitioner.

Motivational and interpersonal dynamics

In Chapter 4, we explored the various motivational dynamics of rape. Whilst much of this research has not focused specifically on strangers, Greenall and West (2007, 2008) found the MTC:R3 was able to show that even among stranger rapists, various motivational dynamics were apparent, with some more apparent than others. For example, the sexual types (i.e., opportunistic and sexual non-sadistic) accounted for 63.4%, the sadistic types (sexual sadistic) 24.4%, and the angry/violent types (i.e., angry and vindictive) 12.2%. Viewed another way, these findings suggest that sexual gratification, be it of an opportunistic, non-sadistic, or sadistic nature, is the driving force for over three-quarters (75.7%) of stranger rapes, including those committed by men with a mental illness (87%) and a personality disorder (87.5%) (see Table 5 in Greenall & West, 2007, p. 160). This finding builds on previous research which suggests *'sexual release'* was the main motivation for sexually aggressive men, most of whom targeted strangers (Langevin *et al.*, 1988).

In Chapter 4, we also explored the various interpersonal dynamics of rape and the behavioural themes (or 'modes of interaction', see Canter & Heritage, 1990) that exist between the offender and his victim. Although Greenall and West (2007, 2008) replicated the methodology of these earlier studies, their more broader interpretation of the results suggested the interpersonal dynamics of stranger rape can be captured by one of two *'superordinate'* themes relating to sex and violence (see Table 9.3). This is not to say that all cases will be *'pure'* examples of one or the other, as combinations or *'mixed'* cases indicative of anger or sadism will occur. Rather, they key point is that even stranger rapes reflect the sexual and violent themes, which motivational typologies have traditionally highlighted (see Table 4.2). Whilst these findings apply to offences of rape (some of which include sexual assaults and sexual assaults by penetration), we can use them to hypothesise that similar factors drive and underpin non-penetrative sexual assaults that occur in pubs, clubs, university campuses, and public locations.

Future implications?

As with other types of stranger sexual violence, a key consideration in relation to contact sexual offences relates to whether these men will re-offend, and if so, will they commit similar offences or escalate into more serious acts of sexual violence? Whilst any type of sexual re-offending is a matter of concern, with contact sexual offenders, any repetition or escalation is a matter of serious concern due to the impact such assaults have on others.

Table 9.3 Sexual and violent stranger rapes

	Sexual rapes	Violent rapes
Offence behaviours as per Greenall and West (2007)	Include verbal contact by an intoxicated man brandishing a weapon, several sexual acts, verbal threats, or minimal violence, compliments, spending time with the victim afterwards, and some apologising for their actions.	Include a surprise attack, aggressive indecent assault, being bitten, held by the throat, bound and/or gagged, raped, and abandoned.
Case Example	In the early hours, a man offers a lone female a lift. She accepts and gets into his car, expecting a lift home. He drives her to a secluded location, where he locks the door, quickly reclines her seat, and begins to kiss and fondle her. Then, at knifepoint, he threatens her, orders her to undress, and rapes her whilst still kissing and fondling her.	A man was rubbing his penis and approached a woman in a field. She attempted to run off, but he jumped onto her, wrestled her to the floor, and started punching her in the face, telling her to "fucking shut up" or he would kill her. He then dragged her to a secluded part of the field, where he vaginally and anally raped her whilst continuing to make these threats.

Will they do it again?

As with non-contact sexual offenders, this question is explored by examining research which has followed-up sexual offenders after release from prison, secure hospitals, or probation to determine whether they have re-offended during a specified timescale. Notwithstanding the problem of the *'dark figure'* of sexual violence, the research suggests most stranger sexual offenders do not sexually re-offend. For example, Friendship and Beech (2005) report that the four-year sexual reconviction rate in England and Wales ranged from 5% to 12%. Later in their evaluation of a sex offender treatment programme, Mews *et al.* (2017) found that after an average follow-up period of eight years, the sexual recidivism rate ranged from 8% (untreated group) to 10% (treated group). In the US, Alper and Durose (2019) found that 7.7% of sexual offenders who were originally convicted of rape or sexual assault were arrested for rape or sexual assault within nine years of release. However, in a review of previous studies, Przbylski (2015) found that rates of sexual recidivism increased with the length of time sexual offenders were followed up in the community, as sexual recidivism rates of sex offenders ranged from about 5% after three years to about 24% after 15 years. Although these and other studies include mixed victim–offender relationship types, a study by Hood *et al.* (2002) illustrated the recidivism rates of stranger sexual offenders and found them to be smaller. Among stranger sexual offenders who had targeted adults, 2.9% were reconvicted and imprisoned for any sexual offence after four years, rising to 5.3% after six years. The potentially violent nature of these men was shown by the fact that 17.6% were reconvicted and imprisoned for any sexual or violent offence after four years, declining slightly to 15.8% after six years.

Criminal profiles of stranger sexual offenders

Whilst we can reasonably hypothesise that stranger sexual offenders will mostly not sexually re-offend, that still leaves us with an important issue to consider, namely, what role does sexual violence play in the criminal histories of stranger sexual offenders?

Research suggests most stranger rapists have diverse criminal histories, but most do not have previous sexual convictions. For example, Davies et al. (1997; 1998) found 84% of stranger rapists had a criminal record, and 61% had previously been in custody. Their criminal records covered the full range of offences, including 32% who had previous convictions for sexual violence. Similarly, Greenall and West (2007, 2008) found 98% of stranger rapists had a criminal record, and 71% had previously been in custody. Like Davies et al. (1997; 1998), Greenall and West (2007, 2008) found the criminal records of stranger rapists covered the full range of offences, including 39% who had previous convictions for sexual violence. More recently, Almond *et al.* (2021) found 73.2% of stranger rapists had a criminal record, and although once again this included the full range of offences, only 16.5% had previous convictions for sexual violence. At the higher end of the sexually violent spectrum, Beauregard and Martineau (2017) report that across 13 previous studies of sexual murderers, the numbers with previous convictions for sexual violence range from 12.5% to 29%. More specifically, for our purposes, Greenall and Richardson (2015) found that only 16% of stranger sexual killers had previous convictions for sexual violence.

Along with considering criminal histories, sexual histories are relevant here too, especially given that some contact sexual offences may be indicative of frotteurism or sadism.

For example, among convicted sexual offenders, rates of frotteurism and sadism have ranged from 25% and 11%, respectively (McElroy *et al.*, 1999), to 16.8% and 13.3%, respectively (Dunsieth *et al.*, 2004). However, among a sample of sexually aggressive men, most of whom targeted strangers, Langevin *et al.* (1988) found around a third (31%) had histories of frotteurism, whilst 13% had histories of sadism. Indeed, although the nature of their deviant sexual practices was not specified, Greenall and West (2007, 2008) found that 66% of stranger rapists had histories of adult sexual deviancy.

By exploring the criminal profiles of stranger sexual offenders, we can formulate three hypotheses about stranger sexual offenders. First, most of these men have diverse criminal histories and are therefore generalist rather than specialist offenders (Soothill *et al.*, 2000). This means that any further (or, for that matter, previous) offending may not be limited to sexual violence. Second, only about a third of stranger sexual offenders are sexual recidivists, which means in most cases, their stranger sexual assaults are their first (known) sexual offence. Third, around a third of stranger sexual offenders have histories of frotteurism, and about a fifth have histories of sadism. These findings lead us to consider whether there are any warning signs that may indicate that a stranger sexual offender may re-offend and/or be on an upward offence trajectory.

Warning signs

This is a complex area, and ways in which this can be explored by criminal justice practitioners working with a stranger sexual offender will be explored in more detail in chapters 11–12. For now, there are one or two *'red flags'* that, if evident in an individual's sexual assault of a female stranger, should make criminal justice practitioners sit up and take note. As stated elsewhere in this book, research on recidivism has shown that two factors are especially important when considering the chances of an individual committing further acts of sexual violence, namely sexual deviancy and an antisocial/criminal orientation (Hanson & Bussière, 1998; Hanson & Morton-Bourgon, 2004). In the case of sexual deviancy, if an offence evidenced any of the paraphilic disorders explored in Chapter 6, and/or other behaviours explored in the previous two chapters, that would be a red flag. For example, evidence that the offender derived sadistic pleasure from the violence inflicted and/or stole fetish items (e.g., her underwear) from the victim would be a matter of concern. Another red flag would be evidence that an individual disregards the stranger's sexual offender's dilemma and is prepared to take unnecessary risks to engage in sexual violence. As illustrated with Barry in Box 9.1, it is one thing for a man to grope a woman in a crowded bar or tube train where his identity can be hidden by others around him; it is a different matter when he does this on an individual basis where his identity as her assailant is obvious to his victim. In such cases, we can hypothesise that the sexual gratification he receives from assaulting strangers and his antisocial attitudes override his ability to engage in consequential thinking. Another more recent example is shown in Box 9.2 and shows how a young man was driven to engage in risky behaviour to satisfy his sexual desires.

In the case of an antisocial/criminal orientation, one or two factors are worthy of consideration. As stated in Chapter 6, Canter and Heritage (1990) suggested that some stranger rapes are marked by a criminal interpersonal dynamic. This mode of interaction comprised several behaviours, including, among others, the usage by the offender of blindfolds, gags, restraints, and him wearing a disguise and stealing from the victim. Similar modes of interaction have been found by subsequent studies (e.g., Canter *et al.*,

---

Box 9.2   High-risk behaviour associated with sexual assault

Police hunting a cyclist who slapped a woman's buttocks and showed lewd pictures

Northumbria Police were first contacted by a woman who was approached by a man in his mid-20s on a bicycle, who asked her to look at his phone and showed her a lewd picture before riding off. Since then, several similar incidents have been reported to the police, all taking place in the same area of South Shields and commonly between the hours of 6am and 10am. These have included reports of a male sexually assaulting women by cycling past and slapping them on the buttocks before cycling away. Others report a male engaging a woman in conversation, making lewd comments towards them, or inviting them to look at indecent images of himself on his phone. Every woman has given a similar description of the man, and all incidents are being treated as linked. Officers have now released a CCTV image of a man who may be able to assist with their enquires
Source: www.chroniclelive.co.uk

2003; Häkkänen *et al.*, 2004; House, 1997; Lehmann *et al.*, 2013). More specifically, Lehmann *et al.* (2013) found the criminal mode was significantly predictive of sexual recidivism and also significantly correlated with previous sexual convictions. Therefore, should a stranger sexual offender evidence behaviours suggestive of an antisocial/criminal orientation, such as stealing non-sexual items from his victim, this could be a red flag for further offending and indicate he has previous convictions for acquisitive offending (Almond *et al.*, 2021; Davies *et al.*, 1997; 1998; Häkkänen *et al.*, 2004; Scott *et al.*, 2006; ter Beek *et al.*, 2010). Moreover, should his antisocial/criminal orientation extend to the usage of excessive violence, which is not the source of sadistic pleasure, this too would be a red flag, as the usage of physical violence during a sexual assault is a recognised risk factor for further sexual violence (Boer *et al.*, 2017; Hart *et al.*, 2022), and it could indicate a greater likelihood that the offender in question has previous convictions for violence (Davies *et al.*, 1997, 1998; House, 1997; Jackson *et al.*, 1997; ter Beek *et al.*, 2010).

Conclusions and implications for practice

This chapter has introduced the concept of contact stranger sexual violence and has shown how these offences exist on a continuum, with what might be regarded as '*minor*' non-penetrative sexual touching at one end and penetrative offences like rape at the other. Within this continuum, some offences may be indicative of a deviant sexual preference in the form of a frotteuristic disorder, and others may evidence sexual sadism. As with non-contact sexual violence, our understanding of the prevalence of these offences is hindered by the '*dark figure*' of unknown/unreported incidents, and in the case of rape, the process of attrition. What the research suggests, however, is that serious acts of stranger sexual violence, such as the offences considered in this chapter, are far more widespread in our society than official opinion would have us believe. In support of research which highlights the fear factor associated with stranger sexual violence, this chapter has shown that these offences really can happen to any woman anytime, anywhere, including public locations and her own home.

When trying to understand why some men sexually assault adult female strangers, the research summarised in Chapter 4 suggests that sexual and violent dynamics underpin these offences. However, more recent research suggests that sexual gratification is the driving force in most cases (Greenall & West, 2007, 2008). What this means is that contact stranger sexual violence is an offence driven by internal (psychological) drives rather than external (social) factors (Schlesinger, 2004a, 2004b). Despite this, research suggests that stranger sexual offenders mostly do not sexually re-offend, and their sexual assault of a female stranger was, in most cases, their first (known) sexual offence. However, it is important to note that stranger sexual offenders are mostly generalist offenders with diverse criminal histories. Therefore, any further (or previous) offending may not be limited to sexual violence. Consequently, criminal justice practitioners are dealing with someone who is more than just a sexual offender.

10 Stranger sexual femicide

The sexual killing of women by male strangers

That day I just reached critical mass, and something had to give, and when everything exploded, it got everything out of my system, which sounds horribly fatuous considering a girl had to lose her life.

(A sexual killer explaining his offence to West, 2000b)

Introduction

Femicide is a type of homicide which involves the killing of women (Radford & Russell, 1992). Most femicides are committed by men, and among the contexts and circumstances in which they occur, one of them is sexual. The reasons why some men sexually assault and kill women have taxed the minds of scholars and practitioners for centuries. In the late 1800s, for example, when Jack the Ripper was inflicting his homicidal sexual desires onto the prostitutes of Victorian London, he was described by Von Krafft-Ebing as a *"psycho-sexual monster"* (1894, p. 64). More recently, cases like Ted Bundy in the USA, the Yorkshire Ripper Peter Sutcliffe, and of course Colonel Williams and Pawel Relowicz discussed in Chapter 7 are just a few examples of men whose crimes have included the sexual killing of women. Although these killings are very rare, criminal justice practitioners need to understand them because not even these crimes are a uniform construct. Rather, the differing motivational and interpersonal dynamics mean these killings are as heterogeneous as any other type of sexual violence.

Chapter aims

This chapter explores what is, without question, the most serious and most feared form of stranger sexual violence. This starts by exploring how this form of sexual violence is defined, which is not easy. Then the prevalence of these killings is explored, which is equally difficult. Exploring what typically happens within these killings and why is an easier task given the growing body of research. However, exploring what implications these killings may have for future offending is another difficult task. One factor which carries over from other forms of sexual violence is the fact that some killings evidence sexual deviancy, which, as we know, is an important risk factor for further sexual violence (Boer *et al.*, 2017; Hart *et al.*, 2022).

DOI: 10.4324/9781003217763-12

Definition: *What is this crime?*

When trying to answer this straightforward question, we encounter three problems: (1) these killings have no universal label; (2) these killings are not defined under English Law; and (3) despite their obvious deviousness, these killings are not formally defined as a clinical construct. Each problem will now be illustrated.

What is this crime called?

Whilst Von Krafft-Ebing (1894) used the label *'lust murder'* to describe these killings, subsequent researchers have used several others. These include sadistic lust murder, sadistic murder, rape murder, sexual murder, mutilation murder, and sexual homicide (e.g., see Griffiths, 2013). The existence of multiple labels to refer to what is essentially the same (or very similar) type of crime illustrates what Schlesinger calls the *"problem of definition and terms"* (2004b, p. 2) within this body of research. However, another problem relates to the fact that much of this research includes different victim types (e.g., Chan & Heide, 2009), and so these labels can refer to the sexual killing of men, women or children, strangers, or known. Feminist writers such as Russell (1992) suggested an alternative label to the gender-neutral *'homicide'* was required to highlight the killing of women. Since then, the label *'femicide'* has been used to capture what the World Health Organization (2012) describes as the *"intentional murder of women because they are women"* and in a context which Cecchi *et al.* (2023) suggest involves a man's failure to recognise a woman's right to self-determination. Given that a fundamental feature of this failure to recognise a woman's right to self-determination involves a lack of sexual consent, some researchers (e.g., Pietsch, 2015; Zara *et al.*, 2022) and organisations (e.g., Canadian Femicide Observatory for Justice and Accountability, 2024) use the label *'sexual femicide'* when highlighting the sexual killing of women. In this chapter, therefore, sexual homicide is used as a gender-neural label, and sexual femicide refers to the sexual killing of women.

Legal definitions

Unlike the other sexual offences in earlier chapters, sexual homicide is not defined under English Law. Consequently, no one can be convicted of sexual homicide because legally, the offence does not exist. Rather, under English Law, anyone who commits such a crime will be convicted of one of the homicide offences, namely murder or manslaughter. Although these two offences have the same *'actus reus'* (i.e., unlawful killing), the difference between them relates to the killer's state of mind (his *'mens rea'*) at the material time. With murder, the mens rea involves *'malice aforethought'* which is an intention to kill or to cause grievous bodily harm. Although manslaughter has the same mens rea, the killer's culpability is reduced due to various mitigating circumstances, such as diminished responsibility (Homicide Act 1957, as amended by the Coroners and Justice Act 2009) or a loss of control (Coroners and Justice Act 2009) (see Crown Prosecution Service, 2023). Other scenarios that may result in a manslaughter conviction are when a woman dies when a sex game goes wrong (Yardley, 2020). Greenall (2012) suggested that murder and manslaughter have their sexual equivalents, namely sexual murder and sexual manslaughter. Therefore, when trying to understand sexual homicides, criminal justice practitioners should recognise that they can involve different intentions and different states of mind.

Clinical definitions

Although sexual homicides are deviant, they are not defined as paraphilia within DSM-5-TR (American Psychiatric Association, 2022) or ICD-11 (World Health Organization, 2022). Notwithstanding this, sexual homicide is regarded as a paraphilia called 'erotophonophilia'. Although not officially defined, some definitions are available within the research. For example, Arrigo and Purcell define erotophonophilia as "*the acting out of deviant behaviour by means of brutally and sadistically killing the victim to achieve ultimate sexual satisfaction*" (2001, p. 7); Griffiths (2013) defines erotophonophilia as "*a sexual paraphilia in which individuals derive sexual pleasure and arousal from murdering (or imagining they are murdering) someone*"; and Schug and Fradella define erotophonophilia as "*sexual satisfaction from murdering strangers; lust murder*" (2015, p. 321). Although different researchers offer different definitions, we can see that once again, they are all essentially referring to the same (or very similar) type of crime.

Application: Stranger sexual femicide

Although sexual homicides have various labels and definitions, many researchers have used the gender-neutral definition from Ressler *et al.* (1988), as amended by Chan (2015). Along with the gender specific definition proposed by the Canadian Femicide Observatory for Justice and Accountability (CFOJA, 2024), Table 10.1 shows that whether investigating a case of stranger sexual femicide or working stranger sexual killers, criminal justice practitioners are faced with offenders who have engaged in what I have previously

Table 10.1 Research definitions of sexual homicide/femicide

Ressler et al. (1988)	Chan (2015)	CFOJA (2024)
Sexual homicide describes murders with evidence or observations that indicate that the murder was sexual in nature. These include: a Victim attire or lack of attire. b Exposure of the sexual parts of the victim's body. c Sexual positioning of the victim's body. d Insertion of foreign objects into the victim's body cavities. e Evidence of sexual intercourse (oral, anal, or vaginal). f Evidence of substitute sexual activity, interest, or sadistic fantasy.	To classify a homicide as sexual, one of the following criteria must be met: a Physical evidence of pre-, peri-, and/or post-mortem sexual assault (vaginal, oral, or anal) against the victim. b Physical evidence of substitute sexual activity against the victim (e.g., genitalia mutilation, exposure of the sexual parts or sexual positioning of the victim's body, insertion of foreign objects into the victim's body cavities) or in the immediate area of the victim's body (e.g., masturbation) reflecting the deviant or sadistic sexual fantasy of the offender. c Legally admissible offender confession of the sexual motive of the offence that intentionally or unintentionally results in a homicide. d Indication of the sexual element(s) of the crime from the offender's personal belongings (e.g., home computer and/or journal entries).	Sexual violations and sexual violence that result in the death of a woman or girl or occur during the killing of a woman or girl. Sexual femicides may be intentional including, for example, sexual violence perpetrated during armed conflict or against specific groups of women, but they may also be unintentional such as sexual violence perpetrated against women by male partners that results in the woman's death. The sexual violence involved in sexual femicide may range from leaving the victim unclothed, often displayed publicly, to rape and mutilation.

called "*a distinctive form of homicide and an extreme form of sexual violence*" (Greenall, 2012, p. 338). Whilst the popular profile of these killings involves a woman being raped and strangled by a male stranger, we will see these killings present in many ways. However, before we explore the details of what happens within stranger sexual femicides, we need to consider how common they are.

Prevalence: *How common is this crime?*

The fact that sexual homicide is not defined by law means there are no official statistics on the prevalence of these killings. However, research from several countries suggests these killings are very rare, accounting for around 1%–5% of all homicides (De Veauuse Brown & Watson, 2022; Greenall, 2012; James & Proulx, 2014). This figure was recently confirmed by Giorgetti *et al.* (2022), who found 5.6% of Italian femicides were sexual.

Within Great Britain research suggests sexual femicides, especially involving strangers, are very rare indeed. For example, the Femicide Census found that of the 1,425 femicides in Britain during the ten years 2009–2018, 57 (4%) occurred in a context described as '*sexually motivated*'. Although this was the third most common context, there was evidence of sexual violence in 83 (6%) cases. It was also reported that 119 (8%) of the 1,425 femicides were committed by a stranger (Long *et al.*, 2019). What these figures tell us is that each year over this ten-year period, there were on average almost twelve (11.9) stranger femicides, almost six (5.7) sexually motivated femicides, and just over eight (8.3) femicides that included evidence of sexual violence. Although the offender–victim relationship in the sexual cases was not specified, it was in another report by the Femicide Census. In that report, 936 femicides that occurred in England and Wales during the six years 2009–2015 were explored. It was found that 31 (3.3%) women were killed in sexually motivated attacks, 10 of whom by strangers (Brennan, 2017). What these figures tell us is that each year over this six-year period, there were on average just over five (5.2) sexually motivated femicides and less than two (1.7) stranger sexual femicides, meaning the prevalence of stranger sexual femicide during this period was 1.1%. These figures are similar to those of Greenall and Richardson (2015), whose sample of 81 stranger sexual femicides between 1970 and 2010 suggests that on average there were just over two cases per year.

'*Dark figure*' of sexual femicide

As we shall see below, not all killings will be recognised as being sexual, and so even here, a '*dark figure*' (DeLisi *et al.*, 2016) exists. In relation to the Femicide Census findings above, they suggested their figures are likely to be an undercount because there are several factors that contribute to a lack of identification of evidence of sexual violence in femicide cases. For example, police officers and pathologists may lack training to spot indicators of sexual violence, and prosecutors may only proceed with the most serious charge, i.e., murder (Long *et al.*, 2019). Additionally, how many of the thousands of women who go missing each year in Britain might have been the victims of a stranger sexual femicide, but no one knows?

Practical implications

The rarity of stranger sexual femicide has practical implications. First, many criminal justice practitioners may only encounter a few, if any, stranger sexual killers during their careers. Indeed, although the offender–victim relationship or victim's gender was not specified, the rarity of sexual killers within our criminal justice system was illustrated by Beech, Fisher and Ward (2005), who report that only 6% of convicted murderers in British prisons had committed sexually related homicides. By way of illustration, for 13 years working in a forensic medium secure unit, I only encountered a handful of stranger sexual killers or men who wanted to become one (for a case study of one of these men, see Greenall & Millington, 2021). Second, when a stranger sexual femicide occurs, as illustrated by Pawel Relowicz' killing of Libby Squire in 2019 and Metropolitan Police Officer Wayne Couzens' killing of Sarah Everard in 2021, police officers quickly become involved in a high-profile murder investigation, with the media, politicians, and the public demanding swift action. But even police officers may only encounter a few, if any, stranger sexual femicides during their career, and as illustrated in the killing of Rachel Nickel in London in July 1990, mistakes can result in the case remaining in the public eye for years afterwards (Cerfontyne, 2010). Consequently, police officers and other criminal justice practitioners need to understand what happens within these offences to aid their practice and to avoid missing any indicators of sexual violence within a femicide.

Offence details: *What typically happens, when, and where?*

Although studies have summarised the details of what typically happens within sexual homicides (e.g., Carter & Hollin, 2010; Chan, 2017), a study by Greenall and Richardson (2015) focused exclusively on stranger sexual femicides. This and other research build a profile of what typically happens within these offences.

Pre-crime phase

Greenall and Richardson (2015) found that just over half (53%) of the killings occurred in outdoor locations, such as roads, streets, alleyways, fields, or parks. The rest occurred indoors, mostly in the victim's or offender's residence. Among all the locations, the single most common was the victim's residence (31%), a finding which highlights the importance of burglary to our understanding of these killings (Schlesinger & Revitch, 1999). In relation to timing, more killings were committed on a Friday than any other day, and 71% occurred between Thursday and Sunday. Additionally, most killings (54%) commenced between 9pm and 3am. These findings suggest there is a weekend/night-time aspect to many stranger sexual femicides and an association with socialising in public places (e.g., pubs or bars, etc.) and intoxication.

Crime phase

Similar to the findings on stranger rape summarised in the previous chapter, Greenall and Richardson (2015) found that stranger sexual femicides also include a sexual and violent dynamic.

- *Sexual dynamic:* Involved various behaviours that were overtly sexual. These included some women being raped (vaginal, anal, or oral), sexually assaulted by penetration, or sexually assaulted in other ways. Some victims had more than one body orifice sexually penetrated, and others engaged sexually with their assailant during the assault. This engagement included acts such as hugging and/or kissing their assailant and/or undressing themselves. In other killings, the sexual dynamic was more covert and inferred from the way the body was found. For example, some victims were found with their clothing completely or partially removed, leaving them naked, or with their breasts and/or genitalia exposed. In some cases, it was the offenders who undressed their victim. However, the act of undressing victims was not uniform, as whilst the clothing of some victims was undamaged, others had their clothing cut, ripped, or torn.

- *Violent dynamic:* Involved the use of one or more weapons, such as a ligature (the most common), a knife, or a blunt instrument. In many cases, weapons were obtained from the crime scene, whilst in others, weapons were brought by the offender. In several cases, multiple causes of death were recorded, but the most common was asphyxiation by a ligature or manual strangulation. Other women received head injuries or knife injuries in one or more parts of the body. Many cases included expressive violence, as 84% of victim injuries were coded as severe and 14% as extreme.
- *Other behaviours:* Some killers displayed actions aimed at assisting with the killing, such as disabling the victim with a gag or blindfold, tying them up, or disabling their telephone. Other behaviours were precautionary and aimed at avoiding detection, such as wearing a disguise, gloves, or mask, using a false name, disguising their car, wearing a condom, and destroying forensic evidence.

Post-crime phase

After the killing, Greenall and Richardson (2015) found that in a fifth of cases (21%), the offender moved the body from the crime scene to another location. When the victim was abandoned, most offenders (56%) made no effort to hide the body and simply left it exposed for others to find. About a third (35%) made some effort to conceal the body, such as leaving it in water or partially or completely buried. The geographic nature of these killings was later illustrated by Greenall (2018). Here it was found that the distances between the killer's homes and the place where their victim's body was found, which in most cases was also the crime scene, ranged from zero to 106.2 miles (171 km), with a mean of 8.6 miles (13.8 km) and a median of 1.2 miles (1.9 km). Just under one-third (31%) of victims were found within half a mile (0.8 km) of the killer's home, just under half (48%) within one mile (1.6 km), and 59% within two miles (3.2 km). By contrast, a third of victims were found over five miles (8 km) from the killer's home. This included twelve cases that were found over 10 miles (16 km) and one over 100 miles (160 km) from the killer's home.

Comparisons with other types of sexual violence

When considering stranger sexual femicide, a key question is whether these offences are somehow unique. To answer this, we need to consider findings on sexual homicide generally and other types of sexual violence. This comparison suggests that the key features of stranger sexual femicide are similar to those of other types of sexual homicide and sexual violence. For example, previous research into sexual homicide (e.g., Beauregard & Martineau, 2013; De Veauuse Brown & Watson, 2022; Roberts & Grossman, 1993) has found that outdoor locations and the victim's residence are the most popular crime scene locations. Moreover, Grubin and Gunn (1990) found that 27% of rapes that ended with the woman's death had started out as burglaries. As we saw in the previous chapter, these are key locations for stranger rape. In relation to timing, Safarik *et al.* (2002)

found that most sexual homicides (66%) occurred between 8 pm and 8 am. This again reflects research on stranger rape reported in the previous chapter. Other studies of the offence behaviours of sexual killers have found they include a range of sexual, violent, and other (i.e., precautionary) behaviours (e.g., Beauregard & Martineau, 2013; Carter *et al.*, 2017; Eichinger & Darjee, 2021), which again is similar to the findings on stranger rape reported in the previous chapter. Moreover, research into sexual homicide has found that asphyxiation, beatings, and stabbings are common causes of death (Carter & Hollin, 2010; Chan, 2017). Similarly, in their study of imprisoned rapists, Grubin and Gunn (1990) found that among those assaults that ended in the victim's death, most (70%) were caused by strangulation, with others beaten to death or stabbed. Finally, in relation to the geographic nature of stranger sexual femicide, previous studies have found that most sexual homicides occur close to the killer's home (Dern *et al.*, 2005; Safarik *et al.*, 2002), as with stranger rape in the previous chapter. What these findings suggest is that, when viewed in a wider context, stranger sexual femicide bears more than a passing resemblance to other types of sexual homicide and sexual violence. Be that so, does it follow that the reasons why some men commit this offence are similar to why they commit other types of sexual violence?

Motivation: *Why do some men commit this offence?*

This is one of the most complex questions in this book. However, like other types of sexual violence, understanding the motivational and interpersonal dynamics and the contexts and circumstances in which these killings occur can help criminal justice practitioners to find answers to this question.

Motivational dynamics of stranger sexual femicide

Although sexual femicide is an extreme form of sexual violence, research suggests that motivational similarities exist between this and other types of sexual violence. For example, Keppel and Walter (1999) classified sexual homicide into the power-assertive, power-reassurance, anger-retaliatory, and anger-excitation types originally proposed by Groth *et al.* (1977). Although some researchers later suggested this classification of sexual homicide was potentially invalid (e.g., Bennell *et al.*, 2013), the work of Keppel and Walter (1999) remains important to our understanding of these killings for two reasons. First, Keppel and Walter (1999) show that not all sexual killers intend to kill their victims. Second, Keppel and Walter (1999) suggest that, as with cases of rape (see Table 2.1), sexual homicides can be driven by psychological factors relating to sexual desire, anger, or sadism (Table 10.2).

Although several other motivational classifications of sexual homicide followed Keppel and Walter (1999) (e.g., see Chapter 2 in Chan, 2015; Chan & Heide, 2009), a key finding from a growing body of research (e.g., Beech, Fisher, *et al.*, 2005; Beech, Oliver, *et al.*, 2005; Higgs, Carter, *et al.*, 2017; Kerr *et al.*, 2013; Proulx, 2008; Stefanska *et al.*, 2015) has been to support the idea that sexual homicides are driven by the same motivational factors as other types of sexual violence, namely anger, sadism, and a desire to silence the chief witness and potential accuser of a sexual assault. As shown in Table 10.3, we can draw upon this body of research, plus others considered in Chapter 4, to paint a hypothetical profile of three types of stranger sexual femicide. Table 10.3, however, is not attempting to classify individual stranger sexual killers into one type or another, as

Table 10.2 Keppel and Walter's classification of sexual homicide

Sexual types		Angry type	Sadistic type
Power-assertive	Power-reassurance	Anger-retaliatory	Anger-excitation
Dynamics			
Rape is planned, but killing is not. Increasing aggression ensures power and control over the victim, who is eliminated as a potential witness.	Rape is planned, but killing is not. The killer acts out his fantasies and seeks reassurance from his victim about his sexual adequacy.	Rape and killing are planned. Seeks revenge for his anger towards another person by attacking a symbolic victim.	Rape and killing are planned and involve the infliction of pain and terror for the killer's gratification. The luxury of sadism is in the process of killing, not the death.
Homicidal pattern			
Victims are often strangers, chosen by opportunity or surprise, in a public location or after a burglary. Organised offender often leaves the body at the chosen crime scene or moves it to another location.	Victims can be strangers or known, and the offender applies his fantasies to them. No intent to harm or degrade his victim, but if she does not respond as desired, he is panicked into a disorganised homicidal overkill.	Victims often come from areas in which the killer lives or works and are typically a substitute for women who have belittled, humiliated, and rejected him. She is subjected to a violent sexual assault and overkill.	Characterised by a prolonged, bizarre, ritualistic assault based on prior fantasy, supported by a murder kit. Victims may be a stranger who fits his needs for a symbol, such as a nurse, a prostitute, or a student.
Typical suspect			
In his 20s and concerned about his masculine image. Often cruises in his car, carries weapons, and shows an arrogant, condescending attitude towards others.	In his 20s, he is socially isolated and driven by sexual fantasies, which compensate for his real-life sexual inadequacies. Previous convictions may reflect his deviant sexuality.	He was in his 20s and younger than his victim. Has an explosive personality, is impulsive, quick-tempered, and self-centred. His relations with women are conflictual and violent.	Most kill before age 35, but late bloomers or undetected perpetrators may have killed earlier. An organised, intelligent, social man who appears to be law-abiding can deceive others.

Source: Adapted from Keppel & Walter (1999)

some features will inevitably appear within more than one type. Rather, the aim here is for criminal justice practitioners to draw upon these ideas when trying to understand stranger sexual femicides and the men who commit them.

- *Angry stranger sexual femicides:* Are more extreme variants of Groth's angry types and the MTC:R3's pervasively angry/vindictive types. These killings will include expressive violence aimed at hurting the woman, who will be beaten to death and subjected to an overkill. These men will view the world as a dangerous place where violence is required to achieve dominance and control over people, and their assault may have erupted in response to something the woman did or said that enraged him. Whilst the killing may have been intended in many cases, in others it may have been the result of an angry rape that ended in the victim's death.

Table 10.3 Hypothetical profile of three types of stranger sexual femicide

	Anger	Sadism	Sexual desire
Psychological drive	Grievance and resentment towards women.	Enact fantasies of rape, murder, control, domination.	Enact sexual fantasies.
Violence level	Expressive: Victims mostly beaten to death.	Expressive: Victims mostly asphyxiated or stabbed.	Instrumental: Victims mostly stabbed or beaten to death.
Killing reason	Overkill, triggered by something the victim did or said.	Pre-meditated aspect of the assault, or an accident during a sexual assault.	Killing is secondary, related to panic, accident, or witness elimination.
Motivational spectrum	Situational or Catathymic	Compulsive	Situational or Impulsive
Implicit theories	Dangerous world.	Dangerous world and male sex drive is uncontrollable.	Male sex drive is uncontrollable.
Corresponding rapist types	Groth *et al.* (1977) Anger-retaliation. Groth and Birnbaum (1979) Angry rapes. Knight and Prentky (1990a) Pervasively angry or Vindictive.	Groth *et al.* (1977) Anger-excitation. Groth & Birnbaum (1979) Sadistic rapes. Knight and Prentky (1990) Sexual (sadistic)	Groth *et al.* (1977) Power-assertive or Power-reassurance Groth and Birnbaum (1979) Power rapes. Knight and Prentky (1990) Opportunistic or Sexual (non-sadistic).

- *Sadistic stranger sexual femicides:* Are more extreme variants of Groth's anger-excitation and sadistic types and the MTC:R3's sexual (sadistic) type. These killings will evidence similar levels of expressive violence, but here this is the source of sexual pleasure. As such, these men are examples of true sexually motivated killers described by Brittain (1970) and others (e.g., MacCulloch *et al.*, 2000). These pre-mediated assaults will be fantasy-driven and the culmination of a pathway described by MacCulloch *et al.* (1983), as summarised in Chapter 6. The killing, therefore, may be an intentional feature of the sexual killer's plan or an unintended ending to a sadistic rape that went too far. Like their angry counterparts, these men will view the world as a dangerous place where violence is required to achieve dominance and control over people. However, these men will also have a sex drive which they feel they cannot control and which must, in their eyes, be satisfied. The compulsive nature of these killings means there is a high likelihood of repletion (Schlesinger, 2004a, 2004b).
- *Sexually driven stranger sexual femicides:* Are rapes and/or other sexual assaults that went wrong and therefore, are more extreme variants of Groth's power types and the MTC:R3's opportunistic and sexual (non-sadistic) types. Like their sadistic counterparts, these men are driven by their sexual needs, which they feel they cannot control. When the opportunity presents itself, they will assault female strangers in order to satisfy their needs and will aim to use only sufficient force to achieve this. However, once violence is introduced into sexual assault, the outcome is uncertain, and in the heat of the moment, perhaps by accident or in a state of panic, the woman is killed. Alternatively, having satisfied his sexual needs, the assailant concludes that the best way to deal with the stranger's sexual offender's dilemma is to kill the chief witness to his sexual assault.

Interpersonal dynamics of stranger sexual femicide

As with offences of rape, some researchers have explored the interpersonal dynamics of sexual homicide and hypothesised that various behavioural themes exist between sexual killers and their victims. For example, in a study of Australian sexual killers, Kocsis *et al.* (2002b) hypothesised four behavioural themes. First, *predators* planned their violent, sadistic offences, which included evidence of torture. Second, *perverse* offenders organised and attacked their victims to satisfy their bizarre sexual needs, sometimes after the victim's death. Third, *fury* offenders evidenced hatred for women, and their violent assaults were brutal and caused multiple injuries to the victim. Fourth, *rape* offenders intended to sexually assault their victims, and the killing was often an accident. Similarly, in a study of Belgian sexual killers, Gerard *et al.* (2007) hypothesised two behavioural themes. First, *opportunistic-impulsive* killers engage in random violence and respond to urges for immediate sexual gratification when an opportunity arises, leaving the body outdoors once the assault is completed. Second, *sadistic-calculator* killers engage in premeditated violence and take precautions to avoid detection. The sadistic assaults include bindings and torture. In a study of 51 Scottish sexual killers, Darjee and Baron (2018) hypothesise three behavioural themes. First, *sadistic* killings included various sexual and controlling behaviours. Second, *rage* killings included violence resulting in multiple injuries and overkill, reckless behaviour (leaving the weapon at the scene), and fewer sexual behaviours. Third, *criminal* killings included behaviours aimed at avoiding detection, witness elimination, taking items from the crime scene, and general criminality.

Although these studies illustrate the interpersonal dynamics of sexual homicide, they include victims of both genders and different offender–victim relationships. However, in a similar study, Greenall and Wright (2020) focused exclusively on stranger sexual femicides. They found that physical violence within these killings was instrumental or expressive, whilst sexual violence was covert or overt. Of note, however, was the way physical and sexual violence coexisted, as expressive violence coexisted with covert sexual violence and instrumental violence coexisted with overt sexual violence. From this arrangement, four behavioural themes were hypothesised:

Instrumental/overt themes

1 **Rape** killings were highly sexual and included oral, anal, vaginal, or multiple penetrations with instrumental violence.
2 **Impersonal** killings also included instrumental violence and sexual assault by penetration and/or the victim's clothing being ripped or torn.

Expressive/covert themes

3 **Overkill** killings included expressive violence with sharp instruments or other weapons, the infliction of extreme injuries, and covert sexual violence that included other sexual acts.
4 **Controlled** killings also included expressive violence, but with blunt instruments and head injuries, whilst the sexual aspect was inferred by the victim being undressed.

As these studies show, although exploring sexual homicide from a behavioural rather than a motivation perspective, the themes identified have clear overlaps with some of the ideas presented above and add further weight to the idea that most sexual homicides reflect angry, sadistic, and sexually driven dynamics. However, this is not the end of the matter, as to complete our understanding of sexual homicide, we need to briefly consider the contexts and circumstances in which these offences occur.

Context and circumstances of stranger sexual femicide

Whilst consideration of motivational and interpersonal dynamics can help us to understand why and how a man might sexually assault and kill a female stranger, a final consideration involves exploring the contexts and circumstances in which these killings can occur. Greenall (2012) suggested that sexual homicides occur when homicidal and sexual violence combine during an assault. However, these two crimes may not always occur at the same time in a particular killing. Rather, the temporal sequence of them can alter between cases. Recognising this fact and that some sexual killings are not overtly sexual allows us to consider four hypothetical scenarios in which stranger sexual femicide can occur (see Table 10.4).

Table 10.4 captures many of the ideas presented above. For example, scenario one killings may include the sexual types listed in Table 10.3, and scenario two killings may include the angry and sadistic types listed in Table 10.3. However, the merit of Table 10.4 is that it illustrates how some sexual femicides can include other dynamics. For example, scenario three killings may be indicative of necrophilia. This rare paraphilia presents itself in several forms, ranging from men who enjoy having sex with women pretending to be dead to men who can only have sex with dead women (Aggrawal, 2009b). Langevin *et al.* (1988) found evidence of necrophilia in 38% of sexual homicides, whilst Stein *et al.* (2010) found only 16 cases of necrophilia in a sample of 211 sexual homicides. Of note is the fact that in almost half of these 16 cases, victims were raped prior to death, indicating that necrophilia was not the offender's primary motivation. Indeed, Higgs, Stefanska, *et al.* (2017) report that sexual interference with a dead body rarely indicates the presence of necrophilia. In such cases, the killer may be a socially isolated individual who becomes sexually excited by his impulsive, disorganised killing (Greenall, 2012). Another issue raised by Table 10.4 is the fact alluded to above, which is that some sexual homicides contain covert sexual dynamics, which may not be evident at all at the crime scene. Indeed, as Schlesinger (2004b) suggests, not all sexual homicides include the killer achieving an erection, having sexual intercourse, and ejaculating. Consequently, echoing comments made by the Femicide Census above, Ressler *et al.* (1988) previously cautioned that some police officers may not recognise the underlying sexual dynamics of what appear to be either ordinary or motiveless killings. In such cases, the sexual dynamic of these killings may only be determined by post-conviction interviews with the offender.

Table 10.4 Scenarios of stranger sexual femicide

Scenarios	One	Two	Three	Four
Offence details	Sexual violence *then* femicide	Sexual violence *with* femicide	Femicide *then* sexual violence	Femicide with *covert* sexual dynamics
Possible Explanations	Accident, panic, or precaution	Sadism, anger, or misogyny	Necrophilia	To be determined

Source: Adapted from Greenall (2012)

Sexual offenders who kill or killers who sexually offend?

In Chapter 7, we considered whether sexual burglars are sexual offenders who burgle or burglars who sexually offend. Given that not all sexual homicides involve planned killings, a similar question can be asked here, namely, are we dealing with sexual offenders who kill or killers who sexually offend? Although a difficult question to answer, some indications are provided within the research. For example, Keppel and Walter (1999) found that among 2,476 imprisoned sexual homicide offenders in Michigan, most (59%) were sexually driven killings (i.e., power-assertive 38% & power-reassurance 21%) with only about a third driven by anger (i.e., anger-retaliatory 34%), and only a small number driven by sadism (i.e., anger-excitation 7%). From these findings, we could hypothesise that because most sexual homicides (59%) occur in the context of scenario one from Table 10.4 rather than scenario two (41%), most are committed by sexual offenders who kill rather than killers who sexually offend. Support for this comes from a later study by Stefanska *et al.* (2015). They classified 129 British sexual killers and found the deviance (sadistic) group to be the largest (n = 55), followed by the grievance (anger) group (n=40), with the sexually driven group the smallest (n = 34). Whilst these figures may suggest that most cases involved killers sexually assaulting their victims, a closer examination of their findings suggests otherwise. Stefanska *et al.* (2015) found that levels of premeditation were higher among the sexually driven (77%) and deviant (67%) groups. Moreover, Stefanska *et al.* (2015) found that sexually driven killers often reported that their primary motivation was sex, although some were prepared to kill if necessary. Additionally, although the grievance group was the second largest, only 28% were premeditated, as they were found to have occurred in the context of consensual situations and were triggered by something the victim said or did. If stranger sexual killers are mostly sexual offenders who kill rather than killers who sexually offend, what might contribute to this process? The process by which a sexual assault can end in the victim's death was explored by Chéné and Cusson (2007). They found that factors such as alcohol use, the absence of a family or intimate offender–victim relationship, the use of a blunt instrument, and pre-crime anger were responsible for this escalation process. Given that Stefanska *et al.* (2015) found the grievance group had the highest level of intoxication (68%), we can hypothesise that this influenced how they chose to respond to whatever the victim said or did.

Future implications?

As with other types of stranger sexual violence, our concern relates to whether stranger sexual killers will re-offend. As these offences are at the extreme end of the sexual violence spectrum, further escalation is not possible, but re-offending can include other types of offences. Moreover, repetition of similar offences would leave criminal justice practitioners dealing with a nightmare scenario of a serial sexual killer.

Will they do it again?

Although research on the re-offending of sexual killers is limited, some studies have explored this, and the results provide some insight. For example, in Germany, Hill *et al.* (2008) provided post-release follow-up data on 90 sexual killers, with a mean time at risk ranging from 1.8 to 5 years. They found that 47.8% were convicted of a non-violent offence; 28.9% were convicted of any violent offence; 16.7% were convicted of a non-sexual violent offence; 15.6% were convicted of a sexual offence; and 3.3% were convicted for an attempted or completed homicide (two sexual and one non-sexual). Two factors associated with sexual recidivism were committing a sexual homicide younger than age 21 and spending less than 15 years in prison. In the USA, Myers *et al.* (2010) provided post-release follow-up data on 11 juvenile sexual killers. Six of them (55%) re-offended within an average of 4.43 years. Three were convicted of actual or attempted sexual homicide and had admitted to other sexual killings prior to their arrest, meaning they had become serial sexual killers. The other three were convicted of non-sexual offences, including selling drugs, resisting arrest, and parole violations. The six recidivists were found to be significantly more psychopathic than the five non-recidivists, and all three who committed further sexual homicides met the full criteria for sexual sadism. In Scotland, Darjee and Baron (2018) provided follow-up data on 23 sexual killers. They report that 39% had committed minor offences or had breached their conditions of release; 13% had committed a contact sexual offence; 8.7% had committed rape or attempted rape; and 17.4% had committed a homicide or attempted homicide. Whilst these three studies did not focus on stranger sexual killers, these figures suggest that whilst most sexual killers may not commit another sexual offence or a sexual homicide, many of them may commit other types of offences. To understand why this may be so, we need to consider the role of sexual violence in the criminal make-up of these killers.

Criminal profiles of stranger sexual killers

In a study of stranger sexual killers, Greenall and Richardson (2015) found that most (64%) had a criminal record, meaning stranger sexual femicide was an act of recidivism. This finding may not appear too surprising given that large numbers of stranger sexual offenders have previous convictions. However, the opposite finding needs highlighting, namely that 36% did not have any previous convictions, meaning the sexual killing of an adult female stranger was their first (known) offence!

A breakdown of the criminal histories of these men is presented in Table 10.5 and shows that most previous convictions were not of a serious nature, as only a minority had previous convictions for violent (28%) or sexual (16%) offences. When the previous offending of the 52 recidivists were explored in more detail, Greenall and Wright (2015) found that criminal diversity was a major feature. For example, the number of previous convictions held by the recidivists ranged from 1 to 138, with an average of 26 convictions each. The number of offence types from Table 10.5 in their criminal histories ranged from

Table 10.5 Criminal histories of stranger sexual killers

Offence types	Number	Recidivists % (n = 52)	Total sample % (n = 81)
1 Theft	45	87	56
2 Property	24	46	30
3 Violence	23	44	28
4 Police/Courts/ Prisons	23	44	28
5 Fraud	22	42	27
6 Misc.	15	29	18.5
7 Sexual	13	25	16
8 Public Order	12	23	15
9 Weapons	6	12	7
10 Drugs	2	4	2.5

Source: Adapted from Greenall & Richardson (2015)

1 to 8, with an average of 3.6 types each. Only 12 recidivists had previous convictions for one offence type and could therefore be considered specialist offenders prior to their index offence. Among the remaining 40 recidivists, there were on average 4.3 offence types present in their criminal histories. This shows that stranger sexual killers with previous convictions were mostly generalist offenders, evidencing varying degrees of criminal versatility. Even in the area of sexual violence, diversity was evident. For example, when the sexual offences of the 13 men with previous sexual convictions were examined in relation to their sexual femicide offences, it was found that they exhibited sexual behaviours during their sexual femicides that were different from previous sexual offending. These men, therefore, were generalist sexual offenders with a varied sexual offence repertoire.

Conclusions and implications for practice

This chapter has explored what is, without question, the most serious and most feared form of stranger sexual violence. Although sexual homicides have been known and written about for centuries, these offences are still known by various labels; they are neither legally nor clinically defined, and no official statistics are recorded on them. Despite the absence of official statistics, research suggests these killings are very rare. Moreover, the fact that most of these publications report on killings that include offenders and victims of both genders and various ages means that adult male-on-female stranger sexual femicides are indeed very rare. Despite this rarity, research suggests that these killings share several features with other types of sexual violence. These include the sexual and violent behaviours exhibited during these offences, the motivations that drive these offences, the offender-victim interpersonal dynamics within these offences, and the geographic nature of these offences. Indeed, the similarity between sexual femicide and other types of contact sexual violence is illustrated by consideration of the context and circumstances in which these killings occur, as that shows that some sexual femicides started out as lesser sexual offences that ended with the victim's death. Consideration of the motivational and interpersonal dynamics and the contexts and circumstances in which these killings occur can help criminal justice practitioners understand the diversity of sexual femicide and how these killings can:

> involve murder or manslaughter; intentional or accidental killings; rape or other sexual assaults that escalate into homicide; angry and violent assaults in which homicide or serious harm was intended or reasonably foreseen; sadistic assaults where homicidal violence was eroticised; homicides that involve post-mortem sexual behaviour towards the deceased; other displays of sexual deviancy; and other, sometimes motiveless, killings that ultimately are found to contain covert sexual dynamics.
>
> (Greenall, 2012, p. 350)

Armed with this knowledge, criminal justice practitioners can explore the sexual dynamics of a homicide committed by an offender they are working with. If present, this will show that the offender in question is not only a stranger sexual offender but also an offender who is prepared to combine physical and sexual violence in one assault with deadly consequences. This makes them one of the rarest types of stranger sexual offenders and someone who requires a great deal of effort to understand. How this can be achieved with these and other offenders considered within this volume is the focus of volume three.

Part 3

Application to criminal justice practice

11 Forensic case formulation
The key to understanding and intervening

Even the most violent people spend most of their lives not committing violence, so we must ask ourselves, why did they choose to commit specific acts of violence against specific people at specific times, but not other kinds of violence against *other people at other times?*

(Hart & Logan, 2011, p. 94)

Introduction

Whether you are involved in the investigation of stranger sexual violence, work with stranger sexual offenders in prisons or secure hospitals, or manage their risk in the community, the above quote illustrates an important point that every criminal justice practitioner should recognise: Regardless of how frequent or serious, the act of sexually assaulting adult female strangers is but one aspect of a stranger sexual offender's life, and not even the most violent, deviant, or prolific stranger sexual offender does this every day. Therefore, the challenge for criminal justice practitioners is to develop an understanding of the (known or unknown) offender they are dealing with, the nature of his sexual violence, the origins of his propensity to engage in sexual violence, and where this propensity may lead him in the future. In some (perhaps many) cases, we may _never_ objectively know these details and will therefore have to develop one or more evidence-based hypotheses about them. Collectively, these hypotheses should form a narrative about the offender in question and his offending, and this becomes an example of a forensic case formulation. Doing this requires criminal justice practitioners to consider stranger sexual violence from the offender's perspective, and it returns us to where this book began, namely understanding the causes of attacks and their meanings for the perpetrator (MacCulloch *et al.*, 1995).

Chapter aims

This chapter introduces the concept of forensic case formulation and how criminal justice practitioners can use it to enhance their understanding of stranger sexual offenders and their offending, and to communicate this to colleagues. The chapter begins by defining formulation as a process of generating one or more hypotheses about an individual's presentation. In modern forensic practice, this is a structured process with two main approaches. However, the focus of this chapter is the structured professional judgement (SPJ) approach, which will be explored in relation to the assessment and formulation of an individual's history and future risk of sexual violence. The chapter then considers some models of formulation which can be used as a framework to help criminal justice

DOI: 10.4324/9781003217763-14

practitioners to understand how the information obtained about an offender relates to his offending and ways to manage it. Whilst the assessment and formulation of sexual violence have primarily been undertaken by forensic/clinical practitioners working with known offenders, this task can also be undertaken when the identity of the stranger sexual offender is unknown. Therefore, the process of formulation informed by the SPJ approach has the potential to assist criminal investigations into stranger sexual violence.

Definition: *Forensic case formulation*

The concept of formulation is a bit like sexual homicide although the term is widely used in academic/practitioner circles, it has no agreed definition. Indeed, best practice guidelines on working with personality disordered offenders provide not one but two definitions (see Craissati *et al.*, 2020, p. 41). Moreover, these guidelines also distinguish between three types of formulation (ibid., p. 42):

1 *Case formulations:* A statement of understanding about the whole person and the factors that have contributed to their current presentation.
2 *Problem formulations:* A statement of understanding about the origins of a particular problem or offence, as opposed to the whole person.
3 *Risk formulations:* A type of problem formulation that focuses on an individual's potential for future harm to self or others.

A key point here is that just as the various definitions of sexual homicide essentially refer to the same (or very similar) type of crime, the various definitions of formulation essentially refer to the same (or very similar) process. For example, Eells and Lombart (2011) define formulation as generating one or more hypotheses about what causes, triggers, and maintains an individual's psychological, interpersonal, and behavioural problems. Eells and Lombart (2011) advise that formulations can focus on all aspects of an individual's life (e.g., early childhood experiences, socio-cultural influences, attitudes and beliefs about self, others, and the world, etc.) and are open to revision as new information is received. In many cases, the issue being formulated is an individual's psychological presentation (e.g., depression, psychosis, eating disorder, etc.). This process of *clinical* case formulation is aimed at selecting the most effective treatment for that condition (Sturmey, 2009). However, formulating an individual's history and future risk of violence involves the related process of '*forensic*' case formulation (Sturmey & McMurran, 2011). This combines points 1–3 above by developing an understanding of the individual, the problem (e.g., violence), and his risk of further violence. So, whereas clinical case formulation is treatment focused, forensic case formulation is aimed at understanding and managing an individual's risk of violence (see Logan, 2016). However, clinical and forensic case formulations do not exist in isolation, as in cases where an offender presents with one or more of the psychological presentations considered in Chapters 5–6, treatment may be a feature of risk management. Indeed, as Delle-Vergini and Day suggest:

> In the forensic arena, one of the primary purposes of conducting a case formulation is to better understand risk of future offending and the role that treatment can play in managing this risk.
>
> (2016, p. 241)

Application of stranger sexual violence

Hart *et al.* (2011) suggest that forensic case formulation contains several core features. These include the formulation being action-orientated as it aids an understanding of the individual's problem(s); being driven by a relevant theory (see Ward *et al.*, 2006); being individualised to the case in hand; presented in a narrative form; covering past, present, and future events; being testable; producing new knowledge; and being inferential. Drawing upon these ideas, a definition of forensic case formulation for stranger sexual violence is presented below:

- **Forensic case formulation of stranger sexual violence:**
  A process of generating one or more evidence-based, theoretically informed hypotheses about an individual's history of and future risk of engaging in stranger sexual violence, which is presented in a narrative form that can be understood by colleagues from other disciplines, which is subject to revision as new information is received, and which informs one or more interventions aimed at managing that individual's sexual risk to others.

Before the applications of this definition are explored, one of the core features of forensic case formulation suggested by Hart *et al.* (2011) warrants further consideration, as it is key to understanding the mental process of forming a hypothesis.

An inferential process

An inference is the act of drawing a conclusion from known or assumed facts or statements (Oxford English Dictionary: www.oed.com). When describing how inference is a key feature of forensic case formulation, Hart *et al.* (2011) stated that this process goes beyond description, statement of facts, or classification to making predictions that are explained and justified. However, Hart *et al.* (2011) caution that inference has its limitations. We cannot, for example, precisely predict what will happen in the future; our best explanation of events is only one of many possible explanations, and whilst our best explanation may be superior to others, it may prove to be incorrect. Within criminal justice practice, two relevant applications of this inferential/predictive process are criminal investigations, whereby detectives are seeking to identify an unknown stranger sexual offender, and risk assessments of a known stranger sexual offender by forensic/clinical practitioners. The way forensic case formulation can help them both will now be illustrated by reference to the concept of sexual violence risk assessment and formulation.

Sexual violence risk assessment and formulation

Sexual offenders are like any other offenders in that some will re-offend and some will not. Re-offending is an important consideration for all criminal justice practitioners, as it can occur before apprehension/conviction (i.e., with serial offenders) and/or once an offender's engagement with the criminal justice system has ended (i.e., with recidivists). Historically, forensic/clinical practitioners drew upon their professional experience to identify those at risk of further offending. However, the unreliability of such unstructured professional judgements inspired a body of research, which produced some notable findings. For example, as stated in earlier chapters, a history of sexual deviancy is strongly

Table 11.1 Sexual violence risk assessment – Popular ARAIs

SORAG-R	Static-2002R	RM2000
1 Lived with both biological parents until age 16 (except for the death of one parent)	1 Prior sex offences	1 Age at the next opportunity to offend
2 Elementary School Maladjustment	2 Prior sentencing dates	2 Sexual appearances
3 History of alcohol problems	3 Non-contact sex offences	3 Criminal appearances
4 Marital status (at the time of or prior to the index offence)	4 Current non-sexual violence	4 Male victims
5 Criminal history score for non-violent offences	5 Prior non-sexual violence	5 Stranger victims
6 Criminal history score for violent offences	6 Unrelated victims	6 Single
7 Number of previous convictions for sexual offenses	7 Stranger victims	7 Non-contact sex offences
8 History of sex offenses only against girls under 14	8 Male victims	8 Age on release
9 Failure of a prior conditional release	9 Age	9 Violent appearances
10 Age at index		10 Burglary convictions
11 Meets DSM criteria for any personality disorder		
12 Meets DSM criteria for schizophrenia		
13 Phallometric test results		
14 Psychopathy Checklist score		

associated with sexual re-offending (Hanson & Bussière, 1998; Hanson & Morton-Bourgon, 2004). Sexual deviancy is therefore a *'risk factor'* for future sexual violence, and a reasonable hypothesis is that a (known or unknown) sexual offender who evidences this in his offending presents a greater risk of further sexual violence than a sexual offender who does not. Further research in the late 1990s and early 2000s culminated in the identification of additional risk factors that were associated with sexual re-offending. In an official report, Powis (2002) summarised them as being young, male, unmarried, unemployed, having poor education attainment, having a history of substance abuse, and having previous convictions for sexual violence. Factors such as these were incorporated into various protocols (see below) aimed at helping criminal justice practitioners to identify those at risk of sexual re-offending and to do so using evidence-based methods rather than relying on their unstructured professional judgement. These resulting protocols adopt two evidence-based approaches: Actuarial and SPJ.

Actuarial assessments of sexual violence risk

Actuarial risk assessment instruments (ARAIs) are rooted within the nomothetic paradigm and include risk factors statistically associated with further sexual violence. Criminal justice practitioners using an ARAI rate a sexual offender on the number of specified risk factors present in his life. This process yields a numerical score that equates to a risk prediction, usually expressed as a percentage or with high, medium, or low risk labels.

Table 11.1 presents three popular sexual violence ARAIs: the sex offender risk appraisal guide (Harris *et al.*, 2015), static-2002R (Helmus *et al.*, 2021), and the risk matrix 2000 (Thornton *et al.*, 2003). The popularity of such tools is illustrated by the earlier version of static-2002R (i.e., static-99R) being described as *"the most widely used sexual recidivism risk assessment instrument in the world"* (Society for the Advancement of Actuarial Risk Need Assessment, 2021). ARAIs are easy to rate and score and have been used by various criminal justice practitioners, including forensic/clinical psychologists, police, and probation officers (for a review of these and other similar protocols, see Risk Management Authority, 2020).

However, with their focus on historical (static) factors, ARAIs fail to capture any change in an individual's risk presentation over time, as a re-assessment even many years later should result in the same outcome. Moreover, the limited exploration of the index offence (see Chapter 12) means ARAIs fail to help criminal justice practitioners understand the interpersonal or motivational dynamics of the offence and how this may have developed over time or may change (i.e., escalate) in the future. Arguably, two stranger sexual offenders could receive similar ARAI scores from different sexual offences and from similar offences that contained different interpersonal or motivational dynamics. A key reason for this is that ARAIs determine how similar one offender is to the group of offenders upon which the ARAI was based, with all the potential problems this entails as discussed in Chapter 1 (Hart & Cooke, 2013; Hart *et al.*, 2007). Moreover, ARAIs were not designed to assist professional judgements of risk but to replace them with actuarial judgements (Harris *et al.*, 2015). So, just as being the *'wrong'* age and living in the *'wrong'* part of town increases the cost of motor insurance regardless of one's driving ability or the insurance clerk's considerations, an ARAI score determines an offender's sexual violence risk prediction regardless of individual factors or professional considerations. The limited ability of ARAIs to contribute to forensic case formulation led to the development of the SPJ approach.

Structure professional assessments of sexual violence risk

The SPJ approach is considered best practice in the assessment, formulation, and management of violence risk (Department of Health, 2009; Risk Management Authority, 2011). Like their ARAI cousins, SPJ protocols include static risk factors associated with further sexual violence and are therefore similarly rooted within the nomothetic paradigm. However, SPJ protocols do not yield a score. Rather, they help criminal justice practitioners develop hypotheses about an individual and the factors that contributed to his offending. As such, SPJs move away from predicting risk to understanding and managing risk. This focus on the individual means SPJ protocols are also rooted within the idiographic paradigm. Essentially, the SPJ approach aims to combine the actuarial approach with the professional judgements that were replaced by ARAIs, but this time the professional judgements are structured. In effect, the criminal justice practitioner is brought back into the decision-making process, whose importance is confirmed by best practice guidelines:

> Although, like the actuarial tools, these instruments are derived from research evidence, the clinician's discretion is seen as a vital element – especially in relation to formulating the assessment of risk and preparing risk management plans based on the risk factors identified.
>
> (Department of Health, 2009, p. 23)

Table 11.2 Sexual violence risk assessment – SPJ protocols

SVR-20 V2 *(Boer et al., 2017)*	RSVP-V2 *(Hart et al., 2022)*
Psychosocial adjustment	**Nature of Sexual violence (SV) domain**
1 Sexual deviation	N1. Chronicity of SV*
2 Sexual health problems	N2. Diversity of SV*
3 Victim of child abuse	N3. Physical coercion in SV*
4 Psychopathic personality disorder	N4. Psychological coercion in SV*
5 Major mental disorder	N5. Escalation of SV*
6 Substance use problems	**Perpetrator characteristics domain**
7 Suicidal/homicidal ideation	*Psychological adjustment sub-domain*
8 Relationship problems	P1. Problems with minimisation/denial of SV*
9 Employment problems	P2. Attitudes that support or condone SV*
10 Non-sexual offending	P3. Problems with self-awareness
Sexual offending (SO)	P4. Problems with stress or coping
11 Chronic SO	P5. Problems resulting from child abuse
12 Diverse SO	*Mental health sub-domain*
13 Physical harm in SO	P6. Sexual deviance*
14 Psychological coercion in SO	P7. Problems with sexual health*
15 Escalation in SO	P8. Psychopathic personality disorder*
16 Extreme minimisation/denial of SO	P9. Major mental disorder*
17 Attitudes that support or condone SO	P10. Problems with substance use*
Future plans	P11. Problems with sexually violent ideation*
18 Lack of realistic plans	*Social adjustment sub-domain*
19 Negative attitude towards intervention	P12. Problems with intimate relationships*
20 Negative attitude towards supervision	P13. Problems with non-intimate relationships
	P14. Problems with employment
	P15. Problems with antisocial attitudes
	Manageability sub-domain
	P16. Problems with living situations
	P17. Problems with treatment
	P18. Problems with supervision

*Denote items that may be reasonably discernible about an unknown offender.

Table 11.2 presents the latest versions of two popular SPJ sexual violence risk protocols, the SVR-20-V2 (Boer *et al.*, 2017) and RSVP-V2 (Hart *et al.*, 2022). As shown, these protocols are very similar, such that Hart et al. (2022) acknowledge they are equivalent or parallel guidelines. Although different labels are used, the items within them divide into those relating to the offender (i.e., SVR-20-V2 items 1–10 & 18–20; RSVP-V2 items P1–18) and those relating to his sexual violence history (i.e., SVR-20-V2 items 11–17; RSVP-V2 items N1–5). Although the RSVP-V2 contains more risk factors and has a more detailed administration procedure, Hart et al. (2022) advise that experienced criminal justice practitioners should be able to reach similar conclusions about an individual's risk and how to manage it, regardless of which guidelines they use. Given that formal training and usage of the appropriate manual are essential requirements of the SPJ approach, this chapter, like others (e.g., Logan, 2016), can only summarise the procedure illustrated in Table 11.3.

SPJ procedure

Steps 1–2 in Table 11.3 are the same as with ARAIs; information from a variety of sources is gathered relating to the individual's past and current presentation, plus previous and recent offending. Wherever possible, the offender should be involved in providing

Table 11.3 SPJ procedural steps

Steps	Action required
1	Gather and summarise available case information
2	Rate the *presence* of risk factors in the offender's presentation
3	Rate the *relevance* of risk factors to his past/future offending
4	Formulate acts of sexual violence
5	Identify plausible scenarios of future sexual violence
6	Develop scenario focused risk management plans
7	Form conclusory opinions

Source: Adapted from Douglas *et al.*, (2013a), Hart *et al.* (2022)

information, but this may not always be possible if, for example, he refuses or his identity is unknown. This information is then used to decide whether each of the items within the protocol is or was present and to what degree (i.e., yes, possibly, or no). Step three is where the SPJ and ARAI approaches diverge, as here SPJ encourages criminal justice practitioners to use their professional judgement to decide if a particular risk item that is present is also '*relevant*' to the individual's presentation and to what degree (i.e., high, moderate, or low) (Douglas *et al.*, 2013a; Hart *et al.*, 2022; Kropp & Hart, 2015). Essentially, criminal justice practitioners are required to decide whether a functional link exists between the factors judged present in step two and the individual's history and future risk of sexual violence.

Functional link with stranger sexual violence

The concept of a functional link refers to more than a strict '*A causes B*' relationship. Rather, it relates to the extent to which a risk factor is relevant by virtue of having contributed to past violence, being likely to influence an individual's decision to be violent in the future, impairing his ability to employ non-violent responses in given situations, and interfering with attempts to manage his risk. Consideration of relevance is a key feature of the SPJ approach and is regarded as the bridge between the nomothetic and idiographic approaches that underpin it (Douglas *et al.*, 2013b). This relates to the idiographic filter mentioned in Chapter 1 and is based on two factors:

1 Just because a risk factor is present at the nomothetic level does not mean it is ideographically relevant.
2 Just because a risk factor is relevant to one stranger or sexual offender does not mean it is relevant to another.

For example, the presence of sexual deviancy can be indicated by a history of cross-dressing. However, whilst this would be relevant to a case of sexual burglary (e.g., see Colonel Williams in Chapter 7), it would not be relevant to a case of sexual assault (e.g., a man groping a woman in a bar). Similarly, a history of mental illness would be relevant if the offender was driven to sexually offend by the positive symptoms of this illness (see Chapter 5), but it would not be relevant if the onset of mental illness post-dated the sexual offence. In both present and relevant judgements, items can be omitted if there is insufficient information available to the criminal justice practitioner. However, even when sufficient information is available, present/relevant decisions are not always obvious. For example, although Robert's (see Box 8.1) successful employment history suggests an absence of employment problems (i.e., he did not evidence a failure to establish and maintain stable, positive employment), his usage of his employment to find locations to expose himself suggests this type of mobile employment is nonetheless a relevant factor to his history and risk of exhibitionism. Additionally, experienced criminal justice practitioners considering the same information may not agree about the relevance and importance of a particular risk factor (see Box 11.1).

Box 11.1   Case example: The role and relevance of sexual deviancy

This case is taken from my clinical practice in a forensic medium-secure unit

David had several previous convictions for sexual violence against teenage girls and adult women, both known and stranger. He was particularly adept at grooming girls and women and exploiting them sexually. Now under multi-agency (MAPPA) management in the community, it was felt by some that a key risk factor was his fetish for women's clothing, in particular underwear, gloves, and silk scarves. Consequently, as part of his community risk management arrangements, he was forbidden to own or seek to access any such items. In discussion about this with colleagues, opinion was divided as to whether owning these items would constitute a risk factor and increase his risk of sexual violence, or whether they could act as a protective factor by providing a means of satisfying his sexual needs that did not involve victimising girls or women. Who was right and who was wrong? By the time you have read this book, you will hopefully be able to take a look at it yourself.

Approaches to forensic case formulation

Step four of Table 11.3 brings together relevant risk factors and any protective factors that can help an individual to avoid offending in the future (de Vries Robbé & de Vogel, 2013). To achieve this, various models provide a framework for criminal justice practitioners to structure the information and develop hypotheses about the offender and his offence(s). Some models are basic, such as the sexual assault triangle discussed in Chapter 3, which focuses on the motivated offender, the vulnerable victim, and the suitable location (see Figure 3.1). Another similar model comes from criminal law and focuses on an offender having the means, motive, and opportunity to offend (Pendse, 2012). Together, these models can help criminal justice practitioners to consider factors relating to the offender's motive (e.g., sexual, sadistic, or angry – see Chapter 4), his means of executing the assault (e.g., a rape kit), the victim's vulnerability (e.g., walking alone at night), and how the opportunity to commit the assault arose (e.g., how these two came to be in that location at the same time). Although these models can be used to develop hypotheses about these factors, they are limited, and more detailed models are available. Two of the most popular forensic case formulation models are the 5Ps (Weerasekera, 1996) and the 3Ds (Greenall & Millington, 2021) models (see Table 11.4).

The 5Ps model

The 5Ps model is longitudinal as it considers the offender's past, present, and (potential) future presentation. Applied to stranger sexual violence, the presenting problem is the

Table 11.4 Forensic formulation models

5Ps	3Ds
Presenting problem:	Presenting problem is the same.
Stranger sexual violence.	
Predisposing factors:	**Drivers (or motivators):**
Historical experiences that have increased the chances of the individual deciding to sexually assault adult female strangers.	Make stranger sexual violence an attractive or rewarding option for the offender by increasing the perceived benefits of this offence.
Precipitating factors:	**Disinhibitors:**
Events that occurred immediately prior to the incident and which triggered a sexually violent response.	**Make** the stranger sexual offender less likely to be influenced by restraints, because the perceived cost of this offence has decreased.
Perpetuating factors:	**Destabilisers:**
Factors that maintain an individual's risk of engaging in stranger sexual violence in the future.	Disturb the stranger sexual offender's ability to monitor and control his decision-making in relation to stranger sexual violence.
Protective factors:	Protective factors are relevant.
Reduce the chances of future sexual violence.	

Source: Adapted from Douglas *et al.*, (2013a), Hart *et al.* (2022), Kropp and Hart (2015)

index offence, which could be one or more of the offences discussed in volume two. Predisposing factors could include adverse childhood experiences such as abuse, a history of mental disorders or substance abuse, or a deviant sexual preference. Precipitating factors or triggers may include a chance encounter with a suitable victim in a suitable location and/or something the victim did or said. Perpetuating factors can include the core values and beliefs, cognitive distortions, schemas, and implicit theories discussed in Chapter 5, or the continued presence of a mental disorder or a deviant sexual preference. Finally, protective factors can include various internal (e.g., intelligence, empathy), motivational (e.g., employment, positive life goals), and external (e.g., social network, intimate relationships) factors that may reduce the chance of further offending (de Vries Robbé & de Vogel, 2013).

The 3Ds model

The 3Ds model has similar features to the 5Ps in that disinhibitors are similar to predisposing factors and destabilisers are similar to precipitating factors. However, consideration of motive is a strength of this model. Applied to stranger sexual violence, Chapter 4 illustrated the various factors that can drive an individual to engage in sexual violence. However, an individual's decision-making and associated behaviours can also be influenced by disinhibitors and destabilisers. Disinhibitors may include negative attitudes that can excuse or justify sexual violence, a lack of insight into the wrongfulness of sexual violence or the harm it causes, and a lack of guilt or empathy about having committed sexual violence or its impact on others. Essentially, these factors reduce or eliminate anticipatory anxiety related to the prospect of violence, which can be exacerbated by intoxication. Destabilisers may include disturbances in the offender's attention, perceptions, and thinking. This can occur because of chronic drug use, serious mental health problems, or serious stressors that impair the offender's perceptions of a situation and how he feels he should respond (Hart *et al.*, 2022).

Putting SPJ into practice

Once a formulation is complete, step five involves developing one or two future scenarios in which stranger sexual violence may reoccur. This can involve repeat offences, offences with a slight twist, or an escalation (e.g., see Greenall & Millington, 2021). These scenarios may also include references to the nature (i.e., type of violence), severity (i.e., how serious), frequency (i.e., how often), imminence (how soon), and likelihood (i.e., what probability) of the hypothesised violence. Some hypothetical examples of how this may apply to the offences considered in Volume 2 are provided in Table 11.5. For example, the man who steals women's underwear from a washing line may engage in sexual burglary by breaking into a house to steal these items; the sexual burglar may sexually assault the female occupant; the voyeur may move from the street to standing outside his victim's window; the exhibitionist may, like Robert (see Box 8.1), commit a contact sexual offence; the rapist may commit a sexual murder; and the sexual murder may become a serial sexual killer.

Once one or two reasonable scenarios have been developed, step six involves developing one or more strategies to manage them, which, in step 7, are communicated to relevant colleagues. These strategies can include one or more of the following:

1 *Supervision:* Involves placing restrictions on the offender's rights or freedoms to make it harder for him to engage in further acts of stranger sexual violence. Examples include which parts or town he can or cannot visit, which activities he cannot engage in (e.g., no alcohol or drugs) and those he must engage in (e.g., community-based treatments), people he must avoid (e.g., those of a certain age or past victims) and not associate or communicate with (e.g., other known offenders).
2 *Monitoring:* Involves official contact with the offender and other relevant individuals, such as potential victims and other professionals involved in his case. Other options include GPS monitoring, mandatory drug tests, and monitoring his communications (written or electronic) with others. The aim is to identify any changes in his presentation (i.e., warning signs) which may alter his risk formulation.
3 *Treatment:* Involves the offender attending rehabilitative courses aimed at improving his psychosocial functioning in the community. Traditionally, the sexual offender treatment programme was the main intervention offered to sexual offenders (Beech,

Table 11.5 Scenarios of future offending

Original offence	Scenario 1: Similar offence with a twist	Scenario 2: Escalation (more serious)
Sexual theft from garden	Sexual burglary (i.e., from the bedroom)	Sexual burglary plus masturbation at the scene
Sexual burglary	Sexual burglary plus masturbation at the scene	Sexual assault of a female occupant
Voyeurism from the street (e.g., behind a bush)	Voyeurism from the garden (e.g., outside the window)	Enters the house (i.e., a sexual burglary)
Exhibitionism and runs away	Exhibitionism with masturbation or verbal contact with victim	Contact sexual offence
Sexual assault	Attempted rape	Rape
Rape	Rape with more violence or sexual deviancy	Sexual femicide
Sexual femicide	Sexual femicide	Sexual femicide

Oliver *et al.*, 2005), but this changed following the publication of critical research (Mews *et al.*, 2017). Presently, the Ministry of Justice (2022) provides a range of accredited offending behaviour programmes that can be delivered within prisons and the community. These are aimed at helping offenders to address various areas, such as substance abuse, violence, thinking skills, and interpersonal relationships.

4 *Victim safety planning:* In cases of stranger sexual violence, this intervention becomes very difficult, if not impossible, to implement. However, as the RSVP-V2 advises, communication of important information that can help potential victims is one option here (Hart *et al.* 2022). As such, as we shall consider below, this may be a role that can best be performed by the police.

The above arrangements can be imposed as conditions of early release and/or as part of a sexual harm prevention order. Offenders can be managed in the community under MAPPA arrangements (Ministry of Justice, 2023), with recall into custody and/or further convictions being a consequence of a failure to comply. As a forensic psychologist working with sexual offenders in a medium-secure unit, my colleagues and I would often liaise with colleagues within MAPPA. Examples include attending MAPPA meetings to report back the findings of our assessment and formulation of an offender, and in more serious cases, advising MAPPA colleagues that a particular high-risk sexual offender had attended our service for his weekly out-patient appointment and providing regular feedback on his progress.

Application to criminal investigations

Forensic case formulation has traditionally been the preserve of criminal justice practitioners working with known offenders (e.g., see Greenall & Millington, 2021; Logan, 2014). However, the RSVP-V2 states it can be used when the identity of the offender is unknown but when reports of sexual violence are still under investigation. Relevant examples of how/when the RSVP-V2 may be of assistance include when an offender is interrupted during a sexual assault and flees the scene, when a sexual homicide victim is found, and when police are trying to develop or narrow down a suspect pool (Hart *et al.*, 2022). Given that the RSVP-V2 is the latest version of a best practice guideline within this field, police officers investigating a case of stranger sexual violence and/or behavioural investigative advisors assisting them in this task (Alison & Rainbow, 2011) can draw upon the RSVP-V2 and the SPJ approach in the full knowledge that this is defensible/best practice.

An SPJ approach to criminal investigations?

Looking again at Table 11.2, we can see there are several items (marked with an *) that could reasonably be discernible based on the offender's crime scene behaviour and (where possible) accounts from his victim (e.g., see Fossi *et al.*, 2005; Lawrence *et al.*, 2010). Those items relating to the index offence (N1–5) will be explored in the next chapter. However, some perpetrator items could reasonably be discernible. For example, items P1, P2, and P3 could be evidenced from his verbal engagements with his victim, such as blaming her or minimising his actions towards her and admitting he does not know why he offends or cannot help himself. An offender may refer to his abusive parents (P5); he may evidence erectile dysfunction during the assault (P7); he may evidence a lack of concern for his victim's welfare or her pain and suffering (P8); he may evidence odd behaviour or verbal utterances (P9); he may be intoxicated (P10); he may verbalise a dislike of or hatred of women (P12). These examples are not definitive but are aimed at stimulating thought about how the SPJ process could assist criminal investigations into stranger sexual violence by providing hypotheses that could assist with police decision-making. Relevant examples of such decision-making provided by the RSVP-V2 focus on victim safety planning and include whether to issue public warnings about an unknown stranger sexual offender, if police officers believe there is a risk of serious harm that warrants the deployment of extra resources, and what steps police could take to prevent further acts of sexual violence (Hart *et al.*, 2022).

Whilst the idea of assessing an unknown offender may appear counter-intuitive, police officers are involved in the assessment and management of violence risk (College of Policing, 2023a). Although these tasks were once informed by the RM2000 (see Table 11.1), now police use "*a combination of actuarial tools (OSP OASys sexual reoffending predictor), dynamic tools The active risk management system (ARMS) and professional judgement*" (College of Policing, 2023). However, the OSP is an ARAI similar to those in Table 11.1 (HM Prison & Probation Service, 2022) and will therefore have similar limitations. Moreover, although ARMS includes dynamic factors and protective factors (Kewley & Blandford, 2017), its applicability to unknown offenders appears limited. This leaves open the idea that police officers investigating a case of stranger sexual violence could draw upon the RSVP-V2 and SPJ to assist them, perhaps when following the requirements of the national decision model (College of Policing, 2014).

SPJ and the National Decision Model (NDM)?

As Cook (2019) illustrates, the NDM includes tasks which are very similar to those within the SPJ approach. For example, stage one of the NDM involves information gathering relating to the offence in question; stage two involves assessment of a threat and potential risk of harm, which is similar to a forensic assessment of violence risk; and stages 4–5 involve police officers considering their options and taking action, which is similar to scenario planning and taking steps to mitigate and/or manage those scenarios (College of Policing, 2014). Moreover, as Cook (2019) further illustrates, within the 5WH (i.e., $5 \times W + H$ = who, what, where, when, why, and how) principle, the first critical question relates to who the offender is. Whilst usage of the RSVP-V2 will not identify an unknown stranger sexual offender, it could provide detectives with some of the benefits that have long been recognised within the research, namely an enhanced understanding of the offender (Copson, 1995), plus background information and an (ideographic) risk assessment to assist resource prioritisation (Cole & Brown, 2011). So, although forensic case formulation has traditionally been the preserve of criminal justice practitioners working with known offenders, there appears to be no reason why police officers cannot incorporate key features of the SPJ process into their own practice.

Conclusion and implications for practice

This chapter has introduced the concept of forensic case formulation and how it can be applied to stranger sexual violence. Like other topics within this book, formulation has no agreed definition. However, the various definitions essentially refer to the same (or very similar) process. The fact that formulation involves the generation of one or more hypotheses, which may or may not prove to be correct, means it is an inferential process.

In modern criminal justice practice, a key focus of this process relates to the assessment of future violence risk. This involves gathering information about an individual to make decisions about his offending and the risk of further offender, and two evidence-based approaches exist to guide this process. The actuarial and SPJ approaches both include historical (static) risk factors. However, whilst the actuarial approach is singularly rooted in the nomothetic paradigm and was originally designed to replace professional judgement, the SPJ approach seeks to combine the nomothetic and ideographic paradigms, and it requires criminal justice practitioners to utilise their professional judgement. This is achieved by focusing criminal justice practitioners on the offender in question and by considering the relevance of particular risk factors to the case in hand. To assist this process, various formulation models are available to provide structure and to help criminal justice practitioners to develop a hypothetical narrative that seeks to explain the offender's past, present, and (potential) future risk of sexual harm to others. Armed with this knowledge, criminal justice practitioners can develop strategies to mitigate or manage a stranger sexual offender's potential future risk. Finally, whilst forensic case formulation has primarily been the preserve of forensic/clinical practitioners working with known offenders, there is no reason why the SPJ approach cannot be used by police officers when following the steps of the NDM.

Further considerations

Whilst this chapter has introduced forensic case formulation, interested readers are advised to note that formulations exist on different levels and formulation standards have been proposed (see Craissati *et al.*, 2020, pp. 42–48). For example, level one formulations comment on patterns of behaviour, provide the most important information, offer a psychological explanation, provide a basis for future decisions, and are about a paragraph long. Level two formulations provide a developmental perspective, provide a psychological explanation of the problem and what may maintain it based on collaboration with the offender, offer options for the future, and are 2–3 paragraphs long. Level three formulations provide a full case formulation, are written for the purpose of official hearings after the completion of therapy, and are essentially discharge reports. Whilst levels one and two formulations can be provided by staff with training and support, level three formulations are expected from staff who have received specialist training. Good practice guidelines are designed to ensure that written formulations adhere to certain quality standards. These standards include, for example, clarity as to the purpose of the formulation, stating the information source, a clear presentation of the problem at hand that is succinct and easily understood by colleagues, and a clear set of recommendations (e.g., see Greenall & Millington, 2021; Logan, 2014). Finally, whilst this chapter has primarily focused on the stranger sexual offender, the other important aspect of stranger sexual violence, namely the index offence, has for far too long not received adequate attention. This leads us to the next and penultimate chapter of this book, which highlights the need for criminal justice practitioners to undertake a full index offence analysis.

12 Index offence analysis

A guide for criminal justice practitioners

Those meaningful differences and the functions of the index offence can be revealed by a thorough index offence analysis

(West & Greenall, 2011, p. 147)

Introduction

The previous chapter introduced the concept of forensic case formulation and illustrated how it can be used to help criminal justice practitioners to develop hypotheses about a stranger sexual offender and his offences. In this chapter, we continue with this theme, but here the focus is exclusively on the index offence. A simple point needs to be stated here, which is that a fundamental feature of the process of developing an understanding of a stranger sexual offender and his history and potential future risk of sexual violence is to develop an understanding of how and why his stranger sexual assault occurred where and when it did. This process involves going beyond nomothetic considerations about why _men_ sexually assault adult female strangers to ideographic investigations and assessments which seek to answer the key question that lies at the heart of this book:

> Why and how did this man, commit this sexual offence, against this female stranger, at this time, and in this location?

(See Box 3.1)

Drawing upon research considered in earlier chapters, this chapter considers ways in which criminal justice practitioners can answer this key question. Accordingly, a key argument of this chapter is that criminal justice practitioners should incorporate an evidence-based analysis of the index offence into their practice, and this should be an integral feature of forensic case formulation. Unfortunately, it appears that a detailed analysis of an index offence is not a routine task for many criminal justice practitioners. However, this chapter offers a means by which this can be achieved. In doing this, this chapter does _not_ aim to tell you how to do your job. Indeed, many of you may already incorporate an evidence-based analysis of the index offence into your practice. If so, this chapter may offer you some ideas as to how that process might be improved. If not, this chapter can help to get you started.

Chapter aims

This chapter introduces the concept of index offence analysis (IOA; West & Greenall, 2011). The chapter starts by defining some key terms so that experienced practitioners

DOI: 10.4324/9781003217763-15

and beginners are talking about the same things. The chapter then presents the problem that needs to be addressed, which is that anecdotal evidence suggests an evidence-based analysis of the index offence is not a routine task within criminal justice practice. This is not just a British problem, as researchers from overseas have raised similar concerns. The chapter then presents the solution to this problem, namely IOA. This will be explained and illustrated with a real-case example (see Box 12.1). Finally, the chapter concludes by considering some of the benefits of incorporating IOA into criminal justice practice.

Box 12.1 Case example of a stranger rape incident

Miss Williams & Mr Jones

One Saturday evening (circa 10pm), Miss Williams was assaulted and raped by Mr Smith. The assault took place a few streets away from the 'red light district' of a large English city. Imagine you are a police officer tasked with investigating this offence or a forensic/clinical practitioner tasked with assessing Mr Smith. As you collect more information about this incident, you conduct an IOA, and the following account becomes apparent.

Pre-crime phase

Miss Williams was walking home after being at work in a local shop when she was approached by Mr Smith, who was intoxicated and walking home with a friend after being out socialising with him. Upon noticing Miss Williams, Mr Jones left his friend and approached her. He said hello, and then, believing Miss Williams to be a prostitute, he offered her money for sex. Miss Williams refused, advised him he was mistaken, and tried to walk away.

Crime Phase

When she refused, Mr Smith grabbed Miss Williams and dragged her into a nearby wooded area. Once there, he tried to wrestle Miss Williams to the floor, and during the struggle, Mr Smith put his hand over Miss Williams' mouth to stop her from screaming. She attempted to defend herself by biting his finger, causing it to bleed. In response, Mr Smith slapped her across the face, swore at her, and threatened to hit her again if she did not do as he wanted. She then pinned her arms down and grabbed her by the neck, causing Miss Williams to suffer a temporary loss of consciousness, during which he removed her knickers and had vaginal intercourse without Miss Williams' consent.

Post-crime phase

Miss Williams' next recollection of the event is of Mr Smith standing over her, telling her not to report him to the police. He then stole her knickers, threw the money he had earlier offered her onto the floor next to her, and left. Miss Williams was left with swelling and bruising to her face and scratches to her neck and stomach.

Definitions: *Key terms*

An index offence is the offence in question committed by an offender. So, if you are a detective investigating a rape in your area, the index offence is rape. If you are a probation officer working with an arsonist in the community, the index offence is arson. However, if the detective becomes aware of another offence (e.g., a man exposing himself) having occurred shortly before the rape in the same area and wonders whether the two offences may have been committed by the same offender, exhibitionism becomes another index offence, and a separate IOA is required. Similarly, if the arsonist has an earlier conviction for sexual assault and the probation officer wants to know more about it, the sexual assault becomes another index offence and a separate IOA is required. Whilst these examples may be self-evident, the key point to note is that, on many occasions, the index offence is the offence(s) that brought an offender into contact with the criminal justice system, this may not always be so if other/older offences become the focus of attention. Whilst more detail about the IOA the detective and probation officer may conduct will be presented throughout this chapter, for now we can note that IOA refers to *"the formal and structured examination of the events, circumstances, and behaviours that occurred before, during, and after the ... [index offence] ..."* (West & Greenall, 2011, p. 144).

IOA draws influence from and has similarities with other areas of applied forensic/clinical psychology that examine problematic behaviour. Examples include functional analysis (Daffern, 2011) and chain analysis (Linehan, 2015). However, two areas that have directly influenced the development and application of IOA are the SPJ approach to violence risk assessments considered in the previous chapter and Investigative Psychology (Canter & Youngs, 2009). For example, like SPJ, IOA provides a formal and structured framework that guides the analysis; IOA provides a list of topics to consider within that analysis; and IOA encourages criminal justice practitioners to draw upon multiple sources of information whilst completing that analysis, including their professional judgement (West & Greenall, 2011). Similarly, like Investigative Psychology, IOA focuses on the salient features of a crime by examining primary sources of information, it distinguishes between offenders based on a detailed examination of their offence behaviours, and it uses this information and the available research to develop evidence-based inferences about offenders and their offending (Greenall, 2014). However, to understand why IOA is required, we need to consider the problem it is designed to address.

The problem

IOA is designed to address a problem within forensic/clinical practice, which was articulated by my colleague and clinical mentor, Dr Adrian West, who, drawing upon his experience of assisting the police in the investigation of serious violent crime (West, 2001), suggested that *"many clinicians, whatever their professional background, do not routinely review crime scene data or witness depositions during the course of their involvement with offender/patients..."* (West, 2000a, p. 220).

My experience with secure hospitals led me to concur with this observation. And although it cannot be said that crime scene information and victim/witness depositions are never available to forensic/clinical practitioners, from my experience, they are not a common feature. Moreover, from my experience, accounts of the index offence are sometimes *'cut and pasted'* from previous reports, which may support Dr West's further observation that *"all too often it is easier to believe the offender than to read the witness depositions or observe the crime scene"* (West, 2000, p. 220).

Dr West and I encountered examples of the potential dangers of this during two assessments in secure hospitals. One man who was of no fixed abode had raped and murdered an elderly woman. That day, he visited a local Vicar, for assistance, who was reportedly not very helpful. However, when we read the transcript of the police interview with the Vicar retrieved from the archive, he stated that he had assisted this man by giving him food and directions to where he wanted to go next. It was whilst following these directions that he encountered his victim. In another case, the offender was adamant that his killing of a female stranger was not sexual. However, examination of crime scene photographs and forensic pathology reports showed there was a clear and unequivocal sexual dynamic to this killing. Although he continued to deny the killing was sexual, the primary evidence provided a basis for our hypothesis that it was a sexual murder.

Supporting evidence

Whilst these accounts may not prove the existence of the problem identified by West (2000), of note is the fact that other researchers have raised similar concerns, both before and since. For example, when writing about forensic psychiatrists in the USA, Dietz stated, *"they usually have a great deal of information about the defendant, but too often lack information about the crime itself"* (1985, p. 210). Several years later, still in the USA, Herman similarly stated, *"in many psychological formulations of the motives of sex offenders, the sexual offence virtually disappears"* (1990, p. 182). In a study of a British medium secure unit, Fallon (2007) may have found an explanation for these omissions, as most staff had not seen witness depositions or crime scene photographs and possessed only a limited awareness of their patients' index offences. It was to address these omissions that my colleague Dr West and I argued that IOA should be a routine task within forensic/clinical practice (see Greenall, 2009; West & Greenall, 2011). However, some years later, researchers in Canada were still finding similar problems. For example, Brankley and Goodwill found that *"while clinicians may read police reports to gain a sense of the offender, crime scene behaviours are rarely a required component of case conceptualization"* (2014, p. 16). A key argument of this chapter is that when dealing with stranger sexual violence and stranger sexual offenders, the problem outlined above can be addressed with an IOA.

The solution

The need for an IOA stems from the fact that sexual offenders are very diverse (see Chapter 4). To understand an individual stranger sexual offender, we must conduct a detailed examination of his offence behaviours. That helps us to understand the context and circumstances in which the offence occurred, and the motivational and interpersonal dynamics underpinning it. Indeed, other researchers, especially those who have proposed classification schemes, have taken similar positions. For example, when referring to his motivational spectrum, Schlesinger argued that *"what offenders do– not necessarily what they say or the make-up of their personalities – is most important in understanding the motivational dynamics of their behavior"* (2004a, p. 196).

IOA procedure

Drawing upon SPJ and other related research (e.g., Copson *et al.*, 1997), the IOA procedure involves several sequential stages (see Figure 12.1), which guide the process of

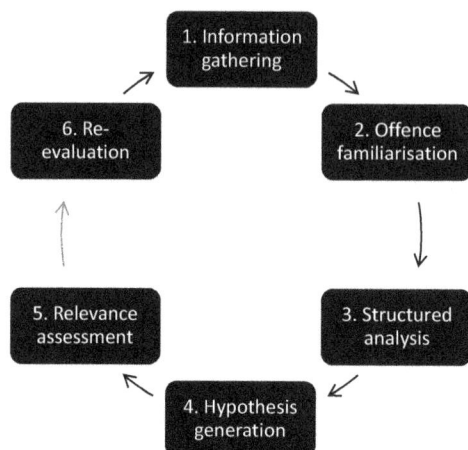

Figure 12.1 Stages of an index offence analysis

understanding an index offence. Stage one involves gathering as much information as possible about the index offence, victim, and offender. Examples include reports from probation, social work, mental health, police interview transcripts with the offender, the victim, and any witnesses, crime scene information such as forensic pathology reports, and photographic evidence. Even if the offender has been interviewed by police, best practice requires criminal justice practitioners to interview him, so he has the opportunity to provide his account of and explanation for the offence. Step two requires all involved to use the information obtained to become familiar with the basic details of the index offence, such as what happened, where, and when. An important feature of the IOA is that the index offence is not viewed as a unified entity but as an event with a beginning, a middle, and an end. Stage three, therefore, involves a three-phase analysis of the index offence (see Figure 12.2), with the offender's actions in each phase examined in detail. However, the boundaries between the phases are not always strict, and some details may span more than one phase.

Pre-crime phase

This phase examines the actions exhibited by the offender *before* the commission of the index offence (West & Greenall, 2011). The aim is to gain an understanding of the context and circumstances from which the offence arose. This phase can be of long or short duration. For example, in some cases, this phase can be a matter of seconds, with sexual violence being a split-second, impulsive act such as when an intoxicated man decides to grope a woman in a bar. In other cases, this phase may last for hours, days, weeks, or months, during which a great deal of planning and perhaps rehearsals have been undertaken by the offender. Key considerations here include details relating to the location and timing of the offence and how the offender and victim came to be there. Essentially, we are considering how the sexual assault triangle considered within Chapter 3 (see Figure 3.1) came into being and what was happening with and between the offender and victim before the offence commenced. Building on the research covered in earlier chapters and the work of others (e.g., Cook, 2019; Hazelwood & Burgess, 2017), the kind of questions to be considered here may include some (or all) of those in Appendix 2 (Table 1).

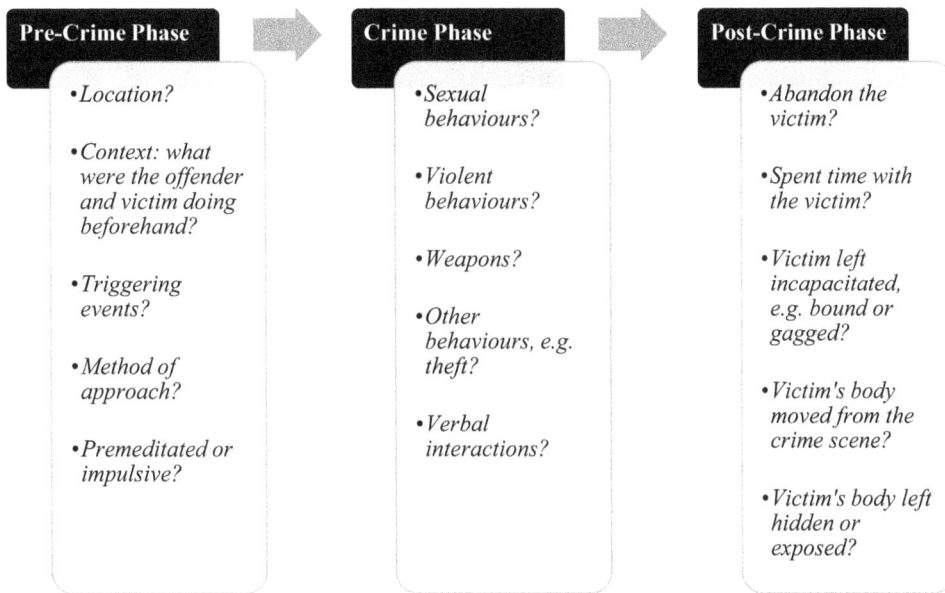

Figure 12.2 Index offence phases

Potential hypotheses

From these questions, one hypothesis could be that the offender made a rational choice (Cornish & Clarke, 2014) to plan, seek out, and target female strangers to sexually assault, and he was in that location for this purpose. Examples include the voyeur hiding behind some bushes to observe a woman undressing in her bedroom, an exhibitionist waiting behind some bushes for a woman to pass so he could expose himself, or a man travelling to a '*red light district*' to target prostitutes. Alternatively, the offence may have occurred during the offender's routine activities (Cohen & Felson, 1979) and was secondary to another act. Examples include Robert taking advantage of opportunities to expose himself on his way to or from work (see Box 8.1), a man who meets a woman in a bar whilst socialising with friends and who follows her with criminal intent, or a prolific burglar who decides to rape a woman he unexpectedly encounters in her home. Related hypotheses may include the offender having followed a premeditated precautionary pathway, an opportunistic convenience pathway, or a premeditated opportunist pathway (see Chapter 2), and whether he used a con, surprise, or blitz attack (see Table 2.1).

Crime phase

This phase examines the actions exhibited by the offender *during* the commission of the index offence (West & Greenall, 2011). The aim is to gain an understanding of what the offender did to his victim whilst carrying out his assault. This phase can also be of long or short duration. For example, in some cases, this phase can be a matter of seconds, such as when an exhibitionist exposes himself and flees. In other cases, this phase may last minutes, hours, or even longer, such as when a full sexual assault occurs or when a woman is sexually assaulted over a long period of time. For example, Colonel Williams' sexual murder of military colleague Marie-France Comeau in November 2009 lasted several hours, whilst his sexual murder of Jessica Lloyd in January 2010 commenced at her home in Belleville and ended almost a day later at the Colonel's cottage in nearby Tweed (Brankley *et al.*, 2014; Watt, 2014). Key considerations here include the sexual, violent, and other behaviours exhibited by the offender. This includes determining how the sexual offence developed, what sexual behaviours were engaged in, what types of violence were involved, and why. Other offender actions are also considered, such as the usage of bindings, the language (complimentary or profane) he used, and whether he stole anything (material or sexual) from his victim. The role played by the victim is also important, not in a blame sense but to try to understand how her responses and behaviours may have influenced the dynamics of the assault. Building on the research covered in earlier chapters and the work of others (e.g., Cook, 2019; Hazelwood & Burgess, 2017), the kind of questions to be considered here may include some (or all) of those in Appendix 2 (Table 2).

Potential hypotheses

Within this phase, hypotheses can be formulated relating to whether violence was instrumental or expressive (Feshbach, 1964). The former may indicate premeditation whilst the latter may indicate that negative emotions such as anger or fear precipitated an impulsive assault (Meloy, 2006). Further hypotheses may relate to the interpersonal nature of the crime and how the offender viewed his victim (Canter & Heritage, 1990), as well as potential motivations that drove the sexual (Groth & Birnbaum, 1979; Knight & Prentky, 1990) and violent (Schlesinger, 2004a, 2004b) aspects of the assault. Such considerations facilitate hypotheses about whether the offender was, for example, a sexual opportunist seeking intimacy and who used violence functionally to restrain an unwilling victim or someone who used gratuitous violence towards a woman he had no concern for to satisfy his sadistic or misogynistic needs. In cases of homicide, these ideas can help formulate hypotheses about whether the death was accidental, intentional and related to anger or sadism, or functional to silence a potential accuser (Kerr *et al.*, 2013).

Post-crime phase

This phase examines the actions exhibited by the offender *after* the commission of the index offence (West & Greenall, 2011). The aim is to gain an understanding of what the offender did once the offence was completed and whether he engaged in any behaviours relating to the avoidance of detection (i.e., forensic awareness). As with the previous two phases, this phase can be of long or short duration. For example, an exhibitionist or rapist may dress himself and run off after completing the sexual assault. However, in other cases, a rapist may spend time with his victim, engage them in conversations, and/ or escort them away from the crime scene (e.g., see Greenall & West, 2007, 2008). Building on the research covered in earlier chapters and the work of others (e.g., Cook, 2019; Hazelwood & Burgess, 2017), the kind of questions to be considered here may include some (or all) of those in Appendix 2 (Table 3).

Potential hypotheses

Within this phase, the offender's behaviour towards his victim may support earlier hypotheses about the interpersonal nature of the offence, such as whether his actions were further evidence of an impersonal assault or a failed attempt at intimacy (Canter & Heritage, 1990). Alternatively, the offender may have left further evidence that the sexual assault contained angry, impersonal, or deviant elements, such as leaving the victim bound/gaged, or stealing sexual items such as her underwear. Along with a possible sexual aspect, leaving the victim incapacitated may also have been designed to delay her ability to alert the authorities. This leads to other possible hypotheses about the offender's knowledge of forensic awareness (Beauregard & Bouchard, 2010; Beauregard & Martineau, 2014; Chopin *et al.*, 2022), which may be related to previous offending and involvement with the criminal justice system. If a homicide occurs, an impulsive killing may be further evidenced by the fact that the body was left at the crime scene, or a pre-meditated killing may be further evidenced by the offender taking active steps to conceal the killing, such as moving the body from the crime scene and/or disposing of it in another location (Lundrigan & Canter, 2001a). Hypotheses such as these and those relating to the pre-crime and crime phases may, in some cases, suggest that the index offence was the culmination of a process whereby the offender has, in recent days, weeks, or months, been enacting a developing and escalating sexual fantasy (MacCulloch *et al.*, 1983). Be that so, this enhanced understanding of what occurred between the offender and victim before, during, and after the offence can provide an indication of what the offender is capable of in the future in similar circumstances.

Idiographic filter

Returning to Figure 12.1, stages 4–5 involve the formulation of individualised hypotheses about the offender and his offence(s). This requires criminal justice practitioners to draw upon research *and* their professional experience and apply *both* to the case at hand. This is another example of IOA drawing influence from SPJ by ensuring there is a clear role for professional judgement within the IOA process. As stated in the previous chapter, SPJ includes consideration of relevance. When considering relevance SPJ is concerned with the degree to which a particular factor was or may in the future be causally relevant to the perpetration of violence (e.g., a violent offender is only violent when intoxicated), and similar sentiments apply here. That is, it is not simply about applying one or more findings to the case in hand because the research suggests it might apply, but using professional judgement and the idiographic filter (see Figure 12.3) to determine the <u>*relevance*</u> of that finding to the case in hand.

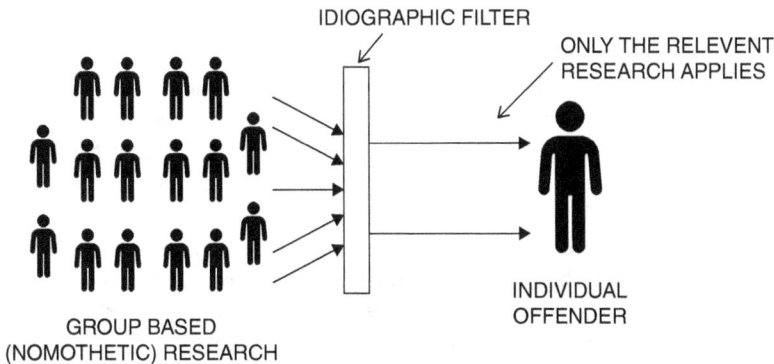

Figure 12.3 Idiographic filter

For example, research suggests that men who use violence during rape have a greater likelihood of having previous convictions for violence (Davies *et al.*, 1998; House, 1997; Jackson *et al.*, 1997), and those who steal from their victim have a greater likelihood of having previous convictions for acquisitive offences (Davies *et al.*, 1998; Häkkänen *et al.*, 2004; Scott *et al.*, 2006; ter Beek *et al.*, 2010). Whilst these findings are clear at the nomothetic level, their ideographic relevance would still need to be considered. For example, was the violence instrumental or expressive and related to anger or sexual arousal (see Chapter 4). Returning to the case of Mr Jones, the fact that he was intoxicated, strangled, and then stole from Miss Williams may suggest he has prior convictions for violence (ter Beek *et al.*, 2010) and acquisitive offending. However, the fact that he stole her underwear and thought she was a prostitute are equally important factors from my experience working with sexual offenders. This leads to stage six, which involves re-evaluation, because hypotheses are only as good as the information that supports them, and they should be reviewed when new information is received.

Benefits of incorporating IOA into criminal justice practice

Returning to the previous chapter, we can see that a key feature of SPJ protocols such as those in Table 11.2 is their inclusion of several risk factors that examine various aspects of the offence, including its link with previous sexual violence. The SVR-20-V2 (Boer *et al.*, 2017) and RSVP-V2 (Hart *et al.*, 2022) both encourage practitioners to consider various factors that could have been evidenced within the index offence. Examples include sexual behaviours such as sexual deviancy, chronicity/frequency, multiplicity/diversity, and escalation. Additionally, various violent behaviours are included, such as physical/psychological harm/coercion. Although SPJs give more consideration to the index offence, to be able to assess an offender's risk using this approach, a reasonably detailed knowledge of the index offence is required. To put it another way, how can criminal justice practitioners assess violence risk using SPJs if they do not have reasonably detailed knowledge of the index offence? Clearly, they cannot, and therefore, undertaking such assessments requires a means by which a reasonably detailed knowledge of the index offence can be obtained. This highlights the need for a formal, structured means of analysing an index offence, which maps the chain of events which led to the offence occurring.

A clinical protocol

Within forensic/clinical practice an IOA-informed knowledge and understanding of what a stranger sexual offender did during their index offence will help criminal justice practitioners formulate meaningful hypotheses about motive. The need for forensic/clinical practitioners to explore motives was illustrated by Smith (2000a). After applying the MTC:R3 to a sample of mentally ill sexual offenders, he concluded that, along with a clinical evaluation of an individual's psychotic presentation, a consideration of motives such as those within the MTC:R3 provides a framework which can inform clinical opinion about the factors that contributed to the index offence. Indeed, other researchers have similarly shown how the MTC:R3 can illustrate the motivations of mentally disordered rapists, including those who have targeted strangers (e.g., Barbaree *et al.*, 1994; Brown & Forth, 1997; Greenall & West, 2007, 2008; Polaschek, 1997). However, this has '*only*' been possible once the offences have been subjected to a detailed analysis.

Along with consideration of motive, as shown in the previous chapter, criminal justice practitioners are often required to assess an individual's future risk. The need for an IOA to play a part in this process is illustrated by research which suggests the findings of a detailed analysis of a sexual offender's crime scene behaviours can inform the process of risk assessment (see Lehmann *et al.*, 2013). Indeed, the idea that an assessment of risk can be improved by an IOA links into best practice in this area. For example, although relating specifically to Scotland, standard 2 of the Risk Management Authority's guidelines states that risk assessments should:

> provide an explanation of the onset, development, occurrence, and maintenance of the offending behaviour...[and]... should articulate the pattern and nature of past offending, estimate the likelihood and seriousness of future harm, and identify the likely scenarios in which offending may occur.
>
> (2018, p. 18)

Again, this guidance can *only* be followed once the index offence (and other relevant factors considered in Chapter 11) has been subjected to a detailed analysis.

An investigative protocol?

Official police guidance suggests that knowledge of how an individual offended (i.e., his modus operandi or MO) is an important feature of an investigation, as it helps detectives to understand how a particular crime was committed, to identify a series of crimes committed with the same MO, to identify links between crimes and known offenders who use the same MO, and to predict future offending patterns that may enable preventive or protective measures to be taken and/or to enable offenders to be caught in the act (Association of Chief Police Officers, 2012). All of this information can help detectives plan and conduct interviews with suspects and victims (Shepherd & Griffiths, 2021).

A key argument of this chapter is that an IOA of a stranger sexual offence can assist detectives with these tasks. Moreover, by providing a framework to help detectives consider important features of an offence at each stage, IOA is attempting to bring an SPJ approach to criminal investigations. This not only allows but encourages detectives to consider and formulate hypotheses about aspects of the offence, such as whether a particular action (e.g., victim tied up) was functional and aimed at assisting the execution of the offence or present because it satisfied a psychological need, and whether another action (e.g., forced fellatio) was sexual (i.e., occurred before anal sex) or aimed at humiliating and degrading his victim (i.e., occurred after anal sex). Considerations of these finer details can provide detectives with an enhanced understanding of what might be distinctive or *'signature'* behaviours. This, coupled with an enhanced understanding of the behaviours that occur within one or more of the three phases, can help detectives to consider whether two or more stranger sexual offences were committed by the same offender. As illustrated by Grubin *et al.* (2001), a stage-by-stage analysis of stranger sexual offences can help detectives identify behavioural similarities in one or more of the stages, a process that now underpins the practice of crime linkage (see Davies & Woodhams, 2019). Given that official police guidance and inspection reports recommend that cases of stranger sexual violence should be considered as being part of a pattern of serial offending (see Chapter 2), IOA has the potential to make an important contribution in this area. However, IOA can also help detectives in other areas, such as understanding the interpersonal and motivational dynamics of the offence. Given the importance of sexual deviancy (see Chapter 6), it would be useful for detectives to be able to differentiate between an opportunistic sexual offender who uses minimal violence in his assault, and the premeditated sexual sadist who derives sexual pleasure from his actions, as the chances of further offending by these two men may differ, and detectives should understand why. Indeed, although mostly a clinical classification, Knight *et al.* (1998) found the MTC:R3 has investigative potential in the areas of expressive violence, sadism, and premeditation, but an IOA would help this process of understanding.

Conclusion and implications for practice

A key argument of this chapter is that criminal justice practitioners should, as a matter of routine, incorporate an evidence-based analysis of the index offence into their practice. To that end, this chapter has introduced the topic and process of IOA, which is a formal and structured examination of the events, circumstances, and behaviours that occurred before, during, and after the index offence. The benefit of dividing an index offence in this way is that it facilitates a detailed examination of an offender's crime scene actions at each stage. The importance of such a detailed analysis was illustrated by Canter, who advised:

> One central research question, then, is to identify the behaviourally important facets of offences, those facets that are of most use in revealing the salient psychological processes inherent in the offence. These carry great potential for answering questions posed by investigators.
>
> (2000, p. 31)

Although written almost a quarter of a century ago, Canter's advice remains correct and relevant. Crucially, Canter's advice is not limited to criminal investigations, as it applies to other areas of criminal justice practice which involve dealing with stranger sexual violence and stranger sexual offenders. Whether Canter's behaviourally important facets of offences include choice of location or what the offender did or said during the offence, IOA provides a means by which criminal justice practitioners can identify these features, and it encourages them to draw upon relevant research when trying to make sense of them. Without such a process, our knowledge and understanding of stranger sexual violence and stranger sexual offenders will be seriously compromised, as will our ability to respond accordingly to the challenges these types of offences/offenders present.

Final comments

To paraphrase West and Greenall (2011), if criminal justice practitioners give more focus to the circumstances of the offence, their analyses can underpin more informed hypotheses about an individual's offending, and therefore, IOA should be routine within criminal justice practice. If this chapter has not convinced you of this, then perhaps the words of Dietz will:

> Even when there is no living witness, it is often possible to arrive at a clear picture of how the offender and victim encountered one another; whether there was cooperation between them up to a particular point; whether the offender brought a weapon or other preparations (e.g., rope, adhesive tape, handcuffs) with him; whether he attempted penetration and into which orifices; whether he ejaculated; whether the victim was conscious, semiconscious, unconscious, or dead at the time

of various injuries he inflicted; what efforts he made to conceal his identity or the crime; what he took or did not take with him; and how he departed.

(1985, pp. 210–211)

Although these observations were made almost 40 years ago, like Canter's advice above, they remain correct and relevant. Whilst the index offence may not have received adequate attention in the intervening years, this chapter provides a means by which that omission can finally be addressed and such an analysis can be incorporated into criminal justice practice.

Part 4
Conclusion

13 Bringing it all together

No-one ever deserves or asks for sexual violence to happen – not even a little bit. 100% of the blame lies with the perpetrator

(www.rapecrisis.org.uk)

Introduction

Each week, if not every day, in Britain, women are sexually assaulted by men they do not know. As the above quote makes clear, they did not ask for this to happen, and responsibility rests entirely with their assailant. In most cases, these women will have been going about their ordinary business, unaware that a man was watching them and waiting for his opportunity to strike, or that their ordinary business would unexpectedly lead them into the path of a man who would impulsively sexually assault them. This is what Libby Squire and Sarah Everard were doing when they encountered Pawel Relowicz and Wayne Couzens, and what countless other women were and in the future will be doing, before encountering a man they do not know who decides to sexually assault them in any of the ways covered within this book.

Although a statistical minority of all sexual assaults, cases involving strangers warrant special attention. The reason for this is that whilst sexual assaults between known individuals require women to be in the company of men they know, stranger sexual violence can happen to any woman, at any time, at any place, anywhere. This point is not made to be sensational or to instil fear, but to highlight a simple fact that all women should know. Whilst stranger sexual violence has received research attention, the need for a dedicated text like this book was recently illustrated when the Home Affairs Committee of the House of Commons published a report into the investigation and prosecution of rape. Although 20 MPs examined this issue and took evidence from several experts over several sessions, their final 91 page report only mentions the word *'stranger'* once, and only then to dispel a myth (House of Commons Home Affairs Committee, 2022). Whilst this is perhaps understandable given that most women are sexually assaulted by men they know, it means that stranger sexual violence and stranger sexual offenders are again left out of the loop. That ends here with this book!

Who is the stranger sexual offender?

This man has been at the centre of this book, and by now it is clear that contrary to the popular stereotype of him being someone who lurks in the shadows waiting for an unsuspecting lone woman to drag into a dark, secluded place to rape before running off,

DOI: 10.4324/9781003217763-17

his presentation is more complex. This book has shown that stranger sexual offenders include men who steal women's underwear from washing lines or who burgle a house to steal these items, men who secretly observe women engaged in private acts, men who publicly expose themselves to women, men who approach women in parks or other public places, on foot or a bike, and who grope or smack them then flee, men – probably drunken – who group women in bars, men who rape women in public places or burglars who rape them in their own home, and men who sexually assault and kill women, again in public places or in their own home after breaking in. The core features of many of these cases are sexual desire, sexual deviancy, anger, and misogyny, and they will run through many cases of stranger sexual violence, just like the words in a stick of seaside rock. Prior to these offences, stranger sexual offenders would have travelled along various psychological pathways, marked by cautious premeditation, opportunistic impulsivity, or pre-meditated opportunism. They would also have travelled along a physical pathway (or JTC) either intentionally or not, to encounter the women they ended up assaulting. Along these psychological and physical pathways, in addition to the potential influence of sexual deviancy, anger, or misogyny, other factors such as attitudes, core beliefs, a mental disorder, or intoxication may have influenced their decision-making and contributed to the type of sexual violence inflicted on their victim, who may have been his primary or secondary target.

Remember what is irrelevant!

As stated in Chapter 2, an important fact that every criminal justice practitioner should recognise when trying to understand acts of stranger sexual violence is that the absence of a relationship matters tremendously. This point is re-stated here because it highlights a factor that, although very important in many cases of sexual violence, is irrelevant here. As an undergraduate, I engaged in fascinating discussions about the issue of consent within sexual encounters between men and women, emanating from famous cases such as R v Olugboja ([1982] QB 320) and R vs Kaitamaki ([1985] AC 147). And some researchers have explored not only the types of coercion used within such cases but also their negative psychological impact on the victims (e.g., see Kern & Peterson, 2020). However, because these cases and subsequent research are not relevant here, criminal justice practitioners are left trying to understand the actions of men like Pawel Relowicz, Wayne Couzens, and countless others who think it is acceptable to intentionally sexually engage with a woman they do not know, knowing full well she does not want this to happen, then flee the scene, leaving her to pick up the pieces, or not if she dies during the assault. As challenging as cases of stranger sexual violence are in comparison to cases where the man and woman are or were in some kind of relationship, a body of research exists which can help criminal justice practitioners unpick these assaults and formulate hypotheses as to what happened, where, when, how, and why. This book has brought this together to improve your practice.

Tools in your practitioner box

This book has presented you with several tools which you can draw upon in your practice as and when appropriate. Draw upon volume one and consider the factors that may have brought the motivated offender to be in the same place as the vulnerable victim; consider the JTC made by the offender and what anchor points it may have started from; consider the behaviours (sexual, violent, and others) exhibited by the offender during the entirety of the assault; consider the factors that motivated the offence; and consider those factors that contributed to his decision making process. Draw upon volume two to gain a thorough understanding of the offence itself and where it might sit along a trajectory of seriousness. Finally, draw upon volume three and incorporate what you know about the offence with the existing research to develop one or more evidence-based hypotheses. In doing this, rather than viewing the assault as a single, unified incident, break it down into pre-crime, crime, and post-crime phases. This will help you to conduct a more detailed analysis of the assault and to tease out one or more finer details that may contribute to a better overall formulation.

Final considerations for your practice

This book aims to be a guide for criminal justice practitioners, and with that in mind, the final considerations are practice-informed and practice based. Whether you are a police officer investigating a case of stranger sexual violence or another criminal justice practitioner tasked with assessing, formulating, and managing the sexual risk presented by a stranger sexual offender, my advice based on my experience is simple: just as an official report into the investigation and prosecution of rape recommended that police officers should initially consider every stranger rape to be part of a pattern of serial offending (Criminal Justice Joint Inspection, 2012); and just as another official report, this time into online child exploitation, referred to the need to consider each possession offender (i.e., someone who possesses indecent images of children) as a potential contact offender to some extent (Child Exploitation and Online Protection Centre, 2012), then criminal justice practitioners should consider ever stranger sexual offender at the lower end of the offence trajectory as having the potential to escalate their offending pattern upwards. Equally, criminal justice practitioners should explore whether those already at the top of the trajectory originally came from the lower end. Doing this will encourage you to give due consideration to where a stranger sexual offender may go next or where he may have come from. If this book helps you in this task, then it has achieved its primary aim.

Appendix 1
Applying classification to your practice

Chapter 4 summarised some of the most important and influential research, which has sought to address the problem of sexual offender heterogeneity, in relation to motivational and interpersonal differences. But how can criminal justice practitioners apply these ideas within their practice, especially if they do not have access to large amount of information on the offender? What follows is a means by which this can be achieved. The ideas that follow were originally presented in my PhD thesis (Greenall, 2015), although other researchers (e.g., Aggrawal, 2009a) have independently presented similar ideas.[1]

Dimensional view of sexual violence

Chapter 1 suggested that stranger sexual violence exists on a continuum. In most cases, sexual violence includes a combination of sex and violence. As we have seen in earlier chapters, these are not uniform concepts; they too exist along a continuum. Violence can be instrumental or expressive, and sex can be overt or covert. Even when overt, sexual acts can be of an erotic or violent nature. As stated in Chapter 9, my colleague and I found the offence behaviours of stranger rapists generally divide into sexual and violent themes. This led us to suggest this "allows, indeed invites, future research and theoretical conceptualizations of stranger rape, to consider further how these two factors may interact in this crime" (Greenall & West, 2007, p. 160). As stated in Chapter 10, following this my study of stranger sexual killers found their offence behaviours similarly divided into sexual (i.e., overt or covert) and violent (i.e., instrumental or expressive) themes (Greenall & Wright, 2020). So, what does this mean?

Interpersonal circle

Sex and violence are not only dimensional factors, but they are independent of each other. This is evidenced by the fact that individual stranger's sexual assaults can include high or low levels of either, neither or both of these factors. A useful way to capture this dynamic interaction is to utilise an interpersonal circle. Originating from Leary (1957) an interpersonal circle is a two-dimensional representation of an interaction between two or more factors. Relevant examples of how an interpersonal circle has been used include Blackburn (1993) who utilised it to illustrate the dimensional nature of personality disorder, and Knight (2010) who utilised it to illustrate how the MTC:R3 types could be accommodated around three components of impulsivity, sexualisation and violence. Groth and Birnbaum (1979) suggested three patterns of rape – *anger, power, sadism* – are distinguishable from the interaction of sexual and aggressive acts and Kerr *et al.* (2013)

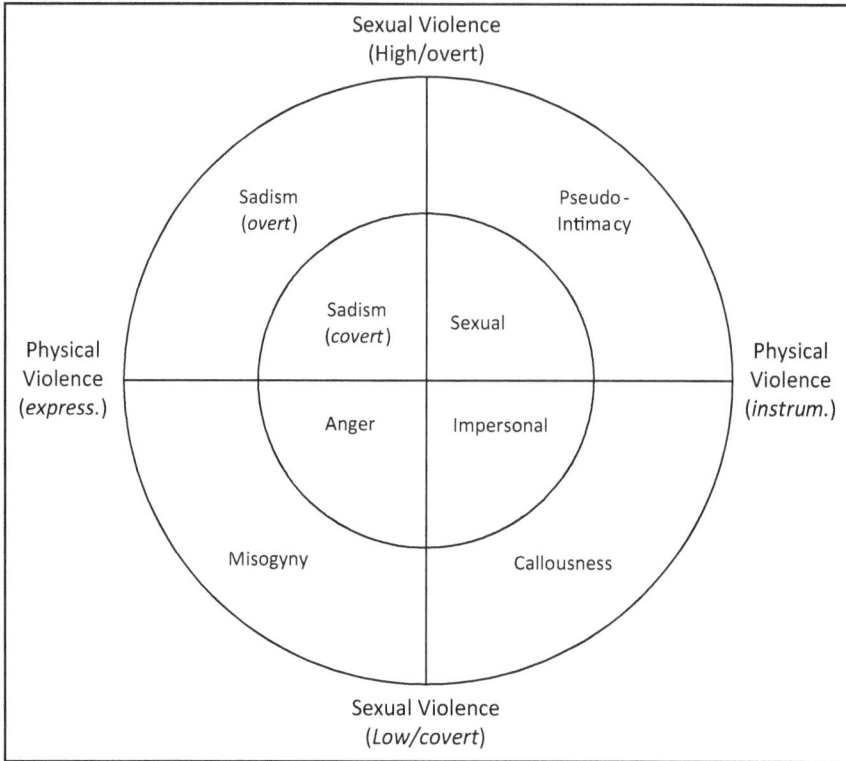

```
                    Sexual Violence
                     (High/overt)




           Sadism                        Pseudo-
           (overt)                        Intimacy


                        Sadism
                        (covert)    Sexual

Physical                                          Physical
Violence                                          Violence
(express.)            Anger      Impersonal       (instrum.)




           Misogyny                      Callousness




                    Sexual Violence
                     (Low/covert)
```

Figure A1.1 A dimensional classification of stranger sexual violence

suggested three motivations – *anger, sadism, sexual/witness elimination* – account for most sexual homicides. However, when sex and violence are arranged on two orthogonal axes within an interpersonal circle (see Figure A1), the interaction of these factors creates a dimensional representation of stranger sexual violence, containing four broad themes. This can be used by criminal justice practitioners to understand the main motivational and interpersonal dynamics within a stranger's sexual assault. Within this model, the 'sex' continuum on the vertical axis can be viewed as being differentiated between overt and covert types and their purpose and meaning (i.e., erotic, or violent) for the perpetrator. The 'violence' continuum on the horizontal axis is differentiated between expressive and instrumental levels and again, their purpose and meaning (i.e., erotic, or violent) for the perpetrator.

Type 1: Sexual/pseudo-intimacy

These assaults contain an overt and subjectively erotic sexual component, which may include several sexual acts. This is coupled with instrumental violence aimed at obtaining and maintaining victim control and compliance. These assaults reflect a sexual motivation similar to those within the MTC:R3 and identified by Groth (see Chapter 4, Table 4.1) and indicate a desire for an erotic experience with the victim. In extreme cases, this manifests itself as what Canter and Heritage (1990) called a desire for pseudo-intimacy. Although violence is instrumental, in extreme cases, it can result in homicide either by accident or intentionally to avoid detection (Kerr *et al.*, 2013).

Type 2: Impersonal/callousness

These assaults contain a covert and unerotic sexual component, coupled with instrumental violence. Although the violence satisfies the same functions and may produce the same outcome as in type one cases, the reduced sexual component suggests these assaults contain what Canter and Heritage (1990) called an impersonal sexual dynamic. That is, although one or more sexual acts may be perpetrated by the offender, levels of subjective eroticism are low indicating the offender was engaging with someone whom he regarded as an object of no concern (Canter, 1994). In extreme cases, this may amount to a callous even psychopathic disregard for the victim, who is akin to an instrument of masturbation (Simon, 2008). Moreover, because the violence serves the same purpose as in type one cases, in extreme cases, deaths may occur for similar reasons but be more of an impersonal killing (Greenall & Wright, 2020).

Type 3: Anger/misogyny

These assaults contain a covert and unerotic sexual component, coupled with expressive violence. Although one or more sexual acts may be perpetrated by the offender, levels of subjective eroticism are low; they are primarily aimed at humiliating and demeaning the victim, rather than sexually gratifying the offender. The level of violence is gratuitous and exceed that required to obtain and maintain victim control and compliance. As such these assaults reflect an angry motivation similar to those within the MTC:R3 and identified by Groth (see Chapter 4, Table 4.1), which in more extreme cases reflect vindictiveness, misogyny, and grievance (Beech *et al.*, 2005; Beech, Oliver, *et al.*, 2005). The angry/vindictive nature of these assaults may be further indicated by the presence of verbal aggression, such as profanities or derogatory phrases.

Type 4: Sadism

These assaults contain an overt and subjectively erotic sexual component similar to type one cases and may therefore include several sexual acts. This is coupled with coupled with expressive violence similar to type three cases. Here the combination of high levels of sex and violence reflects a sadistic motivation similar to those within the MTC:R3 and identified by Groth (see Chapter 4, Table 4.1) and others (e.g., House, 1997). In more extreme (overt) cases, violence can result in the victim's death and make the offender a sadistic sexual killer (Brittain, 1970; Kerr *et al.*, 2013).

Although the above model is theoretical, it nonetheless illustrates how the dynamic interaction of sex and violence can lead to different types of stranger sexual violence. As such it has the potential to be of practical use to criminal justice practitioners who need to determine the following to apply it within their practice.

1 *Violent dynamic:* Determine the level of violence within the offence, considering any victim resistance, i.e., was the level of violence sufficient to obtain and maintain victim compliance (i.e., sexual/impersonal) or was it gratuitous (i.e., anger/sadism).
2 *Sexual dynamic:* Determine the subjective needs satisfied by any sexual acts perpetrated by the stranger sexual offender, i.e., were they perpetrated for erotic (i.e., sexual/sadism) or non-erotic (i.e., impersonal/anger) purposes.
3 *Other dynamics:* Consider the subjective aspect of any non-violent, non-sexual acts, and what the offender was seeking to gain out of them. For example, was theft from

the victim sexually motivated (i.e., her underwear, etc.), impersonal (i.e., stole money after simply asking for it), or designed to humiliate (i.e., stole money and told the victim she might as well pay for his services). Was any profanity (whore, bitch, etc.) designed to enhance his sexual arousal or demean and humiliate his victim?

A guide not a diagnosis

The above is not meant to be a diagnostic tool, but a guide for criminal justice practitioners. In using this, they are encouraged to draw upon their knowledge and experience and the research and combine this with the results of a full index offence analysis (see Chapter 12) and determine the main motivational and interpersonal dynamics underpinning the offence. This will provide a better understanding of the stranger sexual assault in question and the offender who committed it.

Notes

1 Dr Michael R Davis also presented similar ideas at the 15th International Conference of The International Academy of Investigative Psychology, 8-10 April 2014, at London Southbank University. So, the fact that three researchers unknown to each other all had the same idea, suggests it has some merit.

Appendix 2
Index offence analysis: Questions for each phase

Pre-crime phase

Examines the actions exhibited by the offender *before* the commission of the index offence, and below are some questions to consider.

Table A2.1 Pre-crime phased questions

Location and timing
1   How suitable was the location for the offender to sexually assault a female stranger, i.e., was it an isolated, quiet location which afforded him some degree of privacy, or did he take risks by assaulting a woman in an unsuitable location?
2   If the location was specifically chosen, what might this choice indicate about any previous reconnaissance or planning?
3   What time did the offence occur, and does that shed any light on how and why the offender and victim came to be there at that time? For example, if the offence occurred in an isolated location late at night, what might have brought the offender and victim to that location at that time?
4   If the location is close to residential areas, perhaps the offender and victim may have only travelled a short distance? If not, they may have had to travel further. If so, how/why might they have made this journey at this time?
5   Are there any other potential anchor points nearby which may have drawn the offender and victim to that location, e.g., bars, clubs, shops, gyms, etc.?
6   Have there been any other similar incidents in or around that location recently?

Victim details
1   What was the victim's age and ethnicity, and are they similar to the offender?
2   What was the victim doing just before the offence?
3   Did anything about the victim (e.g., activity, location, occupation, intoxication, and being alone) increase her chances of being attacked?
4   How did the victim come to be in the offender's company, i.e., was their meeting spontaneous or was she specifically selected?
5   Was the victim the offender's primary target, or was her victimisation secondary to another event or incident at that time, if so, what?
6   What role, if any, did she play in the pre-assault interactions with her assailant?
7   Did the victim offer any physical or verbal resistance? If so, how did the offender respond to this?

(Continued)

Table A2.1 Pre-crime phased questions

Offender details
1   *What activities was the offender involved in prior to the offence?*
2   *Did the offender take any steps to hide his identity from his victim?*
3   *How did the offender initially engage with his victim?*
4   *What type of conversation (if any) occurred between the offender and victim?*
5   *How did the offender gain control of his victim to carry out the assault, i.e., threats, force, deception, and incapacitation?*
6   *If the offender had a weapon, what type and where did he get it from?*
7   *If he had a weapon or other items that could constitute a 'rape kit', why would he be in that location at that time with these items on his person?*

Crime phase

Examines the actions exhibited by the offender <u>*during*</u> the commission of the index offence, and below are some questions to consider.

Table A2.2 Crime phase questions

Location:
1   *Did the offence take place in the same location as the pre-crime phase, or did the offender move the victim to another location before attacking her?*

Offender:
Violent behaviours
1   *Did the offender issue verbal threats or profanity? If so, what did he say?*
2   *Did the offender use physical violence? If so, what did this involve, and was it sufficient to gain victim control (i.e., instrumental) or excessive (i.e., expressive)?*
3   *Did the offender display unusual violence, e.g., biting, burning, or choking the victim?*
4   *Were weapons brandished or used by the offender?*
5   *Has the offender a history of carrying/collecting/using weapons?*
6   *If a homicide, what killed the victim, and were there any post-mortem injuries?*
7   *Was the violence and/or the victim's fear sexually arousing to the offender?*

Sexual behaviours
8   How soon did the offence become sexual?
9   *How was the sexual aspect of the assault started?*
10   *What type of sexual behaviour(s) did the offender inflict upon his victim? Were they of a deviant nature?*
11   *Did the offender experience sexual dysfunction?*
12   *Did the offender wear a condom?*
13   *Did the offender display behaviours such as shaving his victim or taking photographs?*
14   *Did the offender insert foreign objects into the victim's vagina or anus?*
15   *Did the offender use bindings, a gag, or similar materials to restrict his victim's movements? If so, were they deployed in a functional way to facilitate the assault or used as props to enhance the offender's sexual arousal?*
16   *Was the assault based on sexual/violent fantasies? If so, how long had the offender experienced them? Had they developed over time? Did the offence live up to them?*
17   *If a homicide, did the offender sexually assault his victim after her death?*

(*Continued*)

Table A2.2 Crime phase questions

Other behaviours

18 *What type of conversation (if any) occurred between the offender and victim?*
19 *Did the offender compliment his victim and/or apologise for his behaviour?*
20 Did the offender reveal any personal information about himself? If so, what and why?
21 Did the offender ask the victim to reveal personal information about herself? If so, what and why?
22 *Did the offender steal anything from his victim? If so, what?*
23 *Was the offender intoxicated with alcohol and/or drugs at the material time?*
24 *How long did this phase last?*

Victim:

1 *Was the victim intoxicated with alcohol and/or drugs at the material time?*
2 *Did the victim sustain any injuries? If so,*
   a *Were they minor (i.e., did not require medical attention), more serious (i.e., required medical attention), or life-threatening?*
   b *Were they defensive injuries sustained whilst she was defending herself from her assailant (i.e., around her hand and/or arms) or where they located near one or more specific parts of her body, e.g., the neck, face, breasts, legs, or vagina?*
3 *Was the victim forced to sexually engage with her assailant, e.g., hugging, kissing, masturbating him, or engaging in sexualised talk?*
4 *Did the victim offer any physical or verbal resistance? If so, how did the offender respond to this?*

Post-crime phase

Examines the actions exhibited by the offender *after* the commission of the index offence, and below are some questions to consider.

Table A2.3 Post-crime phase questions

Offender:

1 *Did the offender leave the scene immediately after the assault was completed, or did he spend time with the victim afterwards?*
2 *Did the offender engage in any verbal interactions, such as complimenting his victim, apologising for his behaviour, exchanging contact details, or seeking another meeting?*
3 *Did the offender leave his victim incapacitated in any way, e.g., bound or gagged?*
4 *Did the offender attempt to destroy and/or remove any evidence from the crime scene or engage in other behaviours aimed at avoiding detection?*
5 *Did the offender try to stop the victim from reporting the offence?*
6 *If a homicide, was the victim killed during this phase?*
7 *If a homicide, did the offender move the body to another location, attempt to hide the body, or was it left in such a way as to convey a message to others?*

References

Abel, G. G., Becker, J. V., Cunningham-Rathner, J., Mittelman, M., & Rouleau, J. L. (1988). Multiple paraphilic diagnoses among sex offenders. *Journal of the American Academy of Psychiatry and the Law*, 16(2), 153–168. http://jaapl.org/content/jaapl/16/2/153.full.pdf

Abel, G. G., & Rouleau, J. L. (1990). The nature and extent of sexual assault. In W. L. Marshal, R. D. Laws, & H. E. Barbaree (Eds.), *Handbook of sexual assault: Issues, theories, and treatment of the offender* (pp. 9–21). Plenum Press.

Abracen, J., Looman, J., & Anderson, D. (2000). Alcohol and drug abuse in sexual and nonsexual violent offenders. *Sexual Abuse*, 12(4), 263–274. https://doi.org/10.1177/107906320001200403

Ackerman, J. M., & Rossmo, D. K. (2015). How far to travel? A multilevel analysis of the residence-to-crime distance. *Journal of Quantitative Criminology*, 31(2), 237–262. https://doi.org/10.1007/s10940-014-9232-7

Adhami, E., & Browne, D. P. (1996). *Major crime enquiries: Improving expert support for detectives*. Home Office Police Research Group, Special Interest Series Paper 9.

Aggrawal, A. (2009a). *Forensic and medico-legal aspects of sexual crimes and unusual sexual practices*. CRC Press. https://doi.org/10.1201/9781420043099

Aggrawal, A. (2009b). A new classification of necrophilia. *Journal of Forensic and Legal Medicine*, 16(6), 316–320. https://doi.org/10.1016/j.jflm.2008.12.023

Aggrawal, A. (2009c). References to the paraphilias and sexual crimes in the Bible. *Journal of Forensic and Legal Medicine*, 16(3), 109–114. https://doi.org/10.1016/j.jflm.2008.07.006

Ahlers, C. J., Schaefer, G. A., Mundt, I. A., Roll, S., Englert, H., Willich, S. N., & Beier, K. M. (2011). How unusual are the contents of paraphilias? Paraphilia-associated sexual arousal patterns in a community-based sample of men. *The Journal of Sexual Medicine*, 8(5), 1362–1370. https://doi.org/10.1111/j.1743-6109.2009.01597.x

Ahlmeyer, S., Kleinsasser, D., Stoner, J., & Retzlaff, P. (2003). Psychopathology of incarcerated sex offenders. *Journal of Personality Disorders*, 17(4), 306–318. https://doi.org/10.1521/pedi.17.4.306.23969

Alison, L., & Rainbow, L. (Eds.). (2011). *Professionalizing offender profiling: Forensic and investigative psychology in practice*. Routledge. https://doi.org/10.4324/9780203809259

Alison, L. J., & Stein, K. L. (2001). Vicious circles: Accounts of stranger sexual assault reflect abusive variants of conventional interactions. *The Journal of Forensic Psychiatry*, 12(3), 515–538. https://doi.org/10.1080/09585180127391

Almond, L., McManus, M., Bal, A., O'Brien, F., Rainbow, L., & Webb, M. (2021). Assisting the investigation of stranger rapes: Predicting the criminal record of U.K. stranger rapists from their crime scene behaviors. *Journal of Interpersonal Violence*, 36(3–4), NP2005-2028NP. https://doi.org/10.1177/0886260518756118

Alper, M., & Durose, M. R. (2019). *Recidivism of sex offenders released from State Prison: A 9-year follow-up (2005–14)*. U.S. Department of Justice. Retrieved from: https://www.bjs.gov/index.cfm/content/data/index.cfm?ty=pbdetail&iid=6566

American Psychiatric Association. (2022). *Diagnostic and statistical manual of mental disorders* (5th ed., text revision). American Psychiatric Association. https://doi.org/10.1176/appi.books.9780890425787

Amir, M. (1971). *Patterns in forcible rape*. The University of Chicago Press.

Arrigo, B. A., & Purcell, C. E. (2001). Explaining paraphilias and lust murder: Toward an integrated model. *International Journal of Offender Therapy and Comparative Criminology, 45*(1), 6–31. https://doi.org/10.1177%2F0306624X01451002

Association of Chief Police Officers. (2011). *Investigating burglary: A guide to investigative options and good practice*. National Policing Improvement Agency. Retrieved from: https://www.npcc.police.uk/documents/crime/2011/201109CBAInvBurGP.pdf

Association of Chief Police Officers. (2012). *Practice advice on core investigative doctrine* (2nd ed.). National Policing Improvement Agency.

Astion, M. (2008). Differences between stranger and known assailant sexual assaults: Using medical provider data to describe and compare the nature and context of sexual crime perpetrated by strangers and known assailants. Research and Policy Analysis Division, Massachusetts Executive Office of Public Safety and Security.

Ault, R. (2021). Number of flashers and sexual voyeurs where you live in Cambs revealed. *Cambridgeshire Live [online]*, October 11th. Retrieved from: https://www.cambridge-news.co.uk/news/local-news/number-flashers-sexual-voyeurs-you-21796159

Ault, R., & Duffy, T. (2021). Liverpool is now a hotspot for indecent exposure according to latest figures. *Liverpool Echo [online]*, October 9th. Retrieved from: https://www.liverpoolecho.co.uk/news/liverpool-news/liverpool-now-hotspot-indecent-exposure-21800230

Ault, R., & Kitching, S. (2021). Hull's flashing and voyeurism crimes and how many offenders were prosecuted. *Hull Daily Mail [online]*, October 13th. Retrieved from: https://www.hulldailymail.co.uk/news/hull-east-yorkshire-news/hulls-flashing-voyeurism-crimes-how-6039105

Barbaree, H. E., Seto, M. C., Serin, R. C., Amos, N. L., & Preston, D. L. (1994). Comparisons between sexual and nonsexual rapist subtypes: Sexual arousal to rape, offense precursors, and offense characteristics. *Criminal Justice and Behavior, 21*(1), 95–114. https://doi.org/10.1177/0093854894021001007

Barker, M. J. (2018). *The psychology of sex*. Routledge.

Bartels, R. M., & Gannon, T. A. (2011). Understanding the sexual fantasies of sex offenders and their correlates. *Aggression and Violent Behavior, 16*(6), 551–561. https://doi.org/10.1016/j.avb.2011.08.002

Bartol, C. R., & Bartol, A. M. (2013). *Criminal & behavioral profiling*. Sage.

Bártová, K., Androvičová, R., Krejčová, L., Weiss, P., & Klapilová, K. (2021). The prevalence of paraphilic interests in the Czech population: Preference, arousal, the use of pornography, fantasy, and behavior. *The Journal of Sex Research, 58*(1), 86–96. https://doi.org/10.1080/00224499.2019.1707468

Baur, E., Forsman, M., Santtila, P., Johansson, A., Sandnabba, K., & Långström, N. (2016). Paraphilic sexual interests and sexually coercive behavior: A population-based twin study. *Archives of Sexual Behavior, 45*(5), 1163–1172. https://doi.org/10.1007/s10508-015-0674-2

Beauregard, É., & Bouchard, M. (2010). Cleaning up your act: Forensic awareness as a detection avoidance strategy. *Journal of Criminal Justice, 38*(6), 1160–1166. https://doi.org/10.1016/j.jcrimjus.2010.09.004

Beauregard, É., & Martineau, M. (2013). A descriptive study of sexual homicide in Canada: Implications for police investigation. *International Journal of Offender Therapy and Comparative Criminology, 57*(12), 1454–1476. https://doi.org/10.1177/0306624X12456682

Beauregard, É., & Martineau, M. (2014). No body, no crime? The role of forensic awareness in avoiding police detection in cases of sexual homicide. *Journal of Criminal Justice, 42*(2), 213–220. https://doi.org/10.1016/j.jcrimjus.2013.06.007

Beauregard, É., & Martineau, M. (2017). *The sexual murderer: Offender behavior and implications for practice*. Routledge.

Beauregard, É., Proulx, J., & Rossmo, D. K. (2005). Spatial patterns of sex offenders: Theoretical, empirical, and practical issues. *Aggression and Violent Behavior, 10*(5), 579–603. https://doi.org/10.1016/j.avb.2004.12.003

Beech, A., Fisher, D., & Ward, T. (2005b). Sexual murderers' implicit theories. *Journal of Interpersonal Violence, 20*(11), 1366–1389. https://doi.org/10.1177/0886260505278712

Beech, A., Oliver, C., Fisher, D., & Beckett, R. (2005a). *STEP 4: The sex offender treatment programme in prison: Addressing the offending behaviour of rapists and sexual murderers.* Her Majesty's Prison Service.

Beech, A. R. (2010). Sexual offenders. In J. M. Brown & E. A. Campbell (Eds.), *The Cambridge handbook of forensic psychology* (pp. 102–110). Cambridge University Press.

Bennell, C., Bloomfield, S., Emeno, K., & Musolino, E. (2013). Classifying serial sexual murder/murderers: An attempt to validate Keppel and Walter's (1999) model. *Criminal Justice and Behavior, 40*(1), 5–25. https://doi.org/10.1177/0093854812460489

Bennett, G. (2018). Knickers thief carried out obscene act with woman's bra in her home. *Bristol Post, [online], December 17th*. Retrieved from: https://www.bristolpost.co.uk/news/bristol-news/knickers-thief-carried-out-obscene-2329119

Blackburn, R. (1993). *The psychology of criminal conduct: Theory, research and practice.* John Wiley & Sons Ltd.

Blackburn, R. (2000). Treatment or incapacitation? Implications of research on personality disorders for the management of dangerous offenders. *Legal and Criminological Psychology, 5*(1), 1–21. https://doi.org/10.1348/135532500167921

Blackburn, R., Logan, C., Donnelly, J., & Renwick, S. (2003). Personality disorders, psychopathy and other mental disorders: Co-morbidity among patients at English and Scottish high-security hospitals. *The Journal of Forensic Psychiatry & Psychology, 14*(1), 111–137. https://doi.org/10.1080/1478994031000077925

Blanchard, R., & Hucker, S. J. (1991). Age, transvestism, bondage, and concurrent paraphilic activities in 117 fatal cases of autoerotic asphyxia. *British Journal of Psychiatry, 159*(3), 371–377. https://doi.org/10.1192/bjp.159.3.371

Boer, D. R., Hart, S. D., Kropp, P. R., & Webster, C. D. (2017). *Manual for version 2 of the sexual violence risk-20: Sructured professional judgement guidelines for assessing and managing risk of sexual violence.* Protect International Risk and Safety Services Inc.

Bolton, W., Lovell, K., Morgan, L., & Wood, H. (2014). *Meeting the challenge, making a difference: Working effectively to support people with personality disorder in the community.* Department of Health.

Bonnycastle, K. D. (2012). *Stranger rape: Rapists, masculinity, and penal governance.* University of Toronto Press.

Booth, B. (2010). Mentally disordered sexual offenders. In K. Harrison (Ed.), *Managing high risk sex offenders in the community: Risk management, treatment and social responsibility* (pp. 193–208). Willan. https://doi.org/10.4324/9781843929697

Bownes, I. T., O'Gorman, E. C., & Sayers, A. (1991). Rape - A comparison of stranger and acquaintance assaults. *Medicine, Science and the Law, 31*(2), 102–109. https://doi.org/10.1177/002580249103100203

Brankley, A. E., & Goodwill, A. M. (2014). Optimizing case conceptualization of sex offender needs: The utility of behavioural crime scene analysis. *Psynopsis: Canada's Psychology Magazine, 36*(1), 15–16.

Brankley, A. E., Goodwill, A. M., & Reale, K. S. (2014). Escalation from fetish burglaries to sexual violence: A retrospective case study of former Col., D. Russell Williams. *Journal of Investigative Psychology and Offender Profiling, 11*(2), 115–135. https://doi.org/10.1002/jip.1406

Brantingham, P. J., Brantingham, P. L., & Anderson, M. A. (2017). The geometry of crime and crime pattern theory. In R. Wortley & M. Townsley (Eds.), *Environmental criminology and crime analysis* (2nd ed., pp. 98–115). Routledge.

Brantingham, P. L., & Brantingham, P. J. (1981). Notes on the geometry of crime. In P. J. Brantingham & P. L. Brantingham (Eds.), *Environmental criminology* (pp. 27–54). Sage Publications, Inc.

Brennan, D. (2017). *Femicide census: Profiles of women killed by men*. Retrieved from: www.femicidecensus.org.uk

Brittain, R. P. (1970). The sadistic murderer. *Medicine, Science and the Law*, 10(4), 198–207. https://doi.org/10.1177/00258024700100040

Brookman, F. (2005). *Understanding homicide*. Sage Publications Ltd.

Brown, L. (2017). Getting groped is just part of a normal night out. *BBC News [online]*, July 18th. Retrieved from: https://www.bbc.co.uk/news/newsbeat-40633487

Brown, S. L., & Forth, A. E. (1997). Psychopathy and sexual assault: Static risk factors, emotional precursors, and rapist subtypes. *Journal of Consulting and Clinical Psychology*, 65(5), 848–857. https://doi.org/10.1037/0022-006X.65.5.848

Brownmiller, S. (1975). *Against our will: Men, women and rape*. Fawcett Books.

Bureau of Justice Statistics. (2021). *Special topics*. Retrieved January 2, 2024 from https://www.bjs.gov/index.cfm/content/dataonline/content/pub/ascii/content/data/content/index.cfm?ty=tp&tid=97

Caledon/Dufferin Victim Services. (2023). *Safety plan: Stranger violence*. Retrieved January 2, 2024 from https://www.cdvs.ca/a/uploads/Stranger-Violence-Safety-Plan%20(1)_1478098760.pdf

Campbell, J., & Corcoran, S. (2021). Libby squire murder: Accused Pawel Relowicz and his history of voyeurism and sex crimes in Hull's Avenues. *Hull Daily Mail, [online]* January 13th. Retrieved from: https://www.hulldailymail.co.uk/news/hull-east-yorkshire-news/libby-squire-murder-accused-pawel-4882281

Canadian Femicide Observatory for Justice and Accountability. (2024). *Subtypes of femicide*. Retrieved January 2, 2024 from https://femicideincanada.ca/what-is-femicide/subtypes-of-femicide/

Canter, D. (1994). Criminal shadows: Inside the mind of the serial killer. Harper Collins Publishers.

Canter, D. (2000). Offender profiling and criminal differentiation. *Legal and Criminological Psychology*, 5(1), 23–46. https://doi.org/10.1348/135532500167958

Canter, D. (2003). *Mapping murder: The secrets of geographical profiling*. Virgin Books.

Canter, D., Bennell, C., Alison, L. J., & Reddy, S. (2003). Differentiating sex offences: A behaviorally based thematic classification of stranger rapes. *Behavioral Sciences & the Law*, 21(2), 157–174. https://doi.org/10.1002/bsl.526

Canter, D., & Fritzon, K. (1998). Differentiating arsonists: A model of firesetting actions and characteristics. *Legal and Criminological Psychology*, 3(1), 73–96. https://doi.org/10.1111/j.2044-8333.1998.tb00352.x

Canter, D., & Gregory, A. (1994). Identifying the residential location of rapists. *Journal of the Forensic Science Society*, 34(3), 169–175. https://doi.org/10.1016/S0015-7368(94)72910-8

Canter, D., & Heritage, R. (1990). A multivariate model of sexual offence behaviour: Developments in 'offender profiling'. I. *The Journal of Forensic Psychiatry*, 1(2), 185–212. https://doi.org/10.1080/09585189008408469

Canter, D., & Larkin, P. (1993). The environmental range of serial rapists. *Journal of Environmental Psychology*, 13(1), 63–69. https://doi.org/10.1016/S0272-4944(05)80215-4

Canter, D., & Youngs, D. (2008a). *Applications of geographical offender profiling*. Ashgate.

Canter, D., & Youngs, D. (2008b). *Principles of geographical offender profiling*. Ashgate.

Canter, D., & Youngs, D. (2009). *Investigative psychology: Offender profiling and the analysis of criminal action*. John Wiley & Sons Ltd.

Carter, A. J., & Hollin, C. R. (2010). Characteristics of non-serial sexual homicide offenders: A review. *Psychology, Crime & Law*, 16(1–2), 25–45. https://doi.org/10.1080/10683160802621933

Carter, A. J., Hollin, C. R., Stefanska, E. B., Higgs, T., & Bloomfield, S. (2017). The use of crime scene and demographic information in the identification of non-serial sexual homicide. *International Journal of Offender Therapy and Comparative Criminology*, 61(14), 1554–1569. https://doi.org/10.1177/0306624X16630313

Castellini, G., Rellini, A. H., Appignanesi, C., Pinucci, I., Fattorini, M., Grano, E., Fisher, A. D., Cassioli, E., Lelli, L., Maggi, M., & Ricca, V. (2018). Deviance or normalcy? The relationship among paraphilic thoughts and behaviors, hypersexuality, and psychopathology in a sample of university students. *The Journal of Sexual Medicine, 15*(9), 1322–1335. https://doi.org/10.1016/j.jsxm.2018.07.015

Cecchi, R., Masotti, V., Sassani, M., Sannella, A., Agugiaro, G., Ikeda, T., Pressanto, D. M., Caroppo, E., Schirripa, M. L., Mazza, M., Kondo, T., & De Lellis, P. (2023). Femicide and forensic pathology: Proposal for a shared medico-legal methodology. *Legal Medicine, 60*, 102170. https://doi.org/10.1016/j.legalmed.2022.102170

Cerfontyne, R. (2010). *André Hanscombe complaint: Commissioner's report.* Independent Police Complaints Commission.

Chan, H. C. (2015). *Understanding sexual homicide offenders: An integrated approach.* Palgrave Macmillan.

Chan, H. C. (2017). Sexual homicide: A review of recent empirical evidence (2008 to 2015). In F. Brookman, E. R. Maguire, & M. Maguire (Eds.), *The handbook of homicide* (pp. 105–130). John Wiley & Sons Inc. https://doi.org/10.1002/9781118924501.ch7

Chan, H. C., & Beauregard, É. (2016). Non-homicidal and homicidal sexual offenders: Prevalence of maladaptive personality traits and paraphilic behaviors. *Journal of Interpersonal Violence, 31*(13), 2259–2290. https://doi.org/10.1177/0886260515575606

Chan, H. C., Beauregard, É., & Myers, W. C. (2015). Single-victim and serial sexual homicide offenders: Differences in crime, paraphilias and personality traits. *Criminal Behaviour & Mental Health, 25*(1), 66–78. https://doi.org/10.1002/cbm.1925

Chan, H. C., & Heide, K. M. (2009). Sexual homicide: A synthesis of the literature. *Trauma, Violence, & Abuse, 10*(1), 31–54. https://doi.org/10.1177/1524838008326478

Chen, Y. Y., Chen, C.-Y., & Hung, D. L. (2016). Assessment of psychiatric disorders among sex offenders: Prevalence and associations with criminal history. *Criminal Behaviour and Mental Health, 26*(1), 30–37. https://doi.org/10.1002/cbm.1926

Chéné, S., & Cusson, M. (2007). Sexual murderers and sexual aggressors: Intention and situation. In J. Proulx, É. Beauregard, M. Cusson, & A. Nicole (Eds.), *Sexual murderers: A compasrative analysis and new perspectives* (pp. 71–86). John Wilrey & Sons, Ltd.

Chesterman, P., & Sahota, K. (1998). Mentally ill sex offenders in a regional secure unit. I: Psychopathology and motvaton. *The Journal of Forensic Psychiatry, 9*(1), 150–160. https://doi.org/10.1080/09585189808402185

Child Exploitation and Online Protection Centre. (2012). A picture of abuse: A thematic assessment of the risk of contact child sexual abuse posed by those who possess indecent images of children. Retrieved from: https://www.ceop.police.uk/safety-centre/

Chopin, J., Paquette, S., & Beauregard, É. (2022). Is there an "expert" stranger rapist? *Sexual Abuse, 34*(1), 78–105. https://doi.org/10.1177/1079063221993478

Clark, S. K., Jeglic, E. L., Calkins, C., & Tatar, J. R. (2014). More than a nuisance: The prevalence and consequences of frotteurism and exhibitionism. *Sexual Abuse, 28*(1), 3–19. https://doi.org/10.1177/1079063214525643

Clarke, L. (2022). Hundreds of voyeurism and flashing reports in West Yorkshire. *Wakefield Express [online]*, January 10th. Retrieved from: https://www.wakefieldexpress.co.uk/news/crime/hundreds-of-voyeurism-and-flashing-reports-in-west-yorkshire-3521033

Cohen, L. E., & Felson, M. (1979). Social change and crime rate trends: A routine activity approach. *American Sociological Review, 44*, 588–608. https://doi.org/10.2307/2094589

Coid, J., Yang, M., Ullrich, S., Roberts, A., & Hare, R. D. (2009). Prevalence and correlates of psychopathic traits in the household population of Great Britain. *International Journal of Law and Psychiatry, 32*(2), 65–73. https://doi.org/10.1016/j.ijlp.2009.01.002

Cole, T., & Brown, J. (2011). What do senior investigating police officers want from behavioural investigative advisers? In L. Alison & L. Rainbow (Eds.), *Professionalizing offender profiling: Forensic and investigative psychology in practice* (pp. 191–205). Routledge. https://doi.org/10.4324/9780203809259

College of Policing. (2014). *National decision model*. Retrieved January 2, 2024 from https://www.college.police.uk/app/national-decision-model/national-decision-model

College of Policing. (2023a). *Identifying, assessing and managing risk*. Retrieved January 2, 2024 from https://www.college.police.uk/app/major-investigation-and-public-protection/managing-sexual-offenders-and-violent-offenders/identifying-assessing-and-managing-risk

College of Policing. (2023b). *Universities offering a professional policing degree*. Retrieved January 2, 2024 from https://www.college.police.uk/career-learning/joining-new-pc/universities-offering-professional-policing-degree

Connor, L., & Jeffay, J. (2015). Knicker thief shouts sexual comments through woman's letterbox before stealing her underwear from washing line. *Daily Mirror, [online]*, April 13th. Retrieved from: https://www.mirror.co.uk/news/uk-news/knicker-thief-shouts-sexual-comments-5512987

Cook, T. (2019). *Blacksone's senior investigating officer's handbook* (5th ed.). Oxford University Press.

Copson, G. (1995). *Coals to Newcastle? Part 1: A study of offender profiling.* Home Office Police Research Group, Special Interest Series Paper 7.

Copson, G., Badcock, R., Boon, J., & Britton, P. (1997). Editorial: Articulating a systematic approach to clinical crime profiling. *Criminal Behaviour and Mental Health*, 7(1), 13–17. https://doi.org/10.1002/cbm.142

Cornish, D. B., & Clarke, R. V. (Eds.). (2014). *The reasoning criminal: Rational choice perspectives on offending*. Transaction Publishers.

Craissati, J. (2009). Attachment problems and sex offending. In A. R. Beech, L. A. Craig, & K. D. Brown (Eds.), *Assessment and treatment of sex offenders: A handbook* (pp. 13–37). John Wilery & Sons Ltd. https://doi.org/10.1002/9780470714362

Craissati, J. (2019). *The rehabilitation of sexual offenders: Complexity, risk and desistance.* Routledge.

Craissati, J., & Blundell, R. (2013). A community service for high-risk mentally disordered sex offenders: A follow-up study. *Journal of Interpersonal Violence*, 28(6), 1178–1200. https://doi.org/10.1177/0886260512468235

Craissati, J., & Hodes, P. (1992). Mentally ill sex offenders. The experience of a regional secure unit. *The British Journal of Psychiatry*, 161(6), 846–849. https://doi.org/10.1192/bjp.161.6.846

Craissati, J., Joseph, N., & Skett, S. (Eds.). (2020). *Practitioner guide: Working with people in the criminal justice system showing personality difficulties* (3rd ed.). HM Prison & Probation Service / National Health Service. Retrieved from: https://www.gov.uk/government/publications/working-with-offenders-with-personality-disorder-a-practitioners-guide

Criminal Justice Joint Inspection. (2012). *Forging the links: Rape investigation and prosecution. A joint review by HMIC and HMCPSI.* HMIC/HMCPSI. https://hmicfrs.justiceinspectorates.gov.uk/publications/forging-the-links-rape-investigation-and-prosecution/

Cross, N. (2023). Criminal justice, actus reus and mens rea. In K. Corteen, R. Steele, N. Cross, & M. McManus (Eds.), *Forensic psychology, crime and policing* (pp. 108–113). Policy Press. https://doi.org/10.51952/9781447359418.ch019

Crown Prosecution Service. (2021). *Rape and sexual offences - Overview and index of 2021 updated guidance*. Retrieved January 2, 2024 from https://www.cps.gov.uk/legal-guidance/rape-and-sexual-offences-overview-and-index-2021-updated-guidance

Crown Prosecution Service. (2023). *Homicide: Murder, manslaughter, infanticide and causing or allowing the death or serious injury of a child or vulnerable adult*. Retrieved January 2, 2024 from https://www.cps.gov.uk/legal-guidance/homicide-murder-and-manslaughter

Daffern, M. (2011). Functional analysis. In K. Sheldon, J. Davies, & K. Howells (Eds.), *Research in practice for forensic professionals* (pp. 216–230). Routledge.

Darjee, R., & Baron, E. (2018). Recent research on sexual homicide in Scotland: Characteristics, crime scene themes, and comparison with non-homicidal sexual aggressors. In J. Proulx,

E. Beauregard, A. Carter, A. Mokros, R. Darjee, & J. James (Eds.), *Routledge international handbook of sexual homicide studies* (pp. 196–218). Routledge. https://doi.org/10.4324/9781315212289-3

Davies, A., & Dale, A. (1995). *Locating the stranger rapist.* Home Office Special Interest Series: Paper 3.

Davies, A., & Dale, A. (1996). Locating the stranger rapist. *Medicine, Science and the Law, 36*(2), 146–156. https://doi.org/10.1177/002580249603600210

Davies, A., Wittebrood, K., & Jackson, J. L. (1997). Predicting the criminal antecedents of a stranger rapist from his offence behaviour. *Science & Justice: Journal of the Forensic Science Society, 37*(3), 161–170. https://doi.org/10.1016/S1355-0306(97)72169-5

Davies, A., Wittebrood, K., & Jackson, J. L. (1998). *Predicting the criminal record of a stranger rapist.* Policing & Reducing Crime Unit: Special Interest Series Paper 12.

Davies, K., & Woodhams, J. (2019). The practice of crime linkage: A review of the literature. *Journal of Investigative Psychology and Offender Profiling, 16*(3), 169–200. https://doi.org/10.1002/jip.1531

De Block, A., & Adriaens, P. R. (2013). Pathologizing sexual deviance: A history. *The Journal of Sex Research, 50*(3–4), 276–298. https://doi.org/10.1080/00224499.2012.738259

de Oliveira Júnior, W. M., & Abdo, C. H. N. (2010). Unconventional sexual behaviors and their associations with physical, mental and sexual health parameters: A study in 18 large Brazilian cities. *Brazilian Journal of Psychiatry, 32*(3), 264–274. https://doi.org/10.1590/S1516-44462010005000013

De Veauuse Brown, N. F., & Watson, A. E. N. (2022). Differences between sexual and nonsexual homicides of women in the United States: Findings from the national violent death reporting system. *Journal of Interpersonal Violence, 37*(23–24), NP21975–NP21999. https://doi.org/10.1177/08862605211064289

de Vries Robbé, M., & de Vogel, V. (2013). Protective factors for violence risk: Bringing balance to risk assessment and management. In C. Logan & L. Johnstone (Eds.), *Managing clinical risk: A guide to effective practice* (pp. 293–310). Routledge.

Dedel, K. (2011). *Sexual assault of women by strangers.* Centre for Problem-Orientated Policing, U.S. Department of Justice.

DeFeo, J. (2020). Noncontact sexual offenses. In J. Proulx, F. Cortoni, L. A. Craig, & E. J. Letourneau (Eds.), *The Wiley handbook of what works with sexual offenders* (pp. 371–385). Wiley. https://doi.org/10.1002/9781119439325.ch21

DeLisi, M. (2019a). Psychopathy and crime are inextricably linked. In M. DeLisi (Ed.), *Routledge international handbook of psychopathy and crime* (pp. 3–12). Routledge. https://doi.org/10.4324/9781315111476

DeLisi, M. (Ed.). (2019b). *Routledge international handbook of psychopathy and crime.* Routledge. https://doi.org/10.4324/9781315111476.

DeLisi, M., Caropreso, D. E., Drury, A. J., Elbert, M. J., Evans, J. L., Heinrichs, T., & Tahja, K. M. (2016). The dark figure of sexual offending: New evidence from federal sex offenders. *Journal of Criminal Psychology, 6*(1), 3–15. https://doi.org/10.1108/JCP-12-2015-0030

Delle-Vergini, V., & Day, A. (2016). Case formulation in forensic practice: Challenges and opportunities. *The Journal of Forensic Practice, 18*(3), 240–250. https://doi.org/10.1108/JFP-01-2016-0005

Department of Health. (2009). Best practice in managing risk: Principles and evidence for best practice in the assessment and management of risk to self and others in mental health services. Department of Health, National Mental Health Risk Management Programme. Retrieved from: https://www.gov.uk/government/publications/assessing-and-managing-risk-in-mental-health-services

Dern, H., Frönd, R., Straub, U., Vick, J., & Witt, R. (2005). *Geographical behaviour of stranger offenders in violent sexual crimes.* Bundeskriminalamt.

Dietz, P. E. (1985). Sex offender profiling by the FBI: A preliminary conceptual model. In M. H. Ben-Aron, S. J. Hucker, & C. D. Webster (Eds.), *Clinical criminology: The assessment and treatment of criminal behaviour* (pp. 207–219). M & M Graphics, Clarke Institute of Psychiatry, University of Toronto.

Dietz, P. E., Hazelwood, R. R., & Warren, J. (1990). The sexually sadistic criminal and his offenses. *Bulletin of the American Academy of Psychiatry and the Law*, *18*(2), 163–178. http://jaapl.org/content/jaapl/18/2/163.full.pdf

Douglas, K. S., Blanchard, A. J. E., & Hendry, M. C. (2013b). Violence risk assessment and management: Putting structured professional judgment into practice. In C. Logan & L. Johnstone (Eds.), *Managing clinical risk: A guide to effective practice* (pp. 29–55). Routledge. https://doi.org/10.4324/9780203106433

Douglas, K. S., Hart, S. D., Webster, C. D., & Belfrage, H. (2013a). *HCR-20ᵛ³: Assessing risk for violence (Version 3) user guide*. Mental Health, Law and Policy Institute, Simon Fraser University.

Doyle, T. (2009). Privacy and perfect voyeurism. *Ethics and Information Technology*, *11*(3), 181–189. https://doi.org/10.1007/s10676-009-9195-9

Drake, C. R., & Pathé, M. (2004). Understanding sexual offending in schizophrenia. *Criminal Behaviour and Mental Health*, *14*(2), 108–120. https://doi.org/10.1002/cbm.576

Duell, M. (2014). 'I love you': Cambridge graduate stands by rapist husband who told his victim he was doing it because 'he didn't get sex from his wife'. *Daily Mail, [online]*, May 7th. Retrieved from: https://www.dailymail.co.uk/news/article-2621567/amp/Woman-stands-rapist-husband-told-victim-doing-didnt-sex-wife.html

Duff, S. (2018). *Voyeurism: A Case Study*. Palgrave Macmillan. https://doi.org/10.1007/978-3-319-97160-5

Dunsieth, N. W., Nelson, E. B., Brusman-Lovins, L., Holcomb, J. L., Beckman, D. A., Welge, J., Roby, D., Taylor, P., Soutullo, C., & McElroy, S. L. (2004). Psychiatric and legal features of 113 men convicted of sexual offenses. *The Journal of Clinical Psychiatry*, *65*(3), 293–300. https://doi.org/10.4088/jcp.v65n0302

Durkin, K. F. (2001). Telephone and sexual deviance. In C. D. Bryant (Ed.), *Encyclopedia of criminology and deviant behavior, volume III: Sexual deviance* (pp. 406–408). Brunner-Routledge.

Eells, T. D., & Lombart, K. G. (2011). Theoretical and evidence-based approaches to case formulation. In P. Sturmey & M. McMurran (Eds.), *Forensic case formulation* (pp. 1–32). John Wiley & Sons, Ltd. https://doi.org/10.1002/9781119977018.ch1

Eichinger, M., & Darjee, R. (2021). Sexual homicide in Australia and New Zealand: A description of offenders, offences and victims. *Psychiatry, Psychology and Law*, *28*(6), 885–908. https://doi.org/10.1080/13218719.2021.1894261

Elkin, M. (2023a). *Sexual offences in England and Wales overview: Year ending March 2022*. Office for National Statistics.

Elkin, M. (2023b). *Sexual offences prevalence and trends, England and Wales: Year ending March 2022*. Office for National Statistics.

Erikson, M., & Friendship, C. (2002). A typology of child abduction events. *Legal and Criminological Psychology*, *7*(1), 115–120. https://doi.org/10.1348/135532502168423

Fallon, A. C. (2007). *Index offence awareness amongst forensic staff working in a medium secure psychiatric service*. Manchester Metropolitan University: Unpublished Master of Science Dissertation.

Fallon, C. (2021). Exclusive: Over 20 indecent exposure reports every day last year, police data shows. *Channel Four News [online]*, October 12. Retrieved from: https://www.channel4.com/news/exclusive-over-20-indecent-exposure-reports-every-day-last-year-police-data-shows

Feist, A., Ashe, J., Lawrence, J., McPhee, D., & Wilson, R. (2007). *Investigating and detecting recorded offences of rape*. Home Office Online Report 18/07.

Feldman, M. P., & MacCulloch, M. J. (1971). *Homosexual behaviour: Therapy and assessment*. Pergamon Press. https://doi.org/10.1016/C2013-0-05589-2

Felitti, V. J., Anda, F., Nordenberg, D., Williamson, D. F., Spitz, A. M., Edwards, V., Koss, M. P., & Marks, J. S. (1998). Relationship of childhood abuse and household dysfunction to many of the leading causes of death in adults: The adverse childhood experiences (ACE) study. *American Journal of Preventive Medicine, 14*(4), 245–258. https://doi.org/10.1016/S0749-3797(98)00017-8

Felson, M. (2017). The routine activity approach. In R. Wortley & M. Townsley (Eds.), *Environmental criminology and crime analysis* (pp. 87–97). Routledger.

Fenton, R. (2017). Understanding the myths that new students hold about sexual violence and domestic abuse is key for prevention. *The Conversation*. Retrieved January 2, 2024 from https://theconversation.com/understanding-the-myths-that-new-students-hold-about-sexual-violence-and-domestic-abuse-is-key-for-prevention-88888

Feshbach, S. (1964). The function of aggression and the regulation of aggressive drive. *Psychological Review, 71*(4), 257–272. https://doi.org/10.1037/h0043041

Firestone, P., Kingston, D. A., Wexler, A., & Bradford, J. M. (2006). Long-term follow-up of exhibitionists: Psychological, phallometric, and offense characteristics. *Journal of the American Academy of Psychiatry and the Law, 34*(3), 349–359.

Fisher, D., & Beech, A. R. (2007). Identification of motivations for sexual murder. In J. Proulx, É. Beauregard, M. Cusson, & A. Nicole (Eds.), *Sexual murderers: A comparative analysis and new perspectives* (pp. 175–190). John Wiley & Sons Ltd.

Fisher, D., & Mair, G. (1998). *A review of classification systems for sex offenders*. Home Office Research and Statistics Directorate, Research Findings No. 78.

Flatley, J. (2017). *Overview of burglary and other household theft: England and Wales*. Office for National Statistics.

Flatley, J. (2018). *Sexual offences in England and Wales: Year ending March 2017*. Office for National Statistics.

Forsyth, C. J. (2001). Voyeurism. In C. D. Bryant (Ed.), *Encyclopedia of criminology and deviant behavior, volume III: Sexual deviance* (pp. 430–433). Brunner-Routledge.

Fossi, J. J., Clarke, D. D., & Lawrence, C. (2005). Bedroom rape: Sequences of sexual behavior in stranger assaults. *Journal of Interpersonal Violence, 20*(11), 1444–1466. https://doi.org/10.1177/0886260505278716

Freund, K. (1990). Courtship disorder. In W. L. Marshal, R. D. Laws, & H. E. Barbaree (Eds.), *Handbook of sexual assault: Issues, theories, and treatment of the offender* (pp. 195–207). Plenum Press.

Freund, K., & Blanchard, R. (1986). The concept of courtship disorder. *Journal of Sex & Marital Therapy, 12*(2), 79–82. https://doi.org/10.1080/00926238608415397

Freund, K., Watson, R., & Rienzo, D. (1988). The value of self-reports in the study of voyeurism and exhibitionism. *Annals of Sex Research, 1*(2), 243–262. https://doi.org/10.1177/107906328800100205

Friendship, C., & Beech, A. R. (2005). Reconviction of sexual offenders in England and Wales: An overview of research. *Journal of Sexual Aggression, 11*(2), 209–223. https://doi.org/10.1080/13552600500063690

Gavin, H. (2019). *Criminological and forensic psychology* (2nd ed.). Sage Publications Ltd.

Gerard, F., Mormont, C., & Kocsis, R. N. (2007). Offender profiles and crime scene patterns in belgian sexual murders. In R. N. Kocsis (Ed.), *Criminal profiling: International theory, research, and practice* (pp. 27–47). Humana Press. https://doi.org/10.1007/978-1-60327-146-2_2

Giorgetti, A., Fais, P., Giovannini, E., Palazzo, C., Filipuzzi, I., Pelletti, G., & Pelotti, S. (2022). A 70-year study of femicides at the Forensic Medicine department, University of Bologna (Italy). *Forensic Science International, 333*, 111210. https://doi.org/10.1016/j.forsciint.2022.111210

Godwin, G. M. (2001). Death by detail: A multivariate model of U.S. serial murderers' crime scene actions. In G. M. Godwin (Ed.), *Criminal psychology and forensic technology* (pp. 125–151). CRC Press LLC.

Grant, J. (2021). Indecent exposure: A serious 'nuisance' offence. *Women's History Review, 30*(7), 1219–1224. https://doi.org/10.1080/09612025.2021.2001147

Green, D. (2022). Hundreds of voyeurism and flashing reports in Sussex. *The Argus [online]*, January 6th. Retrieved from: https://www.theargus.co.uk/news/19829723.hundreds-voyeurism-flashing-reports-sussex/

Greenall, P. V. (2009). Assessing high risk offenders with personality disorder. *British Journal of Forensic Practice*, *11*(3), 14–18. https://doi.org/10.1108/14636646200900018

Greenall, P. V. (2012). Understanding sexual homicide. *Journal of Sexual Aggression*, *18*(3), 338–354. https://doi.org/10.1080/13552600.2011.596287

Greenall, P. V. (2014). *Index offence analysis in forensic clinical settings: A new application of investigative psychology?* 15th International Conference of The International Academy of Investigative Psychology, 8–10 April 2014, London Southbank University.

Greenall, P. V. (2018). Stranger sexual homicide. In J. Proulx, E. Beauregard, A. Carter, A. Mokros, R. Darjee, & J. James (Eds.), *Routledge international handbook of sexual homicide studies* (pp. 154–170). Routledge. https://doi.org/10.4324/9781315212289-3

Greenall, P. V. (2023). Forensic psychology and mental disorder. In K. Corteen, R. Steele, N. Cross, & M. McManus, (Eds.), *Forensic psychology, crime and policing* (pp. 59–64). Policy Press. https://doi.org/10.51952/9781447359418.ch010

Greenall, P. V., & Jellicoe-Jones, L. (2007). Themes and risk of sexual violence among the mentally ill: Implications for understanding and treatment. *Sexual and Relationship Therapy*, *22*(3), 323–337. https://doi.org/10.1080/14681990701391269

Greenall, P. V., & Millington, J. (2021). A sexual murder prevented? A case study of evidence-based practice. *The Journal of Forensic Psychiatry & Psychology*, *32*(5), 759–775. https://doi.org/10.1080/14789949.2021.1889014

Greenall, P. V., & Richardson, C. (2015). Adult male-on-female stranger sexual homicide: A descriptive (baseline) study from Great Britain. *Homicide Studies*, *19*(3), 237–256. https://doi.org/10.1177/1088767914530555

Greenall, P. V., & West, A. G. (2007). A study of stranger rapists from the English high security hospitals. *Journal of Sexual Aggression*, *13*(2), 151–167. https://doi.org/10.1080/13552600701661540

Greenall, P. V., & West, A. G. (2008). Investigating stranger rape. *Forensic Update, British Psychological Society*, *95*(Autumn), 36–41.

Greenall, P. V., & Wright, M. (2015). Exploring the criminal histories of stranger sexual killers. *The Journal of Forensic Psychiatry and Psychology*, *26*(2), 242–259. https://doi.org/10.1080/14789949.2014.999105

Greenall, P. V., & Wright, M. (2020). Stranger sexual homicide: An exploratory behavioural analysis of offender crime scene actions. *Journal of Sexual Aggression*, *26*(2), 163–177. https://doi.org/10.1080/13552600.2019.1606948

Greer, C. (2003). *Sex crime and the media: Sex offending and the press in a divided society*. Willan Publishing.

Griffiths, M. D. (2013). Thrilling killing and the disgust of lust: Erotophonophilia and the psychology of sexual homicide. *Psychology Today*. Retrieved January 2, 2024 from https://www.psychologytoday.com/intl/blog/in-excess/201308/thrilling-killing-and-the-disgust-lust

Grossin, C., Sibille, I., Lorin de la Grandmaison, G., Banasr, A., Brion, F., & Durigon, M. (2003). Analysis of 418 cases of sexual assault. *131*(2), 125–130. Retrieved from: https://www.sciencedirect.com/science/article/pii/S0379073802004279

Groth, A. N., & Birnbaum, H. J. (1979). *Men who rape: The psychology of the offender*. Plenum Press.

Groth, A. N., Burgess, A. W., & Holmstrom, L. L. (1977). Rape: power, anger, and sexuality. *American Journal of Psychiatry*, *134*(11), 1239–1243. https://doi.org/10.1176/ajp.134.11.1239

Grubin, D. (1994). Sexual murder. *The British Journal of Psychiatry*, *165*(5), 624–629. https://doi.org/10.1192/bjp.165.5.624

Grubin, D., & Gunn, J. (1990). *The imprisoned rapist and rape*. Department of Forensic Psychiatry, Institute of Psychiatry.

Grubin, D., H., & Kennedy, H. G. (1991). The classification of sexual offenders. *Criminal Behaviour and Mental Health, 1*, 123–129. https://doi.org/10.1002/cbm.1991.1.2.123

Grubin, D., Kelly, P., & Brunsdon, C. (2001). *Linking serious sexual assault through behaviour.* Home Office Research Study 215.

Häkkänen, H., Lindlöf, P., & Santtila, P. (2004). Crime scene actions and offender characteristics in a sample of Finnish stranger rapes. *Journal of Investigative Psychology and Offender Profiling, 1*(1), 17–32. https://doi.org/10.1002/jip.1

Hammond, L., & Youngs, D. (2011). Decay functions and criminal spatial processes: Geographical offender profiling of volume crime. *Journal of Investigative Psychology and Offender Profiling, 8*(1), 90–102. https://doi.org/10.1002/jip.132

Hanson, R. K., & Bussière, M. T. (1998). Predicting relapse: A meta-analysis of sexual offender recidivism studies. *Journal of Consulting and Clinical Psychology, 66*(2), 348–362. https://doi.org/10.1037/0022-006X.66.2.348

Hanson, R. K., & Morton-Bourgon, K. (2004). *Predictors of sexual recidivism: An updated meta-analysis.* Public Safety Canada. Retrieved from: https://www.publicsafety.gc.ca/cnt/rsrcs/pblctns/2004-02-prdctrs-sxl-rcdvsm-pdtd/2004-02-prdctrs-sxl-rcdvsm-pdtd-eng.pdf

Hare, R. D. (1993). *Without conscience: The disturbing world of the psychopaths among us.* The Guilford Press.

Hare, R. D. (1999). Psychopathy as a risk factor for violence. *Psychiatric Quarterly, 70*(3), 181–197. https://doi.org/10.1023/A:1022094925150

Hare, R. D. (2003). *Hare psychopathy checklist - revised* (2nd ed.). Multi-Health Systems, Inc.

Hare, R. D., Neumann, C. S., & Widiger, T. A. (2012). Psychopathy. In T. A. Widiger (Ed.), *The Oxford handbook of personality disorders* (pp. 478–504). Oxford University Press. https://doi.org/10.1093/oxfordhb/9780199735013.013.0022

Harris, D. A., Pedneault, A., & Knight, R. A. (2012). An exploration of burglary in the criminal histories of sex offenders referred for civil commitment. *Psychology, Crime & Law*, 1–17. https://doi.org/10.1080/1068316X.2012.678850

Harris, D. A., Smallbone, S., Dennison, S., & Knight, R. A. (2009). Specialization and versatility in sexual offenders referred for civil commitment. *Journal of Criminal Justice, 37*(1), 37–44. https://doi.org/10.1016/j.jcrimjus.2008.12.002

Harris, G. T., Rice, M. E., Quinsey, V. L., & Cormier, C. A. (2015). *Violent offenders: Appraising and managing risk* (3rd ed.). American Psychological Association.

Harris, J., & Grace, S. (1999). *A question of evidence? Investigating and prosecuting rape in the 1990s.* Home Office Research Study 196.

Hart, S. D., & Cooke, D. J. (2013). Another look at the (im-)precision of individual risk estimates made using actuarial risk assessment instruments. *Behavioral Sciences & the Law, 31*(1), 81–102. https://doi.org/10.1002/bsl.2049

Hart, S. D., Kropp, P. R., Watt, K. A., Darjee, R., Davis, M. R., Klaver, J., Laws, D. R., & Logan, C. (2022). *RSVP-V2: Version 2 of the risk for sexual violence protocol.* Protect International.

Hart, S. D., & Logan, C. (2011). Formulation of violence risk using evidence-based assessments: The structured professional judgment approach. In P. Sturmey & M. McMurran (Eds.), *Forensic case formulation* (pp. 81–106). John Wiley & Sons, Ltd. https://doi.org/10.1002/9781119977018.ch4

Hart, S. D., Michie, C., & Cooke, D. J. (2007). Precision of actuarial risk assessment instruments: Evaluating the 'margins of error' of group v. individual predictions of violence. *The British Journal of Psychiatry, 190*(49), s60–s65. https://doi.org/10.1192/bjp.190.5.s60

Hart, S. D., Sturmey, P., Logan, C., & McMurran, M. (2011). Forensic case formulation. *International Journal of Forensic Mental Health, 10*(2), 118–126. https://doi.org/10.1080/14999013.2011.577137

Hazelwood, R. R. (2017). Analyzing the rape and profiling the offender. In R. R. Hazelwood & A. W. Burgess (Eds.), *Practical aspects of rape investigation: A multidisciplinary approach* (5th ed., pp. 97–122). CRC Press. https://doi.org/10.1201/9781315316369

Hazelwood, R. R., & Burgess, A. G. (2017). The behavioral-orientated interview of rape victims: The key to profiling. In R. R. Hazelwood & A. G. Burgess (Eds.), *Practical aspects of rape investigation: A multidisciplinary approach* (5th ed., pp. 79–96). CRC Press. https://doi.org/10.1201/9781315316369

Healey, J. (2006). The etiology of paraphilia: A dichotomous model. In E. W. Hickey (Ed.), *Sex crimes and paraphilia*. Pearson Education, Inc.

Hearnden, I., & Magill, C. (2004). *Decision-making by house burglars: Offenders' perspectives*. Home Office, Findings 249.

Heide, K. M. (1992). *Why kids kill parents*. Sage Publications, Inc.

Heil, P., & Simons, D. (2008). Multiple paraphilias: Prevalence, etiology, assessment, and treatment. In D. R. Laws & W. T. O'Donohue (Eds.), *Sexual deviance: Theory, assessment, and treatment* (2nd ed., pp. 527–556). The Guilford Press.

Helfgott, J. B. (2008). *Criminal behavior: Theories, typologies, and criminal justice*. Sage Publications, Inc.

Helmus, L. M., Lee, S. C., Phenix, A., Hanson, R. K., & Thornton, D. (2021). *Static-99R & static-2002R evaluators' workbook*. Society for the Advancement of Actuarial Risk Needs Assessment. Retrieved from: https://www.stopinc.us/STOP/FA2022handouts/Wilson_handouts/a-NEW-Static_Evaluators_Workbook_2021-09-28.pdf

Her Majesty's Inspectorate of Constabulary. (2007). Without consent: A report on the joint review of the investigation and prosecution of rape offences. Her Majesty's Inspectorate of Constabulary.

Herman, J. L. (1990). Sex offenders: A feminist perspective. In W. L. Marshal, R. D. Laws, & H. E. Barbaree (Eds.), *Handbook of sexual assault: Issues, theories, and treatment of the offender* (pp. 177–193). Plenum Press.

Hickman, S. E., & Muehlenhard, C. L. (1997). College women's fears and precautionary behaviors relating to acqaintance rape and stranger rape. *Psychology of Women Quarterly*, 21, 527–547. https://doi.org/10.1111/j.1471-6402.1997.tb00129.x

Higgs, T., Carter, A. J., Tully, R. J., & Browne, K. D. (2017). Sexual murder typologies: A systematic review. *Aggression and Violent Behavior*, 35, 1–12. https://doi.org/10.1016/j.avb.2017.05.004

Higgs, T., Stefanska, E. B., Carter, A. J., & Browne, K. D. (2017). The developmental and criminal histories of subgroups of sexual murderers engaging, or not engaging, in post mortem sexual interference, compared to rapists. *Journal of Criminal Justice*, 53, 92–101. https://doi.org/10.1016/j.jcrimjus.2017.10.001

Hill, A., Habermann, N., Klusmann, D., Berner, W., & Briken, P. (2008). Criminal recidivism in sexual homicide perpetrators. *International Journal of Offender Therapy and Comparative Criminology*, 52(1), 5–20. https://doi.org/10.1177/0306624x07307450

HM Inspectorate of Prisons. (2007). *The mental health of prisoners: A thematic review of the care and support of prisoners with mental health needs*. HM Inspectorate of Prisons.

HM Prison & Probation Service. (2022). *OSAys sexual reoffending predictor (OSP): Guidance for practitioners*. HM Prison & Probation Service. https://insidetime.org/wp-content/uploads/2021/12/Policy-Framework-Implementation-and-use-of-oasys-sexual-reoffending-predictor-osp-May-2021.pdf

Hocken, K., & Thorne, K. (2012). Voyeurisim, exhibitionism and other non-contact sexual offences. In B. Winder & P. Banyard (Eds.), *A psychologist's casebook of crime: From arson to voyeurism* (pp. 243–263). Palghrave Mcmillan.

Hodelet, N. (2001). Psychosis and offending in British Columbia: Characteristics of a secure hospital population. *Criminal Behaviour & Mental Health*, 11(3), 163–172. https://doi.org/10.1002/cbm.385

Hollender, M. H. (1997). Genital exhibitionism in men and women. In L. B. Schlesinger & E. Revitch (Eds.), *Sexual dynamics of anti-social behaviour* (pp. 119–131). Charles C. Thomas Publisher, Ltd.

Holmes, R. M., & Holmes, S. T. (2009). *Profiling violent crimes: An investigative tool* (4th ed.). Sage Publications, Inc.

Hood, R., Shute, S., Feilzer, M., & Wilcox, A. (2002). *Reconviction rates of serious sex offenders and assessment of their risk*. Home Office Findings 164.

Hooley, J. M., Butcher, J. N., Nock, K., & Mineka, S. (2017). *Abnormal psychology* (17th ed.). Pearson Education Limited.

House, J. C. (1997). Towards a practical application of offender profiling: The RNC's criminal suspect prioritization system. In J. L. Jackson & D. A. Bekerian (Eds.), *Offender profiling: Theory, research and practice* (pp. 177–190). John Wiley & Sons, Ltd.

House of Commons. (2018). *Sexual harassment of women and girls in public places*. House of Commons, Women and Equalities Committee, Sixth Report of Session 2017–19. Retrieved from: https://publications.parliament.uk/pa/cm201719/cmselect/cmwomeq/701/701.pdf

House of Commons Home Affairs Committee. (2022). *Investigation and prosecutionn of rape: Eighth report of session 2021–2022*. House of Commons. https://committees.parliament.uk/publications/9600/documents/166175/default/

Jackson, J. L., van den Eshof, P., & de Kleuver, E. E. (1997). A research approach to offender profiling. In J. L. Jackson & D. A. Bekerian (Eds.), *Offender profiling: Theory, research and practice* (pp. 107–132). John Wiley & Sons.

James, J., & Proulx, J. (2014). A psychological and developmental profile of sexual murderers: A systematic review. *Aggression and Violent Behavior*, *19*(5), 592–607. https://doi.org/10.1016/j.avb.2014.08.003

Jones, G., Huckle, P., & Tanaghow, A. (1992). Command hallucinations, schizophrenia and sexual assaults. *Irish Journal of Psychological Medicine*, *9*(1), 47–49. https://doi.org/10.1017/S0790966700013938

Jones, J. S., Wynn, B. N., Kroeze, B., Dunnuck, C., & Rossman, L. (2004). Comparison of sexual assaults by strangers versus known assailants in a community-based population. *The American Journal of Emergency Medicine*, *22*(6), 454–459. https://doi.org/10.1016/j.ajem.2004.07.020

Jones, S., & Chan, H. C. (2019). The psychopathic-sexually sadistic offender. In M. DeLisi (Ed.), *Routledge International Handbook of Psychopathy and Crime* (pp. 398–412). Routledge. https://doi.org/10.4324/9781315111476

Joyal, C. C., & Carpentier, J. (2017). The prevalence of paraphilic interests and behaviors in the general population: A provincial survey. *The Journal of Sex Research*, *54*(2), 161–171. https://doi.org/10.1080/00224499.2016.1139034

Joyal, C. C., & Carpentier, J. (2021). Concordance and discordance between paraphilic interests and behaviors: A follow-up study. *The Journal of Sex Research*, 1–6. https://doi.org/10.1080/00224499.2021.1986801

Joyal, C. C., Cossette, A., & Lapierre, V. (2015). What exactly is an unusual sexual fantasy? *The Journal of Sexual Medicine*, *12*(2), 328–340. https://doi.org/10.1111/jsm.12734

Kahn, R. E., Jackson, K., Keiser, K., Ambroziak, G., & Levenson, J. S. (2021). Adverse childhood experiences among sexual offenders: Associations with sexual recidivism risk and psychopathology. *Sexual Abuse*, *33*(7), 839–866. https://doi.org/10.1177/1079063220970031

Kahneman, D. (2012). *Thinking, fast and slow*. Penguin Books.

Kasmi, Y., Duggan, C., & Völlm, B. (2020). A comparison of long-term medium secure patients within NHS and private and charitable sector units in England. *Criminal Behaviour and Mental Health*, *30*(1), 38–49. https://doi.org/10.1002/cbm.2141

Kaylor, L. E., & Jeglic, E. L. (2019). Exhibitionism. In W. T. O'Donohue & P. A. Schewe (Eds.), *Handbook of sexual assault and sexual assault prevention* (pp. 745–760). Springer International Publishing. https://doi.org/10.1007/978-3-030-23645-8_45

Kaylor, L. E., & Jeglic, E. L. (2021). Non-contact paraphilic disorders and offending. In L. A. Craig (Ed.), *Sexual deviance: Understanding and managing deviant sexual interests and paraphilic disorders* (pp. 171–188). John Wiley & Sons, Inc. https://doi.org/10.1002/9781119771401.ch11

Kelly, T. (2023a). Police professionalisation. In K. Corteen, R. Steele, N. Cross, & M. McManus (Eds.), *Forensic psychology, crime and policing* (pp. 198–203). Policy Press. https://doi.org/10.51952/9781447359418.ch033

Kelly, T. (2023b). Policing and mental health. In K. Corteen, R. Steele, N. Cross, & M. McManus (Eds.), *Forensic psychology, crime and policing* (pp. 251–256). Policy Press. https://doi.org/10.51952/9781447359418.ch041

Keppel, R. D., & Walter, R. (1999). Profiling killers: A revised classification model for understanding sexual murder. *International Journal of Offender Therapy and Comparative Criminology, 43*(4), 417–437. https://doi.org/10.1177/0306624x99434002

Kern, S. G., & Peterson, Z. D. (2020). From freewill to force: Examining types of coercion and psychological outcomes in unwanted sex. *The Journal of Sex Research, 57*(5), 570–584. https://doi.org/10.1080/00224499.2019.1671302

Kerr, K. J., Beech, A. R., & Murphy, D. (2013). Sexual homicide: Definition, motivation and comparison with other forms of sexual offending. *Aggression and Violent Behavior, 18*(1), 1–10. https://doi.org/10.1016/j.avb.2012.05.006

Kewley, S., & Blandford, M. (2017). The development of the active risk management system. *Journal of Criminal Psychology, 7*(3), 155–167. https://doi.org/10.1108/JCP-10-2016-0034

Kind, S. S. (2008). Navigational ideas and the Yorkshire Ripper investigation. In D. Canter & D. Youngs (Eds.), *Principles of Geographical offender profiling* (pp. 21–31). Ashgate.

Kingston, D. A., Olver, M. E., Harris, M., Wong, S. C. P., & Bradford, J. M. (2015). The relationship between mental disorder and recidivism in sexual offenders. *International Journal of Forensic Mental Health, 14*(1), 10–22. https://doi.org/10.1080/14999013.2014.974088

Knight, R. A. (1999). Validation of a typology for rapists. *Journal of Interpersonal Violence, 14*(3), 303–330. https://doi.org/10.1177/088626099014003006

Knight, R. A., & Prentky, R. A. (1990a). Classifying sexual offenders: The development and corroboration of taxonomic models. In W. L. Marshal, R. D. Laws, & H. E. Barbaree (Eds.), *Handbook of sexual assault: Issues, theories, and treatment of the offender* (pp. 23–52). Plenum Press.

Knight, R. A., & Prentky, R. A. (1990b). *MTC:R3 criteria, scales, component rating sheets, and flow chart aids*. Brandeis University.

Knight, R. A., Warren, J. I., Reboussin, R., & Soley, B. J. (1998). Predicting rapist type from crime-scene variables. *Criminal Justice and Behavior, 25*(1), 46-80. https://doi.org/10.1177/0093854898025001004

Knox, P. (2020). Sex fiend search: Cops hunt park sex attacker who preys on lone women after two victims dragged and assaulted in West London. *The Sun [online]*, September 14th. Retrieved from: *https://www.thesun.co.uk/news/12660103/sex-attack-park-west-london-police-search/*

Kocsis, R. N., Cooksey, R. W., & Irwin, H. J. (2002a). Psychological profiling of offender characteristics from crime behaviors in serial rape offences. *International Journal of Offender Therapy and Comparative Criminology, 46*(2), 144–169. https://doi.org/10.1177/0306624x02462003

Kocsis, R. N., Cooksey, R. W., & Irwin, H. J. (2002b). Psychological profiling of sexual murders: An empirical model. *International Journal of Offender Therapy and Comparative Criminology, 46*(5), 532–554. https://doi.org/10.1177/030662402236739

Kropp, P. R., & Hart, S. D. (2015). *SARA-V3: User guide for the third edition of the spousal assault risk assessment guide*. ProActive Solutions Inc.

Langevin, R., Ben-Aron, M., Wright, P., Marchese, V., & Handy, L. (1988). The sex killer. *Annals of Sex Research, 1*(2), 263–301. https://doi.org/10.1007/bf00852801

Långström, N., & Seto, M. C. (2006). Exhibitionistic and voyeuristic behavior in a Swedish national population survey. *Archives of Sexual Behavior, 35*(4), 427–435. https://doi.org/10.1007/s10508-006-9042-6

Lawrence, C., Fossi, J., & Clarke, D. (2010). A sequential examination of offenders' verbal strategies during stranger rapes: The influence of location. *Psychology, Crime & Law, 16*(5), 381–400. https://doi.org/10.1080/10683160902754964

Lehmann, R. J. B., Goodwill, A. M., Gallasch-Nemitz, F., Biedermann, J., & Dahle, K.-P. (2013). Applying crime scene analysis to the prediction of sexual recidivism in stranger rapes. *Law and Human Behavior, 37*(4), 241–254. https://doi.org/10.1037/lhb0000015

Lewis, E. T., & Dwyer, R. G. (2018). Psychosis and sexual offending: A review of current literature. *International Journal of Offender Therapy and Comparative Criminology*, 62(11), 3372–3384. https://doi.org/10.1177/0306624X17740016

Linehan, M. M. (2015). *DBT skills training manual* (2nd ed.). The Guilford Press.

Logan, C. (2014). The HCR-20 version 3: A case study in risk formulation. *International Journal of Forensic Mental Health*, 13(2), 172–180. https://doi.org/10.1080/14999013.2014.906516

Logan, C. (2016). Risk formulation: The new frontier in risk assessment and management. In D. R. Laws & W. O'Donohue (Eds.), *Treatment of sex offenders: Strengths and weaknesses in assessment and intervention* (pp. 83–105). Springer. https://doi.org/10.1007/978-3-319-25868-3_4

Long, J., Wertans, E., Harper, K., Brennan, D., Harvey, H., Allen, R., & Elliott, K. (2019). *Femicide census: UK femicides 2009–2018*. Retrieved from: www.femicidecensus.org

Longpré, N., Guay, J.-P., & Knight, R. A. (2019). MTC sadism scale: Toward a dimensional assessment of severe sexual sadism with behavioral markers. *Assessment*, 26(1), 70–84. https://doi.org/10.1177/1073191117737377

Loveridge-Greene, O. (2021). Women are being injected with date rape drugs in pubs and nightclubs. *Independent [Online]*, October 20th. Retrieved from: https://www.independent.co.uk/news/uk/crime/women-injected-date-rape-nightclubs-b1941634.html

Lowenstein, L. F. (2002). Fetishes and their associated behavior. *Sexuality and Disability*, 20(2), 135–147. https://doi.org/10.1023/A:1019882428372

Lundrigan, S. (2009). *A multivariate model of serial sexual murder*. Anglia Ruskin University: Unpublished Manuscript.

Lundrigan, S., & Canter, D. (2001a). A multivariate analysis of serial murderers' disposal site location choice. *Journal of Environmental Psychology*, 21(4), 423–432. https://doi.org/10.1006/jevp.2001.0231

Lundrigan, S., & Canter, D. (2001b). Spatial patterns of serial murder: An analysis of disposal site location choice. *Behavioral Sciences & the Law*, 19(4), 595–610. https://doi.org/10.1002/bsl.431

Lundrigan, S., & Czarnomski, S. (2006). Spatial characteristics of serial sexual assault in New Zealand. *Australian & New Zealand Journal of Criminology*, 39(2), 218–231. https://doi.org/10.1375/acri.39.2.218

Lundrigan, S., Dhami, M. K., & Agudelo, K. (2019). Factors predicting conviction in stranger rape cases. *Frontiers in Psychology*, 10(526). https://doi.org/10.3389/fpsyg.2019.00526

MacCulloch, M. (1993). Correspondence: The trial of Peter Sutcliffe. *The Journal of Forensic Psychiatry*, 4(3), 583–589. https://doi.org/10.1080/09585189308408226

MacCulloch, M. J., Bailey, J., & Robinson, C. (1995). Mentally disordered attackers and killers: Towards a taxonomy. *The Journal of Forensic Psychiatry*, 6(1), 41–61. https://doi.org/10.1080/09585189508409875

MacCulloch, M. J., Gray, N., & Watt, A. (2000). Brittain's sadistic murderer syndrome reconsidered: An associative account of the aetiology of sadistic sexual fantasy. *The Journal of Forensic Psychiatry*, 11(2), 401–418. https://doi.org/10.1080/09585180050142606

MacCulloch, M. J., Snowden, P. R., Wood, P. J., & Mills, H. E. (1983). Sadistic fantasy, sadistic behaviour and offending. *The British Journal of Psychiatry*, 143(1), 20–29. https://doi.org/10.1192/bjp.143.1.20

Macdonald, S. (2018). *Text, cases and materials on criminal law* (2nd ed.). Pearson.

Marsh, P. J., Odlaug, B. L., Thomarios, N., Davis, A. A., Buchanan, S. N., Meyer, C. S., & Grant, J. E. (2010). Paraphilias in adult psychiatric inpatients. *Annals of Clinical Psychiatry*, 22(2), 129–134.

Marshall, W. L. (2007). Diagnostic issues, multiple paraphilias, and comorbid disorders in sexual offenders: Their incidence and treatment. *Aggression and Violent Behavior*, 12(1), 16–35. https://doi.org/10.1016/j.avb.2006.03.001

Marshall, W. L., & Barbaree, H. E. (1990). An integrated theory of the etiology of sexual offending. In W. L. Marshal, D. R. Laws, & H. E. Barbaree (Eds.), *Handbook of sexual assault: Issues, theories, and treatment of the offender* (pp. 257–275). Plenum Press.

Marshall, W. L., & Marshall, L. E. (2000). The origins of sexual offending. *Trauma, Violence, & Abuse, 1*(3), 250–263. https://doi.org/10.1177/1524838000001003003

Martineau, M., & Beauregard, E. (2016). Journey to murder: Examining the correlates of criminal mobility in sexual homicide. *Police Practice and Research, 17*(1), 68–83. https://doi.org/10.1080/15614263.2014.994215

Matheson, J. (2013). *An overview of sexual offending in England and Wales*. Ministry of Justice, Home Office and the Office for National Statistics.

McCabe, M. P., & Wauchope, M. (2005). Behavioral characteristics of men accused of rape: Evidence for different types of rapists. *Archives of Sexual Behavior, 34*(2), 241–253. https://doi.org/10.1007/s10508-005-1801-2

McCann, J. T. (2000). Borderline personality dynamics, fetishism and burglary in adolescence. *American Journal of Forensic Psychology, 18*(3), 5–15.

McElroy, S. L., Soutullo, C. A., Taylor Jr, P., Nelson, E. B., Beckman, D. A., Brusman, L. A., Ombaba, J. M., Strakowski, S. M., & Keck Jr, P. E. (1999). Psychiatric features of 36 men convicted of sexual offenses. *The Journal of Clinical Psychiatry, 60*(6), 414–420. https://doi.org/10.4088/JCP.v60n0613

McMahon, S., & Farmer, G. L. (2011). An updated measure for assessing subtle rape myths. *Social Work Research, 35*(2), 71–81. https://doi.org/10.1093/swr/35.2.71

McManus, S., Bebbington, P., Jenkins, R., & Brugha, T. (2016). *Mental health and wellbeing in England: Adult psychiatric morbidity survey 2014*. NHS Digital.

McManus, S., Meltzer, H., Brugha, T., Bebbington, P., & Jenkins, R. (2007). *Adult psychiatric morbidity in England, 2007: Results of a household survey*. The NHS Information Centre for Health and Social Care.

McNally, M. R., & Fremouw, W. J. (2014). Examining risk of escalation: A critical review of the exhibitionistic behavior literature. *Aggression and Violent Behavior, 19*(5), 474–485. https://doi.org/0.1016/j.avb.2014.07.001 (Aggression and Violent Behavior)

McNiel, D. E., Eisner, J. P., & Binder, R. L. (2000). The relationship between command hallucinations and violence. *Psychiatric Services, 51*(10), 1288–1292. https://doi.org/10.1176/appi.ps.51.10.1288

Meloy, J. R. (2006). Empirical basis and forensic application of affective and predatory violence. *Australian and New Zealand Journal of Psychiatry, 40*(6–7), 539–547. https://doi.org/10.1080/j.1440-1614.2006.01837.x

Mews, A., Di Bella, L., & Purver, M. (2017). *Impact evaluation of the prison-based core sex offender treatment programme*. Ministry of Justice Analytical Series.

Mind. (2020). *Psychosis*. MIND. Retrieved from: www.mind.org.uk

Ministry of Justice. (2022). *Offending behaviour programmes and interventions*. Retrieved January 2, 2024 from https://www.gov.uk/guidance/offending-behaviour-programmes-and-interventions

Ministry of Justice. (2023). *Multi-agency public protection arrangements (MAPPA): Guidance*. Retrieved January 2, 2024 from https://www.gov.uk/government/publications/multi-agency-public-protection-arrangements-mappa-guidance

Modern Propensities. (1791). Modern propensities; or, an essay on the art of strangling. Illustrated with several anecdotes with memoirs of Susannah Hill and a summary of her trial at the Old-Bailey, September 16, 1791, on the charge of hanging Francis Kotzwarra. Gale ECCO, Print Editions (2010).

Mokros, A., Schilling, F., Eher, R., & Nitschke, J. (2012). The severe sexual sadism scale: Cross-validation and scale properties. *Psychological Assessment, 24*(3), 764–769. https://doi.org/10.1037/a0026419

Moran, R. (1985). The origin of insanity as a special verdict: The trial for treason of James Hadfield (1800). *Law & Society Review, 19*(3), 487–519. https://doi.org/10.2307/3053574

Morrison, S. (2021). Undercover police to patrol bars and clubs under plans to help protect women in wake of Sarah Everard's death. *Evening Standard [Online]*, March 16th. Retrieved from https://www.standard.co.uk/news/uk/undercover-police-nightclubs-bars-protect-women-sarah-everard-b924306.html

Moser, C., & Kleinplatz, P. J. (2020). Conceptualization, history, and future of the paraphilias. *Annual Review of Clinical Psychology, 16*(1), 379–399. https://doi.org/10.1146/annurev-clinpsy-050718-095548

Mulder, R. T. (2021). ICD-11 Personality disorders: Utility and implications of the new model. *Frontiers in Psychiatry, 12*(709). https://doi.org/10.3389/fpsyt.2021.655548

Myers, W. C., Chan, H. C., Vo, E. J., & Lazarou, E. (2010). Sexual sadism, psychopathy, and recidivism in juvenile sexual murderers. *Journal of Investigative Psychology and Offender Profiling, 7*(1), 49–58. https://doi.org/10.1002/jip.113

Myhill, A., & Allen, J. (2002). *Rape and sexual assault of women: The extent and nature of the problem*. Home Office Research Study 237.

National Police Chief's Council. (2017). *New tailored approach to managing registered sex offenders introduced*. Retrieved January 2, 2024 from https://news.npcc.police.uk/releases/new-tailored-approach-to-managing-registered-sex-offenders-introduced

National Policing Improvement Agency. (2010). *Guidance on investigating and prosecuting rape: Abridged edition*. National Policing Improvement Agency.

Nee, C., & Meenaghan, A. (2006). Expert decision making in burglars. *The British Journal of Criminology, 46*(5), 935–949. https://doi.org/10.1093/bjc/azl013

Nitschke, J., & Marshall, W. L. (2018). An evaluation of assessments of sexual sadism. In J. Proulx, E. Beauregard, A. Carter, A. Mokros, R. Darjee, & J. James (Eds.), *Routledge international handbook of sexual homicide studies* (pp. 303–316). Routledge. Retrieved from: https://www.routledgehandbooks.com/doi/10.4324/9781315212289-18

Noguchi, M., & Kato, S. (2010). A case of Williams syndrome with glove fetishism. *Psychiatry and Clinical Neurosciences, 64*(6), 663–663. https://doi.org/10.1111/j.1440-1819.2010.02147.x

Nuttall, A. (2021). Revealed: Scale of flashing and voyeurism in North Wales - and how many offenders went unpunished. *Daily Post [online]*, October 25th. Retrieved from: https://www.dailypost.co.uk/news/north-wales-news/revealed-scale-flashing-voyeurism-north-21889157

Office for Students. (2022). Takling sexual misconduct in universities and colleges. *Insight*, November 15th. Retrieved from: https://www.officeforstudents.org.uk/publications/tackling-sexual-misconduct-in-universities-and-colleges/

Öncü, F., Türkcan, S., Canbek, Ö., Yesilbursa, D., & Uygur, N. (2009). Fetishism and kleptomania: A case report in forensic Psychiatry. *Noro-Psikyatri Arsivi, 46*(3), 125–128. Retrieved from: https://www.proquest.com/scholarly-journals/fetishism-kleptomania-case-report-forensic/docview/225147989/se-2?accountid=48106

Osterburg, J. W., Ward, R. H., & Miller, L. S. (2019). *Criminal investigation: A method for reconstructing the past* (8th ed.). Routledge.

Patrick, W. L. (2017). 4 signs that a stranger poses danger: Not paranoia, but preparedness. How to seperate the helpful from the harmful. *Psychology Today*. Retrieved January 2, 2024 from https://www.psychologytoday.com/us/blog/why-bad-looks-good/201703/4-signs-stranger-poses-danger

Pedneault, A. (2018). Sexually coercive decision making: A rational choice approach. In P. Lussier & É. Beauregard (Eds.), *Sexual offending: A criminological perspective* (pp. 44–62). Routledge.

Pedneault, A., Beauregard, E., Harris, D. A., & Knight, R. A. (2015). Rationally irrational: The case of sexual burglary. *Sexual Abuse, 27*(4), 376–397. https://doi.org/10.1177/1079063213511669

Pedneault, A., Harris, D. A., & Knight, R. A. (2012). Toward a typology of sexual burglary: Latent class findings. *Journal of Criminal Justice, 40*(4), 278–284. https://doi.org/10.1016/j.jcrimjus.2012.05.004

Pendse, S. G. (2012). Ethical hazards: A motive, means, and opportunity approach to curbing corporate unethical behavior. *Journal of Business Ethics, 107*(3), 265–279. https://doi.org/10.1007/s10551-011-1037-0

Phillips, J. (2021). Just one in five London indecent exposure cases lead to convictions. *London News [Online]*, October 11th. Retrieved from: https://londonnewsonline.co.uk/just-one-in-five-london-indecent-exposure-cases-lead-to-convictions/#:~:text=More%20than%202%2C000%20crimes%20of%20flashing%20and%20sexual,54%20offences%20for%20every%20100%2C000%20in%20the%20borough

Phillips, S. L., Heads, T. C., Taylor, P. J., & Hill, G. M. (1999). Sexual offending and antisocial sexual behavior among patients with schizophrenia. *Journal of Clinical Psychiatry*, 60(3), 170–175. https://doi.org/10.4088/JCP.v60n0304

Pietsch, N. (2015). *Sexual femicide.* Learning Network Brief (30). Centre for Research and Education on Violence against Women and Children. Retrieved from: http://www.vawlearningnetwork.ca

Polaschek, D. L. L. (1997). New Zealand rapists: An examination of subtypes. In G. M. Habermann (Ed.), *Looking back and moving forward: 50 years of New Zealand psychology* (pp. 224–231). New Zealand Psychological Society.

Polaschek, D. L. L., & Gannon, T. A. (2004). The implicit theories of rapists: What convicted offenders tell us. *Sexual Abuse*, 16(4), 299–314. https://doi.org/10.1177/107906320401600404

Porter, S., Fairweather, D., Drugge, J., Herve, H., Birt, A., & Boer, D. P. (2000). Profiles of psychopathy in incarcerated sexual offenders. *Criminal Justice and Behavior*, 27(2), 216–233. https://doi.org/10.1177/0093854800027002005

Powis, B. (2002). *Offender's risk of serious harm: A literature review.* Home Office Research, Development and Statistics Directorate. Occasional Paper No 81.

Prentky, R. A., Burgess, A. W., Rokous, F., Lee, A., Hartman, C., Ressler, R. K., & Douglas, J. D. (1989). The presumptive role of fantasy in serial sexual homicide. *American Journal of Psychiatry*, 146(7), 887–891. https://doi.org/10.1176/ajp.146.7.887

Proulx, J. (2008). Sexual murderers: Theories, assessment and treatment. In A. J. R. Harris & C. A. Pagé (Eds.), *Sexual homicide and paraphilias: The correctional services of Canada's expert forum 2007.* Correctional Services of Canada. Retrieved from: https://www.csc-scc.gc.ca/research/shp2007-paraphil12-eng.shtml

Proulx, J., & Beauregard, É. (2008). Decision making during the offending process: An assessment among subtypes of sexual aggressors of women. In A. R. Beech, L. A. Craig, & K. D. browne (Eds.), *Assessment and treatment of sexual offenders* (pp. 181–197). John Wiley & sons Ltd.

Proulx, J., & Sauvêtre, N. (2007). Sexual murderers and sexual aggressors: Psychopathological considerations. In J. Proulx, E. Beauregard, M. Cusson, & A. Nicole (Eds.), *Sexual murderers: A comparative analysis and new perspectives* (pp. 51–69). John Wiley & Sons, Ltd.

Przbylski, R. (2015). *Recidivism of adult sexual offenders.* U.S. Department of Justice. Retrieved from: https://www.ojp.gov/ncjrs/virtual-library/abstracts/recidivism-adult-sexual-offenders

Putwain, D. (2012). Burglary. In B. Winder & P. Banyard (Eds.), *A psychologist's casebook of crime: From arson to voyeurism* (pp. 24–40). Palghrave Mcmillan.

Rabinowitz Greenberg, S. R., Firestone, P., Bradford, J. M., & Greenberg, D. M. (2002). Prediction of recidivism in exhibitionists: Psychological, phallometric, and offense factors. *Sexual Abuse: A Journal of Research and Treatment*, 14(4), 329–347. https://doi.org/10.1177/107906320201400404

Radford, J., & Russell, D. E. H. (Eds.). (1992). *Femicide: The politics of woman killing.* Open University Press.

Rengert, G. F. (2004). The journey to crime. In G. Bruinsma, H. Elffers, & J. de Keijser (Eds.), *Punishment, places and perpetrators: Developments in criminology and criminal justice research* (pp. 169–181). Routledge.

Ressler, R. K., Burgess, A. W., & Douglas, J. E. (1988). *Sexual homicide: Patterns and motives.* Simon & Schuster.

Ressler, R. K., Douglas, J. E., Burgess, A. W., & Burgess, A. G. (1992). *Crime classification manual: The standard system for investigating and classifying violent crimes.* Simon & Shuster Ltd.

Revitch, E. (1978). Sexually motivated burglaries. *Journal of the American Academy of Psychiatry and the Law*, 6(3), 277–283. http://jaapl.org/content/jaapl/6/3/277.full.pdf

Rhodes, W. M., & Conly, C. (1981). Crime and mobility: An empirical study. In P. J. Brantingham & P. L. Brantingham (Eds.), *Environmental criminology* (pp. 167–188). Sage Publications, Inc.

Riedel, M. (1993). *Stranger violence: A theoretical inquiry. Current Issues in Criminal Justice*, Vol. 1. Garland Publishing, Inc.

Risk Management Authority. (2011). *Framework for risk assessment, management and evaluation: FRAME*. Retrieved from: https://www.rma.scot/standards-guidelines/frame/

Risk Management Authority. (2018). *Standards & guidelines: Risk assessment report writing*. Retrieved from: https://www.rma.scot/standards-guidelines/risk-assessment/

Risk Management Authority. (2020). *Sexual offending*. Retrieved January 2, 2024 from https://www.rma.scot/rated/sexual-offending/

Roberts, J. V., & Grossman, M. G. (1993). Sexual homicide in Canada: A descriptive analysis. *Sexual Abuse: A Journal of Research and Treatment*, 6(1), 5–25. https://doi.org/10.1177/107906329300600101

Rossmo, D. K. (1997). Geographic profiling. In J. L. Jackson & D. A. Bekerian (Eds.), *Offender profiling: Theory, research and practice* (pp. 159–175). John Wiley & Sons Ltd.

Rossmo, D. K. (2000). *Geographic profiling*. CRC Press LLC.

Rossmo, D. K. (2018). Geoprofiling serial sexual homicide. In J. Proulx, E. Beauregard, A. Carter, A. Mokros, R. Darjee, & J. James (Eds.), *Routledge international handbook of sexual homicide studies* (pp. 544–561). Routledge. https://doi.org/10.4324/9781315212289-3

Rossmo, D. K., Davies, A., & Patrick, M. (2004). *Exploring the geo-demographic and distance relationships between stranger rapists and their offences*. Home Office, Special Interest series Paper No 16.

Rossmo, D. K., & Rombouts, S. (2017). Geographic profiling. In R. Wortley & M. Townsley (Eds.), *Environmental criminology and crime analysis* (2nd ed., pp. 162–179). Routledge.

Ruparel, C. (2004). *The nature of rape of females in the metropolitan police district*. Home Office Research Findings 247.

Russell, D. E. H. (1992). Preface. In J. Radford & D. E. H. Russell (Eds.), *Femicide: The politics of woman killing* (pp. xiv–xv). Open University Press.

Rye, B. J., & Meaney, G. J. (2007). Voyeurism: It is good as long as we do not get caught. *International Journal of Sexual Health*, 19(1), 47–56. https://doi.org/10.1300/J514v19n01_06

Safarik, M. E., Jarvis, J. P., & Nussbaum, K. E. (2002). Sexual homicide of elderly females: Linking offender characteristics to victim and crime scene attributes. *Journal of Interpersonal Violence*, 17(5), 500–525. https://doi.org/10.1177/0886260502017005002

Salfati, C. G., & Taylor, P. (2006). Differentiating sexual violence: A comparison of sexual homicide and rape. *Psychology, Crime & Law*, 12(2), 107–125. https://doi.org/10.1080/10683160500036871

Sauvageau, A., & Racette, S. (2006). Autoerotic deaths in the literature from 1954 to 2004: A review. *Journal of Forensic Sciences*, 51(1), 140–146. https://doi.org/10.1111/j.1556-4029.2005.00032.x

Schlesinger, L. B. (2004a). Classification of antisocial behavior for prognostic purposes: Study the motivation, not the crime. *The Journal of Psychiatry & Law*, 32(2), 191–219. https://doi.org/10.1177/009318530403200204

Schlesinger, L. B. (2004b). *Sexual murder: Catathymic and compulsive homicides*. CRC Press LLC.

Schlesinger, L. B., & Revitch, E. (1999). Sexual burglaries and sexual homicide: Clinical, forensic, and investigative considerations. *Journal of the American Academy of Psychiatry and the Law*, 27(2), 227–238.

Schug, R. A., & Fradella, H. F. (2015). *Mental illness and crime*. Sage Publications, Inc.

Scott, D., Lambie, I., Henwood, D., & Lamb, R. (2006). Profiling stranger rapists: Linking offence behaviour to previous criminal histories using a regression model. *Journal of Sexual Aggression*, 12(3), 265–275. https://doi.org/10.1080/13552600601090329

Scott, H. (2003). Stranger danger: Explaining women's fear of crime. *Western Criminology Review*, 4(3), 203–214.

Scottish Government. (2022). *Recrded crime in Scotland, 2021–22*. Retrieved from: https://www.gov.scot/publications/recorded-crime-scotland-2021-2022/

Scully, D. (1994). *Understanding sexual violence: A study of convicted rapists*. Routledge.

Seeman, M. V. (2020). Portrait of an Exhibitionist. *Psychiatric Quarterly*, 91, 1249–1263. https://doi.org/10.1007/s11126-020-09810-w

Sentencing Council. (2022). *Burglary offences*. Retrieved January 2, 2024 from https://www. sentencingcouncil.org.uk/sentencing-and-the-council/about-sentencing-guidelines/about-published-guidelines/burglary/

Shepherd, E., & Griffiths, A. (2021). *Investigative interviewing: The conversation management approach* (3rd ed.). Oxford University Press.

Sheridan, L., & Boon, J. (2002). Stalking typologies: Implications for law enforcement. In J. Boon & L. Sheridan (Eds.), *Stalking and psychosexual obsession: Psychological perspectives for prevention, policing and treatment* (pp. 63–82). John Wiley & Sons, Ltd.

Silverman, R. A., & Kennedy, L. W. (1987). Relational distance and homicide: The role of the stranger. *The Journal of Criminal Law & Criminology*, 78(2), 272–308. https://scholarlycom-mons.law.northwestern.edu/jclc/vol278/iss272/273

Sim, J. (1994). Tougher than the rest? Men in prison. In T. Newburn & E. A. Stanko (Eds.), *Just boys doing business? Men, masculinities and crime* (pp. 100–117). Routledge. https://doi.org/10.4324/9781315003566

Singleton, N., Bumpstead, R., O'Brien, M., Lee, A., & Meltzer, H. (2001). *Psychiatric morbidity among adults living in private households, 2000*. The Stationery Office.

Singleton, N., Meltzer, H., Gatward, R., Coid, J., & Deasy, D. (1998). *Psychiatric morbidity among prisoners in England and Wales*. The Stationery Office.

Skinner, B. F. (1953). *Science and human behavior*. The Free Press.

Smith, A. D. (2000a). Motivation and psychosis in schizophrenic men who sexually assault women. *The Journal of Forensic Psychiatry*, 11(1), 62–73. https://doi.org/10.1080/095851800362364

Smith, A. D. (2000b). Offence characteristics of psychotic men who sexually assault women. *Medicine, Science and the Law*, 40(3), 223–228. https://doi.org/10.1177/002580240004000306

Smith, A. D., & Taylor, P. J. (1999). Serious sex offending against women by men with schizophrenia: Relationship of illness and psychotic symptoms to offending. *British Journal of Psychiatry*, 174(3), 233–237. https://doi.org/10.1192/bjp.174.3.233

Smith, J. A., Harré, R., & Van Langenhove, L. (1995). Idiography and the case-study. In J. A. Smith, R. Harré, & L. Van Langenhove (Eds.), *Rethinking psychology* (pp. 59–69). Sage Publications.

Snook, B., Taylor, P. J., & Bennell, C. (2005). Shortcuts to geographic profiling success: A reply to Rossmo (2005). *Applied Cognitive Psychology*, 19(5), 655–661. https://doi.org/10.1002/acp.1142

Society for the Advancement of Actuarial Risk Need Assessment. (2021). *Static-99R users*. Retrieved January 2, 2024 from https://saarna.org/

Soothill, K., Francis, B., Sanderson, B., & Ackerley, E. (2000). Sex offenders: Specialists, generalists - or both? *British Journal of Criminology*, 40(1), 56–67. https://doi.org/10.1093/bjc/40.1.56

Staff, H. (2019). Protecting yourself from stranger rape and date rape. *HealthyPlace*. Retrieved January 2, 2024 from https://www.healthyplace.com/abuse/articles/stranger-rape-and-date-rape-how-to-protect-yourself

Stafford-Clark, D. (1965). *What Freud really said*. Macdonald.

Stefanska, E. B., Carter, A. J., Higgs, T., Bishopp, D., & Beech, A. R. (2015). Offense pathways of non-serial sexual killers. *Journal of Criminal Justice*, 43(2), 99–107. https://doi.org/10.1016/j.jcrimjus.2015.01.001

Stein, M. L., Schlesinger, L. B., & Pinizzotto, A. J. (2010). Necrophilia and sexual homicide. *Journal of Forensic Sciences*, 55(2), 443–446. https://doi.org/10.1111/j.1556-4029.2009.01282.x

Stern, V. (2010). *The stern review: A report by Baroness Vivien Stern CBE of an independent review into how rape complaints are handled by public authorities in England and Wales*. Home Office.

Stinson, J. D., & Becker, J. V. (2011). Sexual offenders with serious mental illness: Prevention, risk, and clinical concerns. *International Journal of Law and Psychiatry*, 34(3), 239–245. https://doi.org/10.1016/j.ijlp.2011.04.011

Stripe, N. (2021). *Nature of sexual assault by rape or penetration, England and wales: Year ending March 2020*. Office for National Statistics.

Stripe, N. (2023). *Crime in England and Wales: Year ending June 2023*. Office for National Statistics.

Sturmey, P. (Ed.). (2009). *Clinical case formulation: Varieties of approaches*. John Wiley & Sons, Ltd. https://doi.org/10.1002/9780470747513

Sturmey, P., & McMurran, M. (Eds.). (2011). *Forensic case formulation*. Wiley-Blackwell. https://doi.org/10.1002/9781119977018

Sugarman, P., Dumughn, C., Saad, K., Hinder, S., & Bluglass, R. (1994). Dangerousness in exhibitionists. *Journal of Forensic Psychiatry*, 5(2), 287–296. https://doi.org/10.1080/09585189408412299

Szumski, F., & Kasparek, K. (2020). Encountering an exhibitionist: The female victim's perspective. *The Journal of Sex Research*, 57(5), 610–623. https://doi.org/10.1080/00224499.2019.1669523

Tarr, C. C. (2016). Pleasurable suspension: Erotic asphyxiation in the nineteenth century. *Nineteenth-Century Contexts: An Interdisciplinary Journal*, 38(1), 55–68. https://doi.org/10.1080/08905495.2015.1105486

Taylor, P. J., Leese, M., Williams, D., Butwell, M., Daly, R., & Larkin, E. (1998). Mental disorder and violence. A special (high security) hospital study. *The British Journal of Psychiatry*, 172(3), 218–226. https://doi.org/10.1192/bjp.172.3.218

ter Beek, M., van den Eshof, P., & Mali, B. (2010). Statistical modelling in the investigation of stranger rape. *Journal of Investigative Psychology and Offender Profiling*, 7(1), 31–47. https://doi.org/10.1002/jip.103

The Psychologist. (2018a). Psychological expert evidence and the Parole Board: 'Psychologists P12 and P1' on the John Worboys case, and communication with the public on complex issues of risk and justice. *The Psychologist*, 31, 2.

The Psychologist. (2018b). Worboys parole case fall-out: Two more contributions to the continuing debate. *The Psychologist*, 31, 2–3.

Thomas, T. (2016). *Policing sexual offences and sex offenders*. Palgrave Pivot.

Thorndike, E. L. (1898). Animal intelligence: An experimental study of the associative processes in animals. *The Psychological Review: Monograph Supplements*, 2(4), 1–109. https://doi.org/10.1037/h0092987

Thornton, D., Mann, R., Webster, S., Blud, L., Travers, R., Friendship, C., & Erikson, M. (2003). Distinguishing and combining risks for sexual and violent recidivism. *Annals of the New York Academy of Sciences*, 989(1), 225–235. https://doi.org/10.1111/j.1749-6632.2003.tb07308.x

Turvey, B. E. (2014). *Forensic victimology: Examining violent crime victims in investigative and legal cintexts* (2nd ed.). Academic Press.

Turvey, B. E. (2016). Investigating fetish burglaries. In B. E. Turvey & M. A. Esparza (Eds.), *Behavioral evidence analysis: International forensic practice and protocols* (pp. 171–176). Academic Press.

Tyrer, P., & Mulder, R. (2022). *Personality disorder: From evidence to understanding*. Cambridge University Press.

U.S. Department of Justice. (1984). *Criminal victimization in the United States, 1982*. Bureau of Justice Statistics.

Vaknin, A. (2018). Sex and personality disorders. *HealthyPlace*. Retrieved January 2, 2024 from https://www.healthyplace.com/personality-disorders/malignant-self-love/sex-and-personality-disorders

Van Patten, I. T., & Delhauer, P. Q. (2007). Sexual homicide: A spatial analysis of 25 years of deaths in Los Angeles. *Journal of Forensic Sciences*, 52(5), 1129–1141. https://doi.org/10.1111/j.1556-4029.2007.00531.x

Vaughn, M. G., DeLisi, M., Beaver, K. M., & Howard, M. O. (2008). Toward a quantitative typology of burglars: A latent profile analysis of career offenders. *Journal of Forensic Sciences*, 53(6), 1387–1392. https://doi.org/10.1111/j.1556-4029.2008.00873.x

Velarde, L. (2014). Geography and individual decision making: Victims and offenders. In B. Hill & R. Paynich (Eds.), *Fundamentals of crime mapping* (2nd ed., pp. 61–78). Jones & Bartlett Learning.

Völlm, B. A., Edworthy, R., Huband, N., Talbot, E., Majid, S., Holley, J., Furtado, V., Weaver, T., McDonald, R., & Duggan, C. (2018). Characteristics and pathways of long-stay patients in high and medium secure settings in England: A secondary publication from a large mixed-methods study [Original Research]. *Frontiers in Psychiatry*, 9(140). https://doi.org/10.3389/fpsyt.2018.00140

Von Krafft-Ebing, R. (1894). *Psychopathia sexualis, with especial reference to contrary sexual instinct: A medico-legal study*. The F. A. Davis Company, Publishers. https://archive.org/details/PsychopathiaSexualis1000006945

Ward, T. (2000). Sexual offenders' cognitive distortions as implicit theories. *Aggression and Violent Behavior*, 5(5), 491–507. https://doi.org/10.1016/S1359-1789(98)00036-6

Ward, T., Polaschek, D. L. L., & Beech, A. (2006). *Theories of sexual offending*. John Wiley & Sons Ltd.

Warr, M. (1988). Rape, burglary, and opportunity. *Journal of Quantitative Criminology*, 4(3), 275–288. https://doi.org/10.1007/BF01072454

Waterhouse, G. F., Reynolds, A., & Egan, V. (2016). Myths and legends: The reality of rape offences reported to a UK police force. *The European Journal of Psychology Applied to Legal Context*, 8(1), 1–10. https://doi.org/10.1016/j.ejpal.2015.04.001

Watt, M. C. (2014). *Explorations in forensic psychology: Cases in criminal and abnormal behaviour*. Nelson Education Ltd.

Weerasekera, P. (1996). *Multiperspective case formulation: A step toward treatment integration*. Krieger.

West, A. G. (2000a). Clinical assessment of homicide offenders. *Homicide Studies*, 4(3), 219–233. https://doi.org/10.1177/1088767900004003002

West, A. G. (2000b). *Sexual homicide: An analysis of the narratives of men who have killed women*. University of Surrey: Unpublished Doctoral Thesis.

West, A. G. (2001). From offender profiler to behavioural investigative advisor: The effective application of behavioural science to the investigation of major crime. *Police Research & Management*, 5(1), 95–108.

West, A. G., & Greenall, P. V. (2011). Incorporating index offence analysis into forensic clinical assessment. *Legal and Criminological Psychology*, 16(1), 144–159. https://doi.org/10.1348/135532510x495124

West, D. J., & Walk, A. (Eds.). (1977). *Daniel McNaughton: His trial and the aftermath*. Gaskell Books.

Willig, C. (2022). *Introducing qualitative research in psychology* (4th ed.). Open University Press.

Wilson, D. (2012). Murder. In B. Winder & P. Banyard (Eds.), *A psychologist's casebook of crime: From arson to voyeurism* (pp. 137–154). Palgrave Macmillan.

Wilson, G., & Alison, L. (2005). Suspect prioritization in the investigation of sex offences: From clinical classification and offender profiling to pragmatism. In L. Alison (Ed.), *The forensic psychologist's casebook: Psychological profiling and criminal investigation* (pp. 68–89). Willan Publishing.

Woodhams, J., & Tonkin, M. (2018). Offender profiling and crime linkage. In G. M. Davies & A. R. Beech (Eds.), *Forensic psychology: Crime, justice, law, interventions* (3rd ed., pp. 283–306). BPS Blackwell.

Woodworth, M., Freimuth, T., Hutton, E. L., Carpenter, T., Agar, A. D., & Logan, M. (2013). High-risk sexual offenders: An examination of sexual fantasy, sexual paraphilia, psychopathy, and offence characteristics. *International Journal of Law Psychiatry*, 36(2), 144–156. https://doi.org/10.1016/j.ijlp.2013.01.007

World Health Organization. (2012). *Understanding and addressing violence against women: Femicide*. World Heath Organization. Retrieved from: https://www.who.int/publications/i/item/WHO-RHR-12.38

World Health Organization. (2022). *International classification of diseases* (11th ed.). Retrieved from: https://icd.who.int/

Wortley, R., & Townsley, M. (Eds.). (2017). *Environmental criminology and crime analysis.* Routledge.

Wright, L. C., & Warner, A. (2020). EMDR treatment of childhood sexual abuse for a child molester: Self-reported changes in sexual arousal. *Journal of EMDR Practice and Research, 14*(2), 90–103. https://doi.org/10.1891/EMDR-D-19-00060

Wunsch, D., Davies, T., & Charleton, B. (2021). *The London rape review 2021: An examination of cases from 2017 to 2019 with a focus on victim technology.* Mayor of London, Office for Policing and Crime.

Yapp, E. J., & Quayle, E. (2018). A systematic review of the association between rape myth acceptance and male-on-female sexual violence. *Aggression and Violent Behavior, 41,* 1–19. https://doi.org/10.1016/j.avb.2018.05.002

Yardley, E. (2020). The killing of women in "sex games gone wrong": An analysis of femicides in Great Britain 2000–2018. *Violence Against Women, 27*(11), 1840–1861. https://doi.org/10.1177/1077801220966956

Yin, R. K. (2018). *Case study research: Design and methods* (6th ed.). Sage Publications, Inc.

Young, B. (2022). Voyeurism and flashing victims 'failed by justice system'. *The Reading Chronicle [online]*, January 5th. Retrieved from: https://www.readingchronicle.co.uk/bestof-berks/19825730.voyeurism-flashing-victims-failed-justice-system/

Young, J. E., Klosko, J. S., & Weishaar, M. E. (2003). *Schema therapy: A practitioner's guide.* The Guilford Press.

Youngs, D. (Ed.). (2013). *Behavioural analysis of crime: Studies in David Canter's investigative psychology.* Ashgate Publishers.

Zara, G., Gino, S., Veggi, S., & Freilone, F. (2022). Sexual femicide, non-sexual femicide and rape: Where do the differences lie? A continuum in a pattern of violence against women. *Frontiers in Psychology, 13.* https://doi.org/10.3389/fpsyg.2022.957327

Zipf, G. (1950). *The principle of least effort.* Addison Wesley.

Index

Note: **Bold** page numbers refer to tables and *italic* page numbers refer to figures.

For Product Safety Concerns and Information please contact our EU
representative GPSR@taylorandfrancis.com
Taylor & Francis Verlag GmbH, Kaufingerstraße 24, 80331 München, Germany

www.ingramcontent.com/pod-product-compliance
Lightning Source LLC
Chambersburg PA
CBHW080132270326
41926CB00021B/4448